Strong in the Struggle

My Life as a
Black Labor Activist

Lee Brown
with Robert L. Allen

ROWMAN & LITTLEFIELD PUBLISHERS, INC.
Lanham • Boulder • New York • Oxford

ROWMAN & LITTLEFIELD PUBLISHERS, INC.

Published in the United States of America
by Rowman & Littlefield Publishers, Inc.
4720 Boston Way, Lanham, Maryland 20706
www.rowmanlittlefield.com

12 Hid's Copse Road, Cumnor Hill, Oxford OX2 9JJ, England

British Library Cataloguing in Publication Information Available

Library of Congress Cataloging-in-Publication Data

Brown, Lee, 1921–
    Strong in the struggle : my life as a black labor activist / Lee Brown with Robert
L. Allen.
        p. cm.—(Voices and visions)
    ISBN 0-8476-9191-8 (alk. paper)
    1. Brown, Lee, 1921– 2. Afro-American labor leaders—Biography. I. Allen,
Robert L., 1942– II. Title. III. Series.

HD8073 .B76 A3 2000
331.88'092—dc21
[B]   00-031107

♾™ The paper used in this publication meets the minimum requirements of
American National Standard for Information Sciences—Permanence of Paper for
Printed Library Materials, ANSI/NISO Z39.48-1992.

In memory of my grandfather, Lee Brown, my first teacher, and Grace, my wife and sister in the struggle.
—Lee Brown

For my mother, Sadie Sims Allen, with love and gratitude for all she has given to me, and for Janet Carter, my best friend and partner in life.
—Robert L. Allen

Contents

Foreword

JULIANNE MALVEAUX

Lee Brown is a bear of a man, a gentle giant with an imposing presence, a ready smile, a gravelly voice, and, most importantly, an unwavering focus and an unwavering commitment to justice. One of Lee's special gifts is his ability to take a meandering conversation and either subtly guide it or bluntly redirect it to the pressing matter of "the people"—the least and the left out, the elderly, the poor, and working people. I thought I knew Lee well because of our mutual involvement in the San Francisco NAACP in the 1980s, but reading his autobiography has given me new appreciation of his walk.

It is also clear that his life fully represents the history of African American workers and activists in the twentieth century, the transformation of our presence from a rural to an urban one, and the impact that the Industrial Revolution, the trade union movement, World War II, and the civil rights movement have had on the way we live and we work. This book is especially important because we have so few worker biographies, so few life stories of "the people" that Lee Brown has always been ready to represent. It is important to see history from this prism, to view our nation's evolution through the life of a man whose voice, strong and authentic, is amplified through this powerful, absorbing, and detail-rich autobiography.

I was especially riveted by Lee Brown's story because it reveals so much hidden history, a story that we ran the risk of losing were it not for the diligence of Lee's scribe, the scholar Robert Allen. It is useful for us to have a work history of an African American man that contrasts sharply with the revisionist vision of the "good old days" of industrial work. And it is important, in the postindustrial context, to be reminded of what work has been for so many people. With the proliferation of technology and the boom of jobs in the computer industry, it is important to remember that, once upon a time, people fought for the right to do backbreaking work and fought to improve the conditions of their employment. When people talk about the "good old days" for workers, they are often referring to the days when people held their jobs for thirty or forty years, starting off in a factory right after high school and working there until they received the gold watch of retirement. They are, perhaps, referring to the days when men with modest educations could find jobs that paid decent wages. Lee Brown's story makes it clear that the good old days weren't good for everyone and that African American men, especially southern African American men, faced an array of challenges even during the economic expansions that came with World War II and the postwar period.

Brown has held an array of jobs—handyman, actor, longshoreman, railway porter, waiter, and union organizer. He worked because he had to, and he was attracted to organizing because it was a way to bargain for fair pay from his employers. Gifted with an innate sense of self and of fair play, Lee Brown never let his work define him. Instead, he struggled to define the terms and conditions of his work and his life and to improve the lives of others.

This book, *Strong in the Struggle,* is an engrossing call and response between Lee Brown, who recounts the facts of his life, and Robert Allen (whose work on Port Chicago clearly influences his understanding of the work status of black men in the World War II era and beyond), who puts Lee's life in a historical context. Using the rich source materials of labor movement and university archives, trial transcripts, and Lee Brown's own file, Allen is able to deepen our appreciation of the struggles and challenges that have shaped Lee Brown's life. The melding of these two black men's voices allows us to appreciate Brown's life and evolution and reminds us that his struggle was the struggle of millions of African American men in the early and middle twentieth century.

Brown emerges as a tenacious man whose understanding of the power of organizing was the pivotal focus in both his work and his civic life. Lee Brown has gathered signatures, organized, picketed, and placed himself in physical jeopardy for the cause of worker rights. He was a top union leader in an interracial union during the time when the South was still segregated, a shop steward and organizer who often involved the community in his union's quest for fair pay. His recollection of the challenges of organizing offers lessons to those who still struggle to bring people together around issues of economic justice. Through it all, this autobiography reveals his thirst for knowledge and appreciation for life lessons, and an optimism that allowed him to make the best of every situation, even the more than two years of jail time he spent on charges of violating the Taft-Hartley Act by being a member of the Communist Party while serving as a union official.

It is one thing to read of the excesses and abuses of the House Un-American Activities Committee in the abstract, or when they focused on internationally known figures and Hollywood stars, but it is quite another to read the way this one black man approached HUAC. Lee Brown's integrity in dealing with HUAC parallels that of Paul Robeson, someone whom Lee both admired and spent time with. Lee refused to answer the committee's questions unless he was allowed to make a statement of his own. Completely unintimidated by the trappings of congressional power, Lee Brown was true to himself and to the cause of freedom.

While this book overflows with history, it also brims over with amusing episodes in Lee Brown's life. He lived a full life, with as much fun as struggle, with the fellowship of engaging friends and colleagues. He overcame the personal tragedy of being separated from his mother at an early age and speaks movingly of the reunion with her, as well as of the relationship with his "sister in the struggle" and wife, Grace. While strength in struggle is the dominant theme in Lee Brown's life, it is a credit to Brown and Allen that Lee's humor, his sense of fun and gentleness, is also a feature in this book.

Words like "hero" and "role model" have become clichés in a media age when the ordinary attempt to distinguish themselves with their trappings and when those who are truly extraordinary have their light obscured by the bells and whistles of common, contemporary fame. The phenomenon reminds me of Paul Laurence Dunbar's 1946 poem, "Not They Who Soar," in which he wrote: "Not they who soar, but they who plod, their rugged way, unhelped, to God, are heroes." Lee Brown is that kind of hero, an ordinary and outstanding man, "heroes, they the soil who trod, not they who soar."

If he has not soared, he has flown, and his light shines, nonetheless. All in all, Lee Brown has lived an exemplary life, and I am grateful to him and to Robert Allen for sharing that life with us in these pages. There are lessons in this life and history, but for me there is also the heartfelt appreciation of a brother in struggle whose commitment to economic justice has been a gift to every life he has touched.

Acknowledgments

A debt of gratitude is owed to the late Vincent Hallinan for first suggesting that this autobiography be written and to Tom Dunphy and the late Grace Oliver Brown for drafting earlier versions of the text. Thanks also to Patricia Scott for suggesting a collaboration between Lee Brown and Robert L. Allen in writing the present version.

For their patient assistance in locating documents and newspaper accounts, we thank Eugene Dennis Vrana, librarian of the International Longshore and Warehouse Union in San Francisco; the librarians of the New Orleans Public Library, Louisiana Branch; the archivists of the U.S. District Court, Eastern District of Louisiana, New Orleans; the archivists of the National Archives, Southwest Region, Fort Worth, Texas; and the staff of the San Francisco Labor Archives at San Francisco State University. Our thanks to Congresswoman Nancy Pelosi and her staff for help in expediting the release of FBI documents under the Freedom of Information Act.

Marcy McGaugh diligently transcribed many hours of taped interviews, and we thank her.

Finally, we want to thank Hasinah Rahim, Doris Ward, the family of the late Rose Robinson, Dr. Arthur Coleman, Harold Treskunoff, the Richardson family of Marcus Book Stores, Dr. David West, Jill Rothenberg, Dean Birkenkamp, and Janet Carter for their support and encouragement.

—L.B.
—R.L.A.

Introduction

ROBERT L. ALLEN

I ring the bell at Lee Brown's apartment building in a housing project in San Francisco's Western Addition neighborhood. He immediately buzzes me in through the metal gate. For the first few months of our meetings he would always look out of his window to check who was there before buzzing me in. Now he says he recognizes me by how I ring the buzzer. He opens the door and waits as I climb the stairs to the third floor. "You in, Bro' Robert?"

"I'm on the way up, Bro' Brown."

At seventy-eight years of age, Lee Brown is tall and husky with light brown skin. His voice is deep and rich. Despite a recent heart attack he is vigorous and animated in discussions, his conversation punctuated by the occasional "oh, brother!" for emphasis. When discussing racist and capitalist adversaries, he adopts an exaggerated scowl, but more often his eyes have a mischievous twinkle and he is quick to laugh.

In his bedroom, which also serves as the living room, a photograph of Elijah Muhammad is displayed prominently over the bed with a Million Man March poster on the adjacent wall. The room is crowded with a bed, an old easy chair, TV, VCR, and four sagging bookcases overflowing with well-thumbed books, newspapers, magazines, and miscellaneous papers. An alcove is crammed with a file cabinet, more books, documents, photographs, and papers. The hundreds of books and pamphlets in his apartment reflect his love of reading and his wide-ranging interests. His collection includes books on labor history, black history, ancient African civilizations, religion, socialism, economics, biography, and philosophy.

1

We do our interviews sitting on two folding chairs at the kitchen table. The table is usually cluttered with a big bowl of fruit in the center, papers scattered around it, and various canned and bottled goods from the welfare department on the table and the floor. He offers me a bottle of ginseng soda. I take a second bottle from the refrigerator for him.

He is a man who delights in good food, though he seldom gets out to restaurants now. A good cook, he enjoys occasionally preparing a favorite dish—savory goat stew—for the pleasure of friends. Each week he looks forward to two meals at a local community center, hoping that they might satisfy his appetite as the trade union struggle fed his spirit.

He believes in dressing to make an impression whenever he leaves his apartment. That means wearing a three-piece brown suit with gold watch and chain in the vest pocket, five or six pens and reading glasses in the coat pocket, several buttons on the lapels, including Africa/Black USA unity pin, NAACP lifetime membership pin, and Local 2/HERE button (Hotel Employees and Restaurant Employees Union). On his head he sports a black leather fez with a map of Africa outlined on its front in green, yellow, and red. He uses a walking cane and wears brown boots. He impresses one as a man who thinks well of himself and is not hesitant to make known his views.

We met through a mutual friend, Patricia Scott, who knew of Lee Brown's efforts to write his autobiography and my interest in African American involvement in social movements. I was immediately fascinated by Lee Brown's story—which he had already started writing with the help of his late wife, Grace, and a friend, Tom Dunphy. He asked if I would help him with the project and I agreed. We both had independently read Nell Irvin Painter's *The Narrative of Hosea Hudson*. We admired this work and it became a model for what we wanted to do.

For more than sixty years Lee Brown has been deeply committed to the struggle for the rights of working people in this country. A largely self-educated man ("doctor of the working class" is how he describes his education), Brown took part in rank-and-file labor struggles on the waterfront of Galveston, Texas, and in railroad labor camps in Arizona in the late 1930s, fought for jobs for black actors in the Hollywood film industry in the 1940s, and campaigned for workers' rights in the great hotels of San Francisco in the 1960s and 1970s.

Brown made history as one of the top leaders of a militant, interracial union in the Deep South during the 1940s and 1950s. He was vice president of Local 207, Warehouse and Distribution Workers' Union (affiliated with the International Longshoremen's and Warehousemen's Union) in New Orleans. Local 207 was a black-led, interracial union of dockworkers who loaded cargo onto river-going barges. Brown also joined the Communist Party, attracted by its open advocacy of trade union and civil rights activism. He would pay a high price for his commitment. In 1957 he was investigated by the House Un-

American Activities Committee. Brown refused to cooperate with HUAC. At the hearings he created a sensation when he adamantly refused to answer any questions unless the committee allowed him to make a statement. (He had planned to pose his own questions to the committee, including, Was Senator Eastland a member of the Ku Klux Klan?) For his insistence on having the right to make a statement, Congressman Bernard Kearney charged Brown with being a defiant, arrogant witness and had him ejected from the hearing.

The following year Lee Brown was charged with violating the Taft-Hartley Act, which prohibited union leaders from being members of the Communist Party. Although he had previously withdrawn his membership in the Communist Party to meet the requirements of the law, he was convicted nonetheless. He became one of the first labor leaders imprisoned during the McCarthyite witch-hunts, and he served one of the longest prison terms of any of the Taft-Hartley victims. He was sentenced to three years' imprisonment at the federal penitentiary at Texarkana, Texas.

Born in 1921 in New Orleans and raised in farming families in rural Louisiana, Lee Brown first joined a common laborers' union at age seventeen when he was working on the dry docks in Galveston, Texas. There he had his first taste of labor struggle when the union called a strike in 1939 for better wages.

Later he worked on the railroads in Arizona. When a foreman unfairly dismissed a worker, Brown told the other workers, "Let's call a meeting. Together we should stand up for this brother." The work stoppage that he organized was successful, and Brown was launched on a lifelong course of militant labor activism.

By the beginning of World War II Lee Brown was in Los Angeles working for RKO Studios and actively involved in the NAACP. He campaigned for better jobs for blacks in the film industry. Along the way he met many famous black actors, including Louise Beavers, Mantan Moreland, and later Paul Robeson, whom he deeply admired. Brown even had a couple of bit parts in films.

After the war he returned to New Orleans and found a job on the docks loading river barges. He joined Local 207 and soon became a shop steward. Local 207 was known for its militancy and consequently was detested by the employers. Moreover, as a union with black and white members and a black president, Andrew Steve Nelson, Local 207 presented a challenge to the racial status quo, a situation especially galling to local and state authorities, and to the federal government as well. Brown's fearlessness and militancy got him chosen as vice president of Local 207.

Like many other black activists at the time, he also joined the U.S. Communist Party. In an effort to decapitate the militant black leadership of Local 207 and end the ILWU presence in New Orleans, both Brown and Nelson were indicted under the anti-Communist provisions of the Taft-Hartley law, the National Labor Relations Act. Nelson was convicted but died before being imprisoned. Brown was convicted and imprisoned at Texarkana.

Serving time in the penitentiary was not easy, but Brown used the time as a learning opportunity, and he was not dissuaded from his politics. When he was released in 1960, he moved to San Francisco and joined Local 110 of the Culinary Workers' Union at the famous Fairmont Hotel, where his rank-and-file activism led to his becoming, to his knowledge, the first union shop steward in a San Francisco hotel. From then until his retirement he was a union organizer and a leader of the struggle against discrimination in employment for black workers in the hotel and restaurant industry in San Francisco. During this period he met and married Grace Oliver, who was also a union activist in the hotel industry.

On coming to San Francisco, Brown resumed a tenuous relationship with the Communist Party. Disillusioned by what he regarded as racism within the party, Brown later drifted away from the CP and joined a black nationalist group. Nevertheless, his fundamental belief that grassroots organizing of all people is the key to social change was instrumental in bringing him back into the CP, where he remained a member for a dozen years. Although he left the party for good in the wake of the collapse of the Soviet Union and the ensuing schisms in the CPUSA, he continues to uphold the ideals of socialism.

Since retiring, Brown has not allowed his militancy to diminish. He has thrown himself into the senior citizen's movement, working with such organizations as the Senior Action Network and Legal Assistance to the Elderly and marching in demonstrations in Sacramento demanding more state aid for seniors.

Lee Brown's story continues a time-honored tradition of African American autobiography stretching back to the slave narratives. Like others in this tradition, it is a story of determined struggle and resistance to oppression, not by an isolated individual but by a person who is rooted in his community and shares the community's travails and struggles; it is an oft-told story of the search for freedom and a better life for self and community.

At the same time Lee Brown's account is an engaging story of a unique individual: a black labor activist in the South, Southwest, and West who worked with several different labor unions, as well as the NAACP, the Communist Party, and black nationalist groups; a militant who was imprisoned for his political beliefs and associations; a Communist who lived to see the collapse of the Soviet Union but remains committed to the struggle for socialism.

For Lee Brown, life and the struggle for change are one and the same. As he put it, "I have dedicated my life in the service of poor people."

Prologue
February 15, 1957

On Friday, February 15, 1957, Lee Brown was summoned to appear before a subcommittee of the notorious House Un-American Activities Committee. The HUAC subcommittee was holding hearings in New Orleans to investigate alleged Communist Party activity. Lee Brown was a leader of a militant waterfront workers union, Local 207 of the International Longshoremen's and Warehousemen's Union (ILWU). The questioners were Richard Arens, HUAC staff counsel, Rep. Edwin E. Willis of Louisiana, chairman, and Rep. Bernard W. Kearney, a committee member from New York. After swearing in and determining that Brown was representing himself, the interrogation proceeded. An excerpt from the transcript:

Arens: Where and when were you born?

Brown: In 1921, May 28.

Arens: Where?

Brown: New Orleans.

Arens: Give us, if you please, just a brief sketch of your education.

Brown: I would like to say one thing, Mr. Chairman, if I may, to the chairman. Are you the chairman?

Willis: All right.

Brown: I would like to say one thing to this committee or any other committee.

Kearney: Mr. Chairman, I suggest that the witness answer the question and not make a speech.

5

Willis: That's right.

Brown: Mr. Chairman, at this point—

Willis: You can answer a very simple question—to give a brief description of your education. That's a very simple question.

Brown: Mr. Chairman, I submit I would like to make a statement before I answer any questions.

Arens: Mr. Chairman, I respectfully suggest the witness be ordered and directed to answer the question.

Willis: I direct you to answer the question; and let me tell you the consequences of that order that I have directed to you: That any attempt on your part to evade questions or to make a speech is out of order. I see you are not represented by counsel. I suppose you know your rights. If any questions are asked of you which you believe honestly might subject you to criminal proceedings, you are entitled to invoke the privilege of the fifth amendment. You can't hedge, pussyfoot, or run around the issues. You are ordered to answer the question.

Brown: Mr. Chairman, I still ask for the privilege under the first amendment to make my statement.

Arens: Mr. Chairman, in view of the fact that he has refused to answer the question with respect to his education and he has been ordered and directed to do so, I propose to interrogate him by other questions on other matters.

Willis: Proceed to another subject. You realize the implications of what I have told you.

Arens: Where are you employed?

Brown: Mr. Chairman, I request to make my statement.

Arens: Mr. Chairman, I respectfully suggest the witness be ordered and directed to answer the question as to where he is employed.

Willis: That's a very simple question, the second simple question, and you are ordered to answer that question. A record is being made of it by the reporter. Since you are not represented by counsel, I will repeat to you that the consequences may be contempt proceedings. I don't know the field counsel will go into, but you will not be permitted to hedge. You are ordered to answer the question, and from now on I will not make any more statements.

Arens: Where are you employed?

Brown: Mr. Chairman, based on the first amendment, I would like to make a statement before I answer any question, period.

Kearney: Mr. Chairman, I suggest that again the witness be directed to answer these questions, and so far as making a statement or a speech, as far as this committee is concerned, I object to it.

Arens: How long have you been employed in your present employment?

Brown: I refuse to answer, period, until I get a chance to make a statement, period.

Arens: Are you vice president of the International Longshoremen's Union in New Orleans?

Brown: I refuse to answer the question until I get a chance to make a statement.

Kearney: Are you a member of the Communist Party?

Brown: I would like to make a statement, period.

Kearney: If you are not a member of the Communist Party, would you tell this committee to that effect?

Brown: I would like to make a statement, period.

Arens: Mr. Chairman, I respectfully suggest the witness now be ordered and directed to answer the questions as to whether or not he is a Communist.

Willis: You are ordered and directed to answer that question.

Brown: Mr. Chairman, I hope you understand it clear and perfect that I am not answering a question until I make a statement, period.

Kearney: Mr. Chairman, may I suggest to this witness you are not scaring this committee.

Brown: You don't frighten me, either.

Kearney: I am not trying to frighten you. We are trying to get you to answer a simple question. In view of his arrogance, Mr. Chairman, I suggest if you can't get any answer from him, you ask the marshal to escort him from the room.

Willis: That will be taken into consideration.

Arens: Mr. Witness, as a prerequisite to obtaining your witness fee, it is necessary for you to affix your signature to the pay vouchers. This is the pay voucher that you will get your witness fee for appearing today. Will you kindly affix your signature?

Brown: I don't sign anything, Mr. Chairman, period.

Arens: Now, Mr. Witness, I lay before you a photostatic copy of a non-Communist affidavit dated July 23, 1951, signed by yourself, here in New Orleans in which you say that you are not a member of the Communist Party or affiliated with the party. Look at that document and tell us, first of all, whether or not that is a true and correct reproduction of your signature.

Brown: Mr. Chairman, I hope I made it clear, I am not answering anything until I make my statement.

Arens: You said in this statement of 1951, and you said it under oath, that you were not a Communist; isn't that true?

Brown: I say I am not answering any question until I make my statement, period.

Arens: Now I lay before you still another affidavit signed by yourself, dated July 15, 1952, and a non-Communist affidavit under the Taft-Hartley Act, in which you say under oath that you are not a Communist. Look at that document which we have marked "Exhibit No. 2" and tell this committee while you are under oath whether or not you signed that document.

Brown: I am not answering anything. I hope I made it clear to you, Mr. Chairman and the rest of the committee, I am not answering any question until I make my statement.

Arens: Now I lay before you still another document signed by yourself, executed under oath, a non-Communist affidavit, in which you say:

"I am not a member of the Communist Party or affiliated with such party. I do not believe in, and I am not a member of nor do I support any organization that believes in or teaches the overthrow of the United States Government by force or by any illegal or unconstitutional methods."

Look at that document now while you are under oath and tell this committee whether or not you executed that document.

Brown: I think I made it clear, Mr. Chairman, and to this committee as a whole, that I am not answering questions until I make my statement.

Arens: Now I lay before you still another document dated June of 1956, signed by yourself, in which you state that you are not a member of the Communist Party. Look at that document which you filed under oath pursuant to the provisions of the Taft-Hartley Act, and tell this committee whether or not that truly and correctly represents your signature.

Brown: I say I am not answering any questions until I make my statement.

Arens: Mr. Chairman, so the record may be perfectly clear, I respectfully suggest to the Chair that this witness now be ordered and directed to answer each and every one of the several questions which I have posed to him with respect to these documents.

Willis: You are now ordered to answer those questions which have to do with your signing these statements relating to your status of being a Communist or non-Communist. You are ordered to answer these questions.

Brown: Mr. Chairman, I think I made the statement clear; I am not intending to answer any questions until I make my statement.

Arens: Mr. Chairman, I respectfully suggest that each of these exhibits which we have just used be appropriately marked and incorporated in the body of the record.

Willis: Let them be so marked and incorporated.

In further testimony Brown was asked to identify various materials presumably produced by the Communist Party and containing mentions of his name. As before, he refused to answer any questions unless he was allowed to make a statement. Then the committee called another witness, Arthur Eugene, and swore him in to testify while Lee Brown was still present.

Arens: Mr. Eugene, will you kindly identify yourself by name, residence, and occupation?

Eugene: Arthur Eugene, Jr. I live here in New Orleans, 2121 St. Anthony Street. My occupation is a warehouseman.

Arens: Mr. Eugene, I expect to interrogate you at length in a few moments, but for the present purpose I should like to ask you, Have you ever been a member of the Communist Party?

Eugene: Yes; I was.

Arens: During what period of time were you a member of the Communist Party?

Eugene: From the period of 1948 until 1956.

Arens: During part of that time, were you working with the Federal Bureau of Investigation furnishing information to your Government?

Eugene: That's right.

Arens: Mr. Eugene, during the course of your membership in the Communist Party, did you know a person as a Communist by the name of Lee Brown?

Eugene: Yes, I did.

Arens: Do you see the person in the courtroom today? Now?

Eugene: Yes, sir.

Arens: Whom you knew as Lee Brown?

Eugene: Yes; I do.

Arens: Would you look him in the eye and point him out to this committee while you are under oath?

Eugene: That is him right here.

Kearney: When you say "that is him right here," you are referring to the witness who is under oath and who has refused to answer all these questions which have been propounded to him by counsel.

Eugene: That is correct.

Arens: Now, Mr. Brown, you have heard the testimony just a moment ago of Arthur Eugene. Is that correct? Did you hear the testimony?

Brown: Mr. Chairman, I refuse to answer any questions until I make my statement.

Arens: Now, Mr. Brown, look at the man at your left who has just identified you as a member of the Communist conspiracy, and while you are under oath look him in the eye and tell this committee, did he lie or did he tell the truth?

Brown: Mr. Chairman, I refuse to answer the question until I make my statement, regardless. I still refuse to answer until I make my statement.

Arens: Are you now a member of the Communist conspiracy designed to overthrow this Government by force and violence?

Brown: Mr. Chairman, I refuse to answer questions until I make my statement. I am not answering any question, period.

Kearney: Are you an American citizen?

Brown: I refuse to answer questions until I make my statement.

Kearney: Aren't you proud to answer that question?

Brown: Until I make my statement.

Kearney: Let me say to the witness, from your answers here, I notice you fail to take advantage of your rights to seek refuge behind any of the amendments you so desire to the Constitution. Do you decline to answer on the grounds of the fifth amendment that to truly answer might incriminate you?

Brown: I refuse to answer any questions.

Kearney: Then I want to say to the witness that, just as soon as we can get together I shall certainly move for a contempt citation, because you are the most arrogant individual I have seen in many a year.

Brown: That don't worry me a bit. That don't worry me what you do. . . .

Kearney: I ask that this witness be escorted from the hearing room. He is one of these defiant, arrogant witnesses that once in a while we run across who has the Commie line in every one of his answers. There is no need of wasting the committee's time with him.

Brown: Mr. Chairman—

Willis: They usually invoke the privilege of the fifth amendment, and then say they do so because there are phantom witnesses and that they are not confronted with their accusers. Here is a very much alive person next to you who, under oath, has subjected himself to the pains and penalties of prosecution if he didn't tell the truth, who has charged you with being a Communist. As a red-blooded American citizen, if you are, here is your chance to stand up and deny that fact if it is not true. What is your answer to that?

Brown: Mr. Chairman, as I have already stated, I refuse to answer the question.

Willis: Mr. Marshal, I suggest you escort the witness out of the room and keep him out of this room throughout these hearings.

That evening the New Orleans States *published an account of the hearing, which is excerpted below:*

Lee Brown, 2017 Jackson, vice president of the International Longshoremen and Warehousemen's local, refused to answer more than 50 questions put to him by the House Un-American Activities subcommittee and was told to leave the hearing room in federal district court.

Brown, after telling his name and address, refused to answer the other questions put to him by the committee and later said he was invoking the First and Fifth amendments to the Constitution as protection.

Rep. Bernard Kearney of New York, committee member, called Brown "one of the most arrogant witnesses to ever appear before this committee."

As each question was put to him, Brown kept repeating: "Mr. Chairman, I hoped I had made it clear that I will not answer any questions until I am permitted to make a statement."

He refused to say whether he is or was a Communist party member, refused to give his occupation, and would not identify document after document placed before him.

Among these were letters written to editors, signed with Brown's name, a reproduction of the Daily Worker, Communist organ, a document bearing the name of the state committee of the Louisiana Communist party, and affidavits in which Brown's signature was put to statements that he was not a Communist.

The dramatic point of Brown's appearance came when Arthur Eugene, who said he was a Communist from 1948 to 1956 and did undercover work for the FBI part of that time, was called to the stand.

Eugene described himself as a warehouseman and resident of 2121 St. Anthony in New Orleans. He appeared as a star witness in the case against Andrew Steve Nelson, former president of the ILWU convicted of falsely swearing he was not a Communist.

Eugene said during the time he was a party member he knew Brown as a fellow party member.

Asked to single out Brown and look him in the eye, Eugene pointed at Brown and said: "That's him right there."

Rep. Edwin W. Willis of St. Martinville, subcommittee chairman, told Brown he did not believe he was honestly using the first and fifth amendments and ordered marshals to evict him from the room.

Brown walked out before marshals had the chance to forcibly eject him, but the federal officials followed him out.

CHAPTER ONE

Childhood

I went to live with my grandfather when I was about three years old. Grandfather owned a farm in Morrow, Louisiana. Grandfather was well-known and was loved and respected by everyone who lived in Morrow. His name was Lee Brown. Everyone called him Uncle Lee Brown. When I was born in the Charity Hospital in New Orleans on May 28, 1921, I was named after him — Lee Brown.

Grandfather was a tall, dark-skinned man with kinda heavy shoulders. He was a large fellow, solid and strong. He always dressed clean and neat. I never saw him in no patches. He told me, "Don't be raggedy. Be neat and clean."

He was also a kindhearted, easygoing man. I never did see him angry. He never got in no fights. Everybody in that little country town liked him. He was always helping people, people that had trouble. He carried his money in a sack, a white sack. I think my grandmother made it. He would lend people money, poor people who needed help. He was always trying to do things for people.

We lived in the countryside among hardworking farmers who was very poor but also very friendly and concerned about each other. Neighbors would come to my grandfather's home every night and they would discuss issues such as farming, church affairs, money problems, and health. Listening to these old people taught me a lot about life and making a living for myself, and especially respect for others.

To me there was no wiser or beloved a man than my grandfather. He loved me a lot too. I remember he used to take me to Bunkie, another little town, and he would buy me toys—a little wagon, marbles, spinning tops. I would bring them back home and then I would give the kids around there some marbles; I would always share with the other kids. He taught me to do that. Even the kids I used to play with, the next-door neighbors, we never did have no fights. He taught me how to get along with people.

Grandfather had a buggy that he used to take me around in. It was a black buggy with red spokes on the wheels and it was pulled by a black horse. Some of the happiest times that I can remember was when I would sit up front alongside my grandfather in his buggy and ride fast across those old dirt roads. I went everywhere with my grandfather. I went to church every Sunday with him. Some Sundays we would go to the church and take food and stay all day talking with the neighbors and exchanging food.

My grandfather would haul freight for different stores. The freight train would stop and leave freight; then he would deliver the freight to the people at four or five stores. He picked it up in his wagon. Two mules pulled that wagon. That was his business, hauling freight. When he went to those stores he didn't bow down, he didn't go in no damn backdoor. He didn't fear no man. I never heard him say "yas, suh" or "naw, suh" to white men like some people did.

On the farm he raised chickens and ducks. He had a few horses and a few mules. No pigs, though. He thought they was unhealthy—too much fat and grease. He used to gather hay from some other place to feed his horses. He didn't grow no crops except for a little truck patch of vegetables to eat—cabbages, tomatoes, potatoes, things like that, and some corn. The farm wasn't no great large one, but it was large enough for him, for what he was doing. Something that he could handle with his own garden tools. Sometimes he hired two, three people 'round there to help him.

He would stand with me by his side, looking over his land, and say to me, "One day this land will be yours." I looked up to him for guidance, wisdom, and knowledge.

In the house grandfather had this long table. I ain't seen no table like that in a long time. Every morning we had our breakfast at this table. He sat me at one end of the table and he sat at the other. He would say a prayer before eating. Now I don't understand this, but in those days they had steak for breakfast. I don't know how they did that; maybe they kept it smoked or something. I know we ate meat and eggs. I remember we ate good. I think I had more than any kid around there, good food, toys. I was the only kid living on the farm. It was just me and my grandfather and Aunt Hannah before she died, and later Aunt Betsy.

My grandmother's name was Hannah. I called her Aunt Hannah. I don't remember her too good. They told me she was a Seminole Indian who came from Florida. She was tall with long black hair that hung to her waist. Aunt Hannah didn't talk very much to anyone but everyone loved her. She was a kind lady.

Those years I lived with my grandfather was the happiest time of my childhood. He was my first teacher.

My grandfather had three sons: Bab, Bud, and Bruce Brown. Bruce Brown was my father. My father was a light-complexioned man and very tall, at six feet seven inches. He wore size fourteen shoes.

Before I was born, my father changed his name to Joseph Brown because the law was after him. Years later I got the story from my sister-in-law, Henrietta, who was married to my half brother, Pete Robinson. She told me that my father and his brothers was robbing them little mixed trains, trains that had one coach car and the rest of them was freight. These mixed trains used to run between the little towns in Louisiana. She once showed me a picture of one of my uncles with a red handkerchief tied around his neck. All three of them was riding together on the train like they was Wild West outlaws. When my father came to New Orleans, he decided to change his name to Joseph, and that's what it says on my birth certificate.

My father was killed when I was very young. On his way to work on the coal boat one morning in 1922, he stepped on a live electric wire that had fallen down on the ground during the night after a terrible thunderstorm. He was killed instantly. I didn't really get to know my father. Little do I know about him, except what I was told.

My mother was born in Bolton, Mississippi. Her name was Janie Davis. Like I said, I was born at the old Charity Hospital in New Orleans. When I was small, my mother received some money from my father's death. She used the money to open a little store. Then she got hold to another man for a while, but he slicked her out of her money and she lost the store and became mentally disturbed. So my grandfather came and got me and took me to live with him at the farm.

One morning later on my mother came to the farm to take me away from my grandfather. When we arrived at the hotel where she was staying, I cried and made such a fuss all night that she was asked by a lady if I was really her son. This lady thought my mother had stolen me. The very next morning my mother took me back to the farm.

Grandfather took good care of me. He used to tell people that he wanted to give me the best education that money could buy. Grandfather never hit me— he never laid a hand on me. He paid a lot of attention to me. When his buggy would roll, I'd be in there. He took me everywhere with him: to the stores, to meet white folks, to church on Sunday. People look up and say, "There comes Uncle Lee—Big Lee and Little Lee." It seemed like people knowed me through him. We was so close; when they saw him they saw me.

Somebody else I remember was Aunt Pauline, who used to live around there with her husband, Uncle Bill. She was a kind of Creole and she didn't speak English. She wore a red handkerchief on her head and had red lips and wore a long dress. My grandfather and I used to pass her on the dirt road and she'd say "bo' jour," and I didn't know what the hell she was saying. I'd break and run. I didn't know she was just saying good morning to me. Her husband, Bill Rieto, fought in the Civil War, and he had a old long gun that I sometimes saw sticking out their window when I passed there. He musta fought in the Union Army. I know he didn't fight for the Confederates, staying around my grandfather, 'cause my grandfather was pretty militant.

One day some neighbor children and I was playing in my yard when suddenly I heard someone scream. Grandfather came out of the barn bent over, blood running down his leg. I don't know how it happened, but he cut his leg while working in the barn. Aunt Hannah came out of the house and helped him get into bed. Aunt Hannah doctored his leg day and night. A hospital that would treat black people was many miles away. Grandfather didn't realize how seriously he was hurt. Months passed; his leg got worse, and he still wasn't seen by a doctor. Things wasn't the same on the farm anymore. The neighbors would leave the house with worried looks on their faces. I soon realized my grandfather's leg wouldn't heal, and it kept getting worse. In the meantime, Aunt Hannah had taken ill and soon she died.

My grandfather hired a housekeeper to take care of us. The housekeeper's name was Betsy. I called her "Aunt Betsy." Later he married her. Little did I know at that time what heartbreak Aunt Betsy would bring to me. It wasn't long after that one night Aunt Betsy woke me up and told me my grandfather had died. I remember hanging on to his neck and screaming. The people that was in the room had to pull me away from him.

My grandfather was a member of the Woodmen of the World. This was the name of a secret order organization, something like the Odd Fellows. He was also a member of the Masons. The men who attended the funeral wore white gloves and carried swords, which was a symbol of the organization. All the women wore white. I was dressed in white too. I was so hurt, and feelings of loneliness and emptiness filled my heart, since my grandfather had been the most important person in my life.

The death of my grandfather was the turning point of my life. I remained with Aunt Betsy on the farm. Betsy was a mean woman with little education or knowledge. Betsy brought her sister, Aunt Alice, to live with us on the farm. Her sister was a mean old woman just like her. Neither of them had any consideration for me or anyone else. Betsy was never pleased with me or anything I tried to do. She used to fuss at me, scold me, and only half feed me.

One evening some men came to the farm. Aunt Betsy had a long conversation with them. Later I found out Aunt Betsy was giving all my grandfather's tools away.

Weeks later a man named Buster Wells, who used to work on the farm for Grandfather, came to live with us on the farm; he also brought his wife. Aunt Betsy gave Buster fifty head of cattle to sell for her. Weeks passed. She was waiting for him to bring the money back, but Buster never came back to the farm. The only news she heard about him was that he had died. Later Buster's wife left the farm. Since Aunt Betsy had no education, men would count her money and shortchange her all the time. Finally all her money was stolen by these people she had trusted.

The remainder of the inheritance grandfather left her was gradually given to her sisters and brothers. Everything that my grandfather had of value was sold or given away. But my grandfather left his land to me and Aunt Betsy. When Aunt Betsy didn't have anything else to sell or give away, she tried to sell my land. But little did she know my grandfather had fixed it so no one could sell it. Finally, Aunt Betsy went to a court in Opelousas to try to sell my land. But the judge told Aunt Betsy that the land couldn't be sold until I reached the age of twenty-one. By that time I would be old enough to decide legally what I wanted to do with the land.

When Aunt Betsy came from court, she was frustrated with me. She went around the farm with frowns all over her face. Then she really started mistreating me. The little food she gave me to eat wasn't served on the long dining room table I was used to eating at. All my toys and clothes disappeared. I never knew whether she gave them away or burned them up. I wasn't surprised anymore over any stupid thing she did. There was times when I would walk around crying and longing for my grandfather. Her sister Alice would often hit me for no reason. My grandfather's friends stopped coming to the farm. They wouldn't have anything to do with such mean women.

Later Aunt Betsy sent me to live with her brother. He was very friendly toward me, more so than his sister. But my visit was cut short. Aunt Betsy came and took me back to the farm. These old ladies gave me little food to eat and mistreated me, and word began to spread throughout Morrow about my situation.

One night in 1927, we had a bad rainstorm. High water was everywhere. All the homes was flooded out with water. People, black and white, received lots of assistance from the Red Cross. When the water kept getting higher, some soldiers came and took everyone to Camp Beauregard. We stayed there three days. When the water went down, we went back to our homes, transported back by the soldiers. On our way back home from Camp Beauregard, we saw dead cattle all along the roads and in people's yards and scattered around their farmhouses. It took weeks before all the dead cattle was burned.

Things began to get better for me. News of my mistreatment reached my cousins who lived in the countryside between LeMoyen and Morrow. My cousin was named Tot Howard and his wife was Rosetta Howard. Tot Howard came to the farm and took me away from Aunt Betsy and her sister, and he took me to live with him and his wife. (At this time, I found out Aunt Betsy didn't want me to leave the farm. She intended to have me stay until I reached the age of twenty-one, so she could try to influence me to sign my land over to her.) Tot Howard and his wife was very poor people, but they tried to do all they could for me.

Tot wanted me in school. I had never attended school before. I was seven and I was very excited about the idea of going to school with kids my own age. This was the beginning of a new experience for me.

All the black children in this small community went to the same school in Morrow. Most of the children was from the families of the Howard people around the same plantation. I went to school three months out of a year. We didn't learn too much in that short length of time. Yet this was quite some experience to look forward to. All of these black families was sharecroppers. Miss Ida Bowers, our teacher, was very respectable and taught one hundred children, which included all primary grades up to the fifth grade. When I became older, I was transferred to another school in LeMoyen. This school was about six miles away.

I walked the six miles every day, in cold weather and in rain. I walked on the railroad tracks with the other black children. We was afraid to walk on the highway because a man had got run over. Black children couldn't ride on the school buses. I realized for the first time I was living in an evil Jim Crow, discriminatory, and racist society. School buses was available only for the white children. This made me want to learn what was behind these problems that existed for black people.

I liked to read. We used to read books like *Bob and Nancy*, and the story of the Tar Baby, and "Little Boy Blue Come Blow Your Horn. The sheep's in the meadow, the cows in the corn." Hell, with stuff like that no wonder I didn't learn nothing in that school!

But I did learn how to read. Reading books became very interesting and enjoyable. After the three months of school was over, I went back to help my cousins. When we wasn't farming, we chopped wood for some white people's homes. The money from chopping wood helped out in the winter months. One thing I couldn't understand was why my cousin didn't chop wood for us and prepare for winter. Instead we would wait until it got real cold, and then we would gather wood every day for the fireplace. But I didn't complain about anything that was done around the place.

The sharecroppers was very poor, but I appreciated what my relatives was doing for me. My appetite was so big I wanted different kinds of food to eat. My cousin Aunt T-Babe (we called our cousins "aunt" and "uncle"; and T-Babe was the nickname for Rosetta, Uncle Tot's wife) made lunch for us everyday to take to school. Sometimes we had potatoes and a cinnamon roll, and sometimes we were eating that damned pork. We didn't know no better. But we ate good. Sometimes Aunt T-Babe made Cha Cha, made out of cabbage, cucumber, pepper, mustard, and green tomatoes. They had a good garden. They had potato banks where they would store the potatoes buried in the ground wrapped in hay and corn silk. They killed their hogs and salted the meat and smoked the meat and made sausage. They would catch fish and smoke the fish. And Aunt T-Babe would bake light rolls. She would let the dough set and rise up and then bake it. And then wrap it up in a piece of cloth to keep it fresh. I remember we didn't have no ice, so we put our drinks in sawdust in a tub. At least that's how I remember it. It's funny how at seventy-eight years old you can remember a lot of things. Seventy-eight ain't too old to remember!

I lived with Uncle Tot and Aunt T-Babe for quite a few years, longer than I stayed with anybody else. They raised me like I was their own child.

One night Uncle Tot and his sister Aunt Bernice went to a small bar in the community. While they was sitting at the table, a drunk white man named Alec Havord came in from the white bar next door and tried to kiss or dance with Aunt Bernice. She refused him, and then he hauled off and slapped her. As soon as this happened, the light in the bar went out. Then a shot rang out in the bar. The white man was shot. Before he died, he called out that Uncle Tot had shot him. This man didn't know who shot him. Uncle Tot didn't have his gun that night. But of course everyone believed Uncle Tot killed this man. White men on horses rode all night in the rural communities looking for Uncle Tot. The neighbors gathered all their children and put them in one house until morning. This went on for three weeks. Uncle Tot escaped the riders' hands by hiding out in a church for two weeks. Later, with the help of friends, he escaped to the train station and made his getaway to Texas. Soon afterward, Aunt T-Babe moved to Evergreen, Louisiana, and took me along. We went to live with her brother. Later we heard that a white man did the killing in the bar that night.

I started school again in Evergreen. I got along fine with the other kids. One time I was playing on some thin ice and fell into a hole. The kids had to pull me out. Another time when my little cousin and I went to a grocery store, I stole a grape and put it in his mouth. When we got home, my cousin told Aunt T-Babe and she gave me a good spanking.

Aunt T-Babe decided it was time for me to get baptized, so I was baptized in the local Baptist church one Sunday morning with three more children. I remember how the preacher gave a long sermon over us, and people be hollering just like it was a funeral. Then the old preacher took me in the water and I thought he was going to preach my funeral. And that water was cold! People just hollering. When the preacher dipped me that last time, people was standing all around in the water and they started to singing "done got over." I remember that good. They took us back to a house and dressed and fed us. I felt like I was some kind of chosen person. For a while I went to church every Sunday and also had Communion.

At about the age of fifteen, I decided it was time for me to go out and find work to help support myself. I was still a young boy but pretty large for my age. I was lucky to find work as a houseboy, working for a German family, although this job didn't turn out too well. The salary was too low for all the work that was required. So I left and went to live with Aunt T-Babe's brother, Dad Jones, and his family, where I worked every day in the fields picking and chopping cotton. With the little money I received I bought some clothes. Dad Jones had a large family, but everyone got to eat a cooked meal and drink milk every morning. He treated me like one of the family.

The field hands' day off was on Saturday. One morning a boy in the neighborhood wanted someone to work in his place, selling meat door-to-door on Saturdays. The job was paying one dollar and fifty cents a day. I took this job and saved enough money to hobo to Melville, Louisiana. I went there looking for other relatives and a cousin named Joe Reece. When I caught the freight train to Melville, other hobos was in the boxcar with me. They told me when the time came to jump off. With a suitcase under my arm and a little money in my pocket, I finally made it to Melville.

Melville wasn't a large town but it had streets and a theater. I started walking down the street asking everyone I met whether they knew anyone by the name of Joe Reece. I happened to see a lady walking on the street and I said, "Lady, can you tell me where Joe Reece lives?"

She said, "He lives out of town." She told me how to get to where he lived and then asked me, "What is your name? You kin to Joe?"

I said, "Yes, my name is Lee Brown."

Then she started mentioning the names of some of the Browns to see if I knew any. I recognized some of the names she mentioned. It turned out this lady was my second cousin. She took me home with her. It so happened she lived only a short distance from Melville. When we arrived at her home, I was introduced to her husband, her daughter, and other relatives. Her name was Esther; my other cousins was Jessie Brown and Henry Brown. I got so excited meeting so many relatives. After dinner we talked about other relatives who lived in different towns. I didn't know any of the relatives mentioned but was glad to hear I had a large family. When time came to go to bed, Cousin Esther prepared a bed in the back of the house. She told me to stay as long as I wanted.

That just goes to show how you can be walking on the street and you just stop some particular person, and it turns out you're related to them. That shows how things can happen. I don't know what you call it. I don't know if I was a chosen man or what, but that's what happened to me.

CHAPTER TWO

On My Own

I didn't want to look for support from my cousin Esther, so the next day I went looking for work and was hired as a houseboy for the LeBlanc family.

My duties included cleaning, shopping, and running errands for Margaret, their daughter. I used to do things like go to the store and buy shoes for her. She'd tell me the size and I'd go get them. I bought her powder, soap, things like that. She probably was too lazy to go herself, so she sent me.

Margaret was in her twenties, a tall, slim brunette. She was going to school. There was three other daughters, but they were older and married and had moved out. Margaret was the only one left in the house. Mrs. LeBlanc was handicapped and couldn't use her left hand.

The LeBlancs was a family of moderate income in this small town. They also had an upstairs maid. I was given a little shack in the back of their house to live in, which was part of my meager wages. The LeBlancs had two grandchildren by another daughter about the same age as I. Their grandchildren and I got along fine together. Mrs. LeBlanc knew the salary she was giving me was small, so she told me to plant a garden in back of the house. The money I earned from selling whatever vegetables I grew would be mine to use for things like movies or pocket change. I grew different kinds of vegetables in my garden. I gave Mrs. LeBlanc's family some vegetables and sold the rest up and down the streets. I pulled a little red wagon filled up to the top with vegetables.

There was times when I got very lonesome in my little shack, especially when the day was over and night began. For a time I did have a German shepherd, Laddie, who followed me everywhere I went, even to the movies. He stayed outside until I came out. I loved this dog. He really was a devoted friend.

One day I was walking along selling my vegetables when a gang of white boys came up to me and wanted to start a fight. I told them I lived at the LeBlancs' home and worked for them. They were surprised to hear this and walked on down the street. I didn't have that trouble anymore.

My salary was two dollars a week plus meals. At first I ate my meals in the backyard under a tree close to the house. They gave me a wooden table and a chair back there. But Margaret didn't like that. Margaret had visited New York and had seen how black and white people lived there, and she explained to her mother that making me eat in the backyard was wrong. Margaret said she didn't believe in discriminating against any race of people. Her mother probably hadn't traveled and didn't know any better. I liked Margaret. She was friendly toward me and she seemed intelligent. If she believed in discrimination, she wouldn't have trusted me going to the store for her. I realized that not all white people was mean and prejudiced; some, like Margaret, tried to be decent toward black people. From then on I ate at the kitchen table and I was treated better than before around the house.

I got acquainted with the black maid who worked upstairs. She did the cleaning and the washing and ironing. I used to give her some of the vegetables from my garden. She was forty years old. She was a very nice lady. She fixed my breakfast every morning.

I worked for the LeBlancs for nearly two years. But I decided to leave to better my condition. The little money I was making wasn't enough. I needed to buy my own clothes and shoes. One day I jumped up and wanted to get to stepping, so I packed my suitcase and left to look for some work that paid more.

I went back to Esther's house and stayed about a month. Esther was nice to me but her daughter and I couldn't get along. Things began to get unpleasant around the house. It seemed to me that Cousin Esther's daughter was mentally disturbed. Often we got into arguments. She slapped me in the face one day. I told Cousin Jessie about how she was acting around the house when everyone was out. He didn't like it and told her never to slap me again. I didn't want to make matters worse, so I left Melville.

I went to a little farm to visit some friends of mine, Annie and Buddy Harris. When I arrived, they was out in the fields planting potatoes. I stayed and helped them plant potatoes for about a week. I felt good helping them with the planting because they was struggling sharecroppers and they appreciated my help.

I left them and stayed for a day or so with Cousin Horace Bertram. When I was leaving, I asked him if he could give me some money for traveling and he gave me a chicken, which I was happy to get. When I was walking down the street, I saw a man coming toward me who was dressed like he was on his way to work. I stopped him and asked if he wanted to buy a chicken. He answered yes. I sold him the chicken for forty cents. With forty cents in my pocket, I went looking for a friend's house to ask him to travel with me and show me the way to Galveston, Texas. I wanted to get to Galveston because I knew Uncle Tot and Aunt T-Babe was now living there.

Oak Tar was my friend's name. When I found Oak Tar, he didn't have any money but he was willing to hobo with me and show me the way. First we hoboed to Opelusas, Louisiana. Then we jumped on a freight train for Galveston. Inside the boxcar it was so cold we had to make a fire. As we traveled, we didn't have anything to eat all the way. When Oak Tar and I finally arrived, the cold wind seemed like it went straight through our bodies. Uncle Tot and Aunt T-Babe was so happy to see me; they hugged and kissed me and fixed us some dinner. When dinner was over, Oak Tar went back to Louisiana.

I spent a few days looking around Galveston. I noticed one day when I was walking down the street that some people was coming out of a building carrying bags of food. I asked the people if I could get some of that food. They told me to go on in and ask for some. When I got inside the building and asked for the food, a lady who was sitting behind a desk told me to sign some papers. When I signed the papers, I got the food—some cornmeal, flour, plums, and grapefruits. I was so glad to get this food I couldn't wait to get home to show Aunt T-Babe and Uncle Tot what I had. When Uncle Tot saw the food, he got very angry at me. Apparently, the building I went into to get the food from was the welfare office. Uncle Tot explained to me I shouldn't go to the welfare office to get food because that food was for people who was out of work and didn't have any other means of support. Even though I didn't quite understand what he was talking about, I didn't go there ever again.

One evening passing the dock, I noticed some men giving away bananas. They gave me some, so I took them. I didn't know what reaction Uncle Tot would have. But he didn't say anything to me about that. I just wanted something different to eat for a change.

It was nice being with my uncle and aunt, but jobs was hard to find. No one was hiring. While I was looking for work, I used to go to the courthouse in Galveston and listen to the cases. I had heard people talking about the courthouse and the law and all, and I was interested. I was also interested because I remembered Uncle Tot's trouble in Louisiana with the white man. Tot got away to Galveston, but the sheriff in Louisiana found out where he was and got the police in Texas to arrest him on his job at the dry docks. They brought him back to Louisiana and put him in jail in Opelusas. I was still living in Louisiana then. But they had to let him out because the white man they claimed Tot killed, his mother came to the courthouse and told them, "Tot did not kill my son." She knew he didn't do it. Some other white man had done it. They had to let Tot go. When he got back to Galveston, the superintendent at the dry docks, a man named Spider, let him have his job back. Tot was a good worker and Spider said, "I don't care if he killed every white man in Louisiana, I want him back on the job!"

So this was one reason I was interested in what went on at the courthouse. I noticed that they had a lot more black folks in there than whites on trial and going to jail for various crimes. It seemed like something was wrong, but I couldn't pinpoint exactly what. I didn't really understand how racism worked at that time, but I knew something was wrong. It wouldn't be until I got into the union that I would understand better. But I could see that black folks was not getting equal justice. And it made me start to thinking.

Every morning for three weeks I would go and line up on the dock for work. All the foremen would come over on a little boat and pick the people they wanted to hire. Todd dry dock was on the other side of the bay. On this particular morning they hired about thirty men, and I was one of them. We were examined and signed up to work as common laborers scaling and painting ships. Each man was given iron-toe shoes and a helmet for safety. Payday was on Fridays.

I was doing common labor—sometimes running the scaling gun or painting. Or I was down in the double hold cleaning out the bottom, which was dangerous work. But I was young and I didn't know how dangerous it was.

Soon I found out that you had to join the union. This was the union of common laborers, a black union. Uncle Tot was a member of the union. Mr. Spriggens, the president, told Uncle Tot, "Your boy is young. You'll have to stand for him to get his book." So Mr. Spriggens signed me up and gave me my black union book.

Later we went on strike for better wages. This was in about 1938. The common laborers was only making thirty-five cents an hour. They put me on the picket line at night. That was my first time on a picket line. The white guys in the other unions—the boilermakers, the carpenters—they respected our picket lines and wouldn't cross the line. I was proud to be in the union and on strike because my Uncle Tot was a strong union man. I remember during the strike Uncle Tot would wake up in the morning and tell Aunt T-Babe, "Hurry up and fix my breakfast, T-Babe; I got to go on duty." That's what he said about going to the picket line; he was proud of it and called it "going on duty." He was picketing during the day and I picketed at night. It was the first time either of us was on a picket line and he inspired me.

The strike lasted three months. When the strike finally was settled, the wages was fifty cents an hour. Afterward, all common laborers joined the union. Now this was my first involvement with any union activity.

Jobs those days was hard for a black man to find, except on farms and plantations, where wages was so low you could barely survive.

I thought about all the black people like my cousins who was sharecroppers for white plantation owners. Black families stayed on some of their land and picked and chopped cotton at just above starvation wages. The living arrangements mostly created hardship, since large families was forced to live in crowded one- and two-room houses. There was no running water, only outdoor toilets, and many people was forced to sleep on floors. Families didn't have enough money to buy new clothing. The white plantation owners sold them hand-me-down clothing.

Some black families moved off the plantations to get jobs in the cities. Some was lucky; others went back to the farm. Black children worked in the fields with little or no education.

The union made me feel that I could do something for poor people like myself and my cousins. The union gave me a way to go forward—to help change things.

The dry dock job lasted six months; then work began to slow down. Mr. Spriggens told the young men that if they wanted to look for work someplace else he would stamp their union book "paid in full" to make it easier to find work. The married men with families stayed working at the dry docks. I got my book stamped and left.

I started working part-time on ships as a screwman. My job was to hook a sling to a crane to help load raw sugar or cotton on the ship. After this I found some part-time work on the railroad in Galveston, helping around the tracks in the yard. They had six or seven men working on the tracks. But this job on the railroad ran out, so I went back looking for work. I was willing to try any kind of work.

I went looking for work all the next week, with no luck. I left Galveston and went to Crosby, Texas, looking for another cousin. I didn't have any luck finding my cousin, so I went walking down the old highway between Crosby and Houston. I had been walking for about an hour, when I spotted a brickyard right off the highway, which was in Green Bayou. I went to the brickyard and asked the foreman if he was hiring. The boss, a German named Bill Schweiner, said he could put on two men. "You know anybody else?" he asked. I thought about Joseph Godrey, my cousin in Galveston who was also out of work. I said to let me go back and get my cousin out of Galveston. I hopped a freight train back to Galveston. That was my transportation. I hit that freight like I owned it.

When my cousin and I returned to Green Bayou, we were put to work. I worked this open field digging up stumps until twelve o'clock noon. By this time I was tired and most of all very hungry. I didn't have any money to buy any food, so a white fellow employee asked if I was hungry. I said I was. He took me to a store for some food and told me he would cover for it until I got paid. I worked in the field the rest of the day.

I didn't have any place to live, but I heard about a boardinghouse that was renting rooms. After work I went to the boardinghouse and inquired about a room. I took the room with board for a dollar fifty per week. My cousin Joseph also stayed there.

George Ware, the man who ran the boardinghouse, had a daughter, Georgia Lee, who lived in Houston. We used to go to Houston, and eventually Joseph married her. She still lives in Houston. Joseph later moved to Alaska and married somebody else and had a son. He died years later in Alaska. They say he choked on a chicken bone. So they said.

The salary at the brickyard was twelve cents an hour. Payday was on Saturday. The next morning when I went to work, the foreman took the field-workers to work in the brickyard. Once I started working inside the brickyard, I realized this work wasn't as hard as the fieldwork.

I worked molding bricks. I was a mud brick maker. You put the mud into something like a mixer. One guy would feed it with the dirt and I be taking it out. It was just like a baking shop. You make three bricks at a time. Put them in the mold, smooth off the top, put the molds on a pallet board, and take them on a buggy to the drying place where they stayed for a couple of weeks. Then they take the bricks to a kiln in a big old building where they burn the bricks. Old Man Henderson was in charge of the kiln.

Old Man Henderson was the one who got me to join the NAACP. Henderson lived in Houston but he'd come and work at the brickyard during the week. On the weekends he'd go back to his family. He used to tell me about the "freedom." I wanted to know about this freedom. In the evening after work he'd tell about how the NAACP was fighting to get freedom. He talked to me and Joseph. We was searching for freedom—young men who wanted to be free. I know I wanted to be free and wanted to join something to get freedom. It was only fifty cents a year to join. This was around 1939. So I got my social security card and my NAACP card that same year.

Most of the single men would go to Houston every Saturday. George Ware would take some of us in his little car. George seemed to have his hand in everything. One Saturday I went to Houston to do some shopping. I went and bought me a pair of trousers and a shirt to put on that Sunday so I'd look sharp. While I was sitting on a bench waiting for George to come back by and pick me up to go back to Green Bayou, I went to sleep. When I woke up, my damn package with my trousers and shirt was gone! I jumped up and looked around. I saw a policeman and asked, "Have you seen anybody with a package?" He said, "I've seen plenty of people with packages, but I can't stop everybody I see with a package." That shows how stupid you can be when you don't have knowledge. I learned the hard way. So that was my loss.

When the fellows finally came back to pick me up, I was upset and angry and I told them about what had happened. They laughed all the way back to Green Bayou.

Meanwhile, I kept on working steadily in the brickyard. I was about eighteen years old now. Everyone on the job thought I was much older. For entertainment after work, I learned how to box, gamble, and drink corn liquor. We used shoot dice and drink. Old Man Bud Springer, an old white guy who worked there, used to make corn liquor and sell it to us. George Ware tried his hand at making corn liquor too.

Mr. Bill, the boss, used to be a fighter. Sometimes I'd play around after work trying to imitate Joe Louis. One day Mr. Bill said, "You got a good stance, Brown Bomber." Everybody on the job called me "Brown Bomber" after Joe Louis. Mr. Bill started training me, and I had some pretty good fights. I had a fight with a white guy and I knocked him out. Then I had a fight with Sonny Boy Bradley and knocked him out. I thought I was hell! Then they brought in Shorty Jeffrey from Beaumont, Texas. He gave me a one-two-three and knocked me out. Shit, the ring was spinning all around. I told Mr. Bill, "Uh, uh, brother. I don't want no more boxing. You can forget about that." He said, "Brown Bomber, you got to get whupped sometimes. That's how you learn." But I was young and I couldn't see it. As long as I was knocking them down that was okay, but when Shorty Jeffrey knocked me out that was it. Maybe I might have made a good fighter but I wasn't ready to go through the hard part.

There was a guy named Red who worked at the other brickyard and had a wife named Lena. Now this guy was very jealous. One Sunday my friend Otsey Pryor came by in his car and picked me up to go to Houston. I had made a good lick that day. I think I had won about fifteen, twenty dollars and I wanted to celebrate. Lena was there so I said, "Come on Lena, you want to go?" I bought her a drink to get her to go with me. So we went up to Houston to get something to eat. When I got back to Green Bayou, somebody said, "Man, Red looking for you. He heard you was out with Lena in Houston." When I heard that, I didn't know what Red might try to do when he got drunk. I went to Old Man Schweiner's house. I told him I wanted to get his shotgun. "What you want a shotgun for, Brown Bomber?"

"Red is looking for me to kill me."

"What did you do?"

"His wife was in a car with Otsey Pryor and me and somebody went and told him."

He said, "Red ain't gonna bother you. Go on back home." Turned out Red wasn't looking for me. People just told me that lie to get me scared. And it did scare me. I didn't run around with Lena no more.

One morning on my day off from work, I was standing in the brickyard in front of the gas burner warming myself. Suddenly my pants caught on fire. The flames was all around my legs. After a few minutes I was able to put the flames out. But my leg was burned so badly I went and asked the brickyard manager if he could send me to see a doctor. The company managers said they couldn't send me to see a doctor because I got burned on my day off and not when I was working.

On my own, I managed to get to Houston to see a black doctor I knew about. I didn't have any money, but when the doctor saw how badly my leg was burned he treated me. The doctor said I could pay him later and I should come back in two weeks. He thought he could get me some insurance money. As days passed, my leg began to get worse. I didn't have any money to travel back and forth to Houston to see the doctor, so I caught a freight train and went back to Galveston. Uncle Tot and Aunt T-Babe sent me to another doctor. It took my leg three months to heal.

Immediately I started looking for a job in Galveston. Jobs still was as scarce as they had been when I first left. So I put in for my unemployment insurance. I worked on odd jobs in hotels, working on trucks and cleaning yards. It took months before I heard from the insurance company. When the answer came by mail, the letter said the company wouldn't pay me any insurance. After getting this answer, I returned to the brickyard.

I was back on the job for a month. Then one of my fellow workers whose name was String took ill. He had been going back and forth to see his doctor. We didn't know the nature of his illness, but his doctor told him not to drink alcohol as long as he was taking shots. One day he went to visit his doctor and had a shot. The same day, he drank some alcohol and died instantly in Houston. We brought his body back to the brickyard. The fellows and I didn't know any of his relatives because he never spoke of any. We took up a collection; each one gave two dollars. We buried his body in a nearby poppy field. I spoke the last words over String's body. I said he was a happy fellow. He always laughed and never had any trouble at the brickyard. I talked about the hair grease he made out of lye that he used to slick down his hair and make it look good. He was a lot of fun, smiling and talking. We would miss old String.

I heard men was needed in Arizona to work on the railroad. I signed up for the job. Before I left, I was examined and given three days to get ready to leave for Arizona. Then I was given a pass to catch a train. I left Houston one night about ten o'clock to go to Gila Bend, Arizona.

When I arrived in Gila Bend, I was sent to a commissary in the train station to buy some food and whatever I needed to take into the camp with me. When I entered the camp, I noticed rows of tents for the workers to sleep in. One of the foremen pointed out a tent for me to sleep in. Then he left. Since it was so quiet and all the men had gone to bed, I went into my tent and went to bed.

Before dawn I could hear a loud whistle blowing in camp. I figured it was time to get up and get dressed for work. When I pulled the entrance of my tent back, I saw the men standing outside of their tents getting ready for breakfast, so I joined them. I introduced myself to some of the men. When breakfast was over, I went to work on the railroad. All the men in camp was black men, except the white timekeeper, the white foreman, and a few Chinese cooks. All the employees were given three meals a day. This was my first time eating Chinese food, and before long it came to be one of my favorite dishes.

I worked on the extra gang, which was a gang of over a hundred men working on the railroad to maintain the tracks. We had to tamp ties and raise the tracks to keep them level. They needed these extra gangs because during the war years there might be eight or nine or more trains a day that would pass along the tracks. I was a flagman. I worked way up on the tracks to signal the trains to slow down. I had my flag and the torpedoes that I used to signal the engineer. When you see a train coming, you put down a red torpedo on the track. When the train hit it and it went off, bam! he would know to slow down. Then you put another one down to slow him down more, and a third meant he should stop. I used my hands to signal to one train how far ahead the next train was.

By ten o'clock in the morning the hot sun was beaming down on my back. No houses to be seen, no people passing by, just me out in this hot desert working on the railroad. When the day was over and the men was back in camp for the night, we sat around together and talked about the things we planned to do when we got home. Sometimes we gambled a little; other times we took trips to Mexico.

The very first time I went to Mexico I had the time of my life. Although I couldn't speak Spanish, I ran into a little Mexican boy who spoke Spanish for me. This little boy was about six years old. He took me any place I thought I wanted to visit. In and out of different restaurants, theaters, and to see plenty of girls. The boy told me that if I didn't like the girls he took me to see, he would take me to see his two sisters and his mother. I didn't like the idea of going to his house, so I told him I would settle for some of the other girls he took me to see. He did all these things for one dollar.

One night I went to a room with a girl, and this little boy was still waiting when I came out. It amazed me how this boy knew his way around town. He walked down the street with me smoking a big cigar. No one seemed to pay any attention to him. When I was ready to leave Mexico, he took me to the immigration office to let the authorities know I was leaving. After my first visit to Mexico, I made several more trips and each time I went this little boy would be waiting for me to show me the town.

My job on the railroad was going alright until one morning 150 black men went out on strike. What happened was that when we knocked off from work every day, we'd put the handcar on the track to get back to camp. This particular day some water had spilled on the seat when the water kegs was loaded, and a black worker named San Antonio saw it and decided to stand up rather than sit in the water. When the white foreman saw San Antonio standing, he told him to sit down. San Antonio said no because there was water on the seat. The foreman told San Antonio again to sit down and again he refused. When we got back to the camp, the foreman told San Antonio he was fired because he had disobeyed the foreman's orders. San Antonio told him, "I wasn't gonna sit in that water no matter whose orders it was."

Now I was watching this and I was already a union man. In fact, I still had my union book. So I got to the boys and I said, "Alright, let's get together tonight and have a meeting." At the meeting I said that we shouldn't go back to work until the foreman put San Antonio back to work. All of them agreed. The next morning the foreman got out there and blew his whistle. We stood by the tracks looking at him but we wouldn't move. "Alright boys, let's go," he said. The boys had already at the meeting said, "Brown, are you going to speak?" And I said, "Oh, yeah, I'll speak." And I showed them my union book. So I told the foreman, "We ain't going until you put San Antonio back to work."

"I can't do that, he's fired now."

I said, "Well, I'm going to call the road master in Yuma." When I said that, shit, the foreman got nervous and said, "Okay, go back to work everybody. I'm gonna put San Antonio back to work." He didn't want to face that road master, the district boss, who could have fired him for not handling the situation. So we got San Antonio back on the job by taking action. I was the only union man out there, but I led the struggle. It was a victory for us.

After this experience was over, I realized that unity with other employees was what made the foreman act. If all employees united together on jobs, there would be less trouble and less firings would come from the employer.

When I came to work on the railroad, I left my sweetheart, Ruth, back in Houston. I had met Ruth through Aunt Bernice. She used to visit Aunt Bernice, who knew Ruth's mama. Bernice invited Ruth there one time when I was visiting and that's how I met her.

As time passed while I was in Arizona, I never heard from Ruth or even got a letter. So I began to worry about her and wanted to see her. I made up my mind I would go back to Houston and try to find Ruth. So I told the foreman I wanted a pass to go home. He gave me a pass and I left Tucson and went back to Houston. When I arrived in Houston I went directly to the house she was living in when I left, but the people living in the house told me she didn't live there any more. Weeks passed. I went everywhere I thought she'd be, with no luck. I never found Ruth. Lonesome and heartbroken, I left Houston and went back to Galveston.

I didn't stay in Galveston very long with the work situation being the same as when I left. Men was still being sent to work on the railroad. When I went to the train station, I sat down on a bench and my mind started wandering concerning what I should do next. I only had one nickel in my pocket. After I sat awhile, I got up from the bench and went and asked the ticket agent if they needed a man on the section gang. The ticket agent looked on a list and asked if I wanted the job. I told him, "Yes, I want the job." After the ticket agent signed me up for the job, he gave me a pass on the train and a letter to get some food from the commissary. I bought a loaf of bread, some cans of beans, a can of wieners, mackerel, and packs of cookies.

I was on my way to Barstow, California, a small town not too far from Los Angeles. As I sat in this small train station waiting for the train to arrive,

I noticed I was sitting next to an old man and his wife. They asked me if I was hungry. I told them I wasn't hungry; I had some food. But they insisted on giving me a slice of watermelon, which I accepted. By this time the train pulled in to the station. Sometime late that night I arrived in Barstow. I stayed in the station all night. The next morning I walked from the little town to the section houses. I gave the foreman my work slip and started to work on the section gang that Monday morning.

A section gang is a group of about six men who maintain a certain section of track. Different section gangs took care of different sections of track. On my section gang we had two brothers and some Spanish guys. The Spanish guys would take me to Mexico every night with long stories about Mexico when we got off work. The two black guys was married. They told me all about Los Angeles and encouraged me to go there. The guys and their wives used to visit Los Angeles frequently on railroad passes. Sometimes they would bring a newspaper back. I was wondering how come they didn't stay in Los Angeles. They was telling me how good it was but here they was on the section gang. Maybe they wanted to get rid of me, I didn't know. Anyway, it got me to thinking about going to Los Angeles.

CHAPTER THREE

Working in Los Angeles

As time passed, Los Angeles kept coming more and more to mind. After working on the railroad job for about three months, I left one morning after being paid. I arrived in Los Angeles at four o'clock that evening. I think this was in the early 1940s. When the train pulled into the station, I was astonished to see how large and beautiful the station looked. I wandered around the station for a while and then I saw a black man standing in the station. I went and asked him if he could tell me where the black people's section of town was. I always liked to be around my people. The man said, "Central Avenue. Catch the Central Avenue streetcar. When you see a crowd of black people, that is Central Avenue!"

In all my excitement in this crowded city, I caught another streetcar but I transferred to the Central car. I stayed on the streetcar until I came to lots of black people on the street. I got off the streetcar at Twelfth and Central Avenue.

A lady was sitting at a table and registering people to vote. I thought she ought to be able to give me some information, so I walked up to her and asked if she knew where I could find a hotel that was renting rooms at a reasonable rate. The lady said, "I have a friend, Mrs. Maude Williams, who is renting rooms." Then the lady said, "I'll give you a note to take to Mrs. Williams, 'cause she's a very good friend of mine." As it happened, the lady at the table was named Mrs. Brown. I have run up on a lot of Browns. So I took the note and went to 1217 South Central Avenue, which was the address. I went to the hotel and gave the note to the lady who was behind the desk. This lady said,

"I know Mrs. Brown; she's a friend of mine. Yes, I have a room for rent." I asked her how much it was and she said three dollars a week. I paid for two weeks. When I paid for the room, the lady gave me a key. I went to my room, hung my clothes in the closet, and went back out onto the streets.

I walked the streets for hours, looking at different parts of Los Angeles. I was looking at different faces to see if I recognized anyone I knew. I didn't recognize anyone, so I just started talking to some fellows on the streets. I saw this one fellow wearing a pair of long-toed shoes, and I thought, "He looks like he might have some knowledge." I asked him what the job situation was. The fellow said, "If you can't find a job, the newspapers carry jobs or ask at the employment agency." He told me about the *Sentinel* newspaper, the black newspaper. The fellow and I began looking through the want ads. Finally, I picked out an employment agency located on Jefferson Avenue. He explained to me what streetcar to take to get there. I went back to my room, put the newspaper on the bed, and wrote my room number on a slip of paper. I knew I could remember where the hotel was because of the Coca Cola plant and the funeral home on Central, but I wasn't sure I'd remember what room. The room number was twelve. Then I went back to the streets to look around Los Angeles some more.

The street on Central Avenue was crowded with black people. Some was shopping, and the bars was crowded inside and out. Children was running up and down the streets. Central Avenue reminded me of some streets in the South. When I finished looking these places over, I decided to go to a movie. I hadn't eaten all day, so I stopped in a restaurant and bought two hamburgers and a Coke. I took my food and ate it in the theater. I stayed until it closed.

As I laid in bed that night, I began to wonder if the people in California would be friendly to work with and what kind of job I might find. After thinking about this for a while, I finally felt so exhausted I fell asleep.

Early the next morning, I woke up feeling rested. When I looked out the window, the weather was foggy. I realized Los Angeles would be a very foggy place to live.

One hour later, I was out on the streets. I went looking for the employment agency. The employment agency office was open on Sunday. When I entered the office, I was astonished to see a black man behind the desk. Naturally, since I had been working on farms and railroads, it was a good feeling to see a black man working behind a desk.

We talked some and I asked if he had any jobs. It turned out that he was from New Orleans too. Then he said he had a job in Corona. The fee was ten dollars. I paid the fee, and then the agent called Corona to find out what type of work they had available. When the agent finished talking on the phone, he told me, "They need a man to work in the dining room of a restaurant and wash dishes." I wanted the job 'cause in a restaurant I could get my food and have money to pay my room rent until I got myself established. He asked if I could leave that evening to live on the premises. I told the agent I could live on the premises and I would take the job.

I went back to the hotel and told Mrs. Williams about the job I had gotten in Corona. She was surprised to hear I had found a job so quickly. She said, "Some people have been living in Los Angeles for years and haven't found a job yet; but you just arrived in California two days ago and you was able to get a job!" I didn't tell her that the agent was my homeboy.

I packed my suitcase to head for Corona, about thirty miles from Los Angeles. I caught a train that evening. When I arrived at the station, I didn't know who was going to pick me up. Then a black couple drove up in a station wagon. The man asked me, "Are you Lee Brown?"

I answered him, "Yes, and are you the one who came to take me to the job?"

The man said, "Yes, I was sent by the boss to take you to Corona." He introduced himself and told me that the lady in the car was his wife and they worked on the Fuller Ranch as cooks.

When I arrived, I didn't have any idea this place was so huge. They called it a ranch but it was really a restaurant—a large house and dining room, with beautiful green grass, which looked like somebody had just finished cutting it. Tall trees were all around. A garden with different kinds of vegetables was growing behind the house. When I went into the house, I was introduced to other black employees: the maid and the waiter. After that they showed me the room where I would stay. After an hour the man and his wife took me back to the station. This happened on a Monday, which I was told was to be my day off. So I went back to Los Angeles, stayed that night, and reported to work Tuesday morning. They paid me twenty-five dollars a week, plus room and board. Besides working in the dining room and washing dishes, I had to help the cook by bringing in vegetables from the garden. Since I took my time coming back, the cook, Henry, started kidding me and calling me "Lightning," and we would laugh about that.

It was two days before I met the owner, Mr. Fuller. I never did see too much of him, but he seemed a nice fellow. The Fuller family entertained frequently. Some parties would last for days. Well-dressed people with furs and diamonds on would come and go all day long. This job was a considerable change from my other jobs.

I worked a month before I got a chance to meet any other people, besides the ones I worked with on the ranch. Mr. Fuller hired a black lady for part-time work. She was friendly from the first time I met her. When she was working on the ranch for a while, she invited me to come to her house on my day off for dinner. I accepted the invitation and went to her house and met her four daughters. I was glad to have met her family because on my days off I wouldn't have to stay on the ranch. Sometimes this lady's daughters would take me shopping. Soon I began looking forward to my days off.

Everything was going along fine on the job, or at least I thought so, until one day the waiter, Mickey, went to town with Mr. Fuller. I didn't think anything about this at the time because Mickey would go with him all the time. But this particular day they was gone all day. I don't know what Mickey said to him but when they got back to the ranch Mr. Fuller said to me, "I'm going to have to let you go. The work is slow." Which I knew was a lie 'cause the work was the same as when I first started. Then I thought maybe Mickey was jealous because the new lady Mr. Fuller had hired was friendly to me.

I didn't ask any questions. I just packed my suitcase and left. I went back to Los Angeles. I didn't waste any time but went to the employment agency. I was sent to another job at a drive-in, working as a porter and washing dishes. This job was paying twenty-five dollars per week. But I needed more money to live on, so I quit the job five months later.

I started feeling discouraged about now 'cause I was finding out a person living in California needed more money to survive than in the South. Rent, clothing, food, and so on was higher than the money the job was paying. Some jobs paid better, but those was the ones that required special skills. I was a common laborer and had to take whatever job I could.

Naturally, I was anxious to find better employment. I was able to find another job from the employment office, working on the Union Pacific dining cars. I made runs on these trains from Los Angeles to Omaha, Nebraska. I made a few runs from Los Angeles to San Diego. At first I worked as a "forty," sometimes called a fourth cook, which actually meant I was a dishwasher. But the chef, who was a brother, and I would get to talking and drinking and have a couple of nips, and he saw that I knowed about food so he said he wanted me to be a "thirty," a vegetable preparer and food server for the waiters, when they was serving breakfast, lunch, and dinner on trains. During the war the help on these trains ate better food than the paying customers.

But I decided I didn't like being a thirty. I wanted to go back to being a forty because the six waiters put all their tips in a cup, and when we got to Omaha they shared the tips with me. I wouldn't have to go to borrow from the commissary because I had some money to buy things. A thirty didn't get any tips. I tried everything, but the chef wouldn't let me go back.

Then the "big boy" used to come around; they called him the traveling chef. He was a brother. He put on white gloves and hit the pots and dishes to see if they was clean. I was kinda glad I was a thirty 'cause I didn't have to be bothered with him again. When I was a forty the chef used to warn me, the "big boy is on here now," which meant "be cautious!"

Sometimes the brothers used to leave with bacon, eggs, butter, chicken when they left the train. But something told me—maybe it was divine knowledge—something told me not to take anything. We had a guy they called Stringbean, another brother. He had taken my place washing dishes. He talked more shit than a radio! I said to myself, Oh, brother! Let me tell you what happened. Stringbean was a railroad detective. Union Pacific was losing all that food and they put Stringbean in there. But something told me to watch out for him. I was lucky. All the other brothers lost their jobs when Stringbean turned them in. I figured something was funny about him; you can tell by the way people act.

On my first run through New Orleans I thought about my mother. I thought about maybe going to New Orleans and trying to find her, but I didn't try to find her at that point.

The railroad job was alright, although the pay was only forty-five cents an hour. My problem was that I couldn't catch any air in the dining car. You couldn't raise the windows to catch some air. I needed air; I was born under the air sign, Gemini. After a while it was hard for me to breathe, since the windows was never pulled up at night when I slept on the train. So I was forced to quit this job. However, I worked six months before I left.

I soon found out Los Angeles was a weak union town; it wasn't organized. The hotels wasn't organized and the restaurants wasn't organized. Where they had unions, like the RKO Studios dining room, the union leadership was weak. Wages was paid according to what employers wanted to pay: low pay, bad working conditions, no pension plans, no sick leave, no health plan for the employees. Who was hurt the most? Black people! And plenty of black people was out of work. Now I know why families left Los Angeles—to try to find work in other cities.

One day I was standing on the streets talking to some fellows. I overheard them talking about work in Hollywood. I went to inquire about the job. It was my luck that this job was still open, working in a restaurant for forty dollars a week plus meals. Mostly black help worked in the kitchen. One black busgirl worked in the dining room. The waiters was white. My job was working in the storage room and cleaning stoves. I handled all the keys to the storage room and helped the head waitress close the restaurant at night.

Working in this restaurant, the Carolina Pine on Melrose Avenue, I found out how prejudiced some white people in California was toward black people. One evening, I'll never forget it, a party of five white people and one black sister came into the restaurant together and sat down at a table. All of them ordered dinner. The white waitress served soup to everybody, except the sister, whose soup wasn't served until after the white people had finished the main course.

The busgirl came into the kitchen and told us what had happened. All the black employees got angry. I got to talking, we got to talking, and talked to the chef and the sous-chef. They was all black people from the South too. I was surprised to see white people still prejudiced in California. I thought I had left all that hate behind in the South. I suggested to the black employees that they come to work one hour early to have a little meeting to discuss what we was going to do. I had a little authority 'cause I was carrying the keys to the storage room.

The regular time to be at work was eleven o'clock. The next morning all the black employees came to work at ten o'clock. We decided that the two cooks and myself should go talk to the owner, Mr. Davis. We told the owner what had happened. He called in the waitress and she went to crying and all that bullshit, talking about she was sorry. Hell, she was prejudiced, that what she was! She should have served all the soup together. She didn't want to serve the black sister. We wanted her fired. We said if she wasn't fired, the other help wouldn't come to work the next morning. She begged and said she was sorry. Mr. Davis told her it was wrong. He told her that she had to serve black people at all times in his place of business. She said she was sorry and that it would never happen again.

All the black employees were standing outside the restaurant waiting until the owner and the rest of us came out to explain what had happened and what the owner intended to do. Mr. Davis said, "This refusal to serve black people will never happen anymore, and I would like all of the employees to come in and go back to work." The black employees talked this over and decided to return to work. The waitress acted much better.

About this time I got called up for the draft. I went before the board and I got classified as 4-F 'cause I couldn't hear. But that was a fake. When I got to the end of the line, the doctor dropped a silver dollar behind me. I heard it but I didn't flinch. I didn't want to go in. Shit, no! I ain't had nothing to fight for. Give me something to fight for. Freedom! I had a little sense. You can overestimate me but don't underestimate me! We wasn't getting freedom, we wasn't getting decent jobs. There was more discrimination there in Los Angeles than there was in New Orleans. I saw some black soldiers and a lot of sailors being shipped down to Long Beach. They came to the Dunbar and the Club Alabam' and the Last Word, bars in the black community.

During World War II, about 1943, there was a lot of racial tension against both blacks and Mexicans in Los Angeles. One time a riot started in Los Angeles between white sailors and Mexicans. During that time there was a men's fashion called the zoot suit, with sharp trousers, a long chain, a long coat, and a hat with a long feather. A lot of Mexicans and some blacks wore zoot suits. A white sailor claimed that a Mexican man wearing a zoot suit had raped his wife. Then the white sailors started attacking every Mexican they came across. The Mexicans started organizing and started fighting back. Then the police started helping the white sailors fight the Mexicans. The white sailors said they were going to come down to Central Avenue and kill all the niggers, and cut all the zoot suits off them.

Then the black zoot suits started helping the Mexicans fight. I heard that the black leaders called on the Mexican government to try to stop the riot. Then the white sailors attacked a girl who was in the ticket box office at the theater on Central Avenue. The black leaders warned the white sailors that if they came past the Lincoln Theater, then black people was going to defend themselves. If the riot didn't stop, they would open fire. No one got killed during the riot.

I think this riot was started to stir up hate and so the police could attack the Mexicans and the blacks. I got caught in the riot while I was trying to come home. The streetcars had stopped running and I was walking down the street. I ended up running down the streets with the black and Mexican zoot suits. The riot lasted four or five days.

Later on, I worked for Frederick Cold Storage loading and unloading boxcars. On this job, I worked with other men loading up boxcars with different kinds of food to be sent overseas for the soldiers. We would send powdered eggs, barrels of whiskey, whatever. But soldiers I talked with said, "We haven't ever seen any whiskey. The whiskey would be for the top brass."

I used to take a hammer and bust them barrels so we could get that good whiskey. The superintendent would look the other way and say, "I don't see nothing." One day the superintendent got so drunk that he started crawling on his knees.

This job went along fine for three months, until one day a black foreman picked up a stick to hit me. I think he must've told me something to do and he didn't figure I was moving fast enough, or something. He was hard and he wanted to be tough. A bad attitude. I overpowered the foreman and took the stick away from him. This black foreman was so proud of his authority over other black workers that his job went to his head. He wouldn't ask his fellow workers on the job, in an intelligent way, to do things, but he demanded things. I hadn't ever had to fight anyone on the job before but knew how to defend myself.

One thing I haven't ever approved of was fighting on the job where I worked. It doesn't make any sense to me. Some blacks with authority, I have seen, treat other blacks on the job worse than any other race. When blacks work on jobs with a little authority over other blacks, they don't have to prove to the bosses that they are not prejudiced. Just treat everyone the same, regardless of race, color, creed! I have seen blacks on jobs lying, harassing, trying to discredit other blacks to get them fired. Don't they know they can also be fired? Lots of black workers let blacks with authority on jobs get away with a lot of mistreatment, because they are black.

After the fight I knew suddenly that this black foreman couldn't be trusted when my back was turned. I called the police to teach him a lesson. The police wanted to take the foreman to jail, but I didn't want them to take him to jail. I told the police there was already too many black people in jails. I only called the police to have them tell the foreman to leave me alone on the job. No job is worth fighting over. When I said this to the police, they didn't make any arrest. The police talked with the foreman and left.

Working in and out of the cold storage kept me with a constant cold, so I soon quit. Next I worked for Triangle Candy Factory as a combination janitor and watchman, which wasn't a bad job. One thing, for sure, no violence ever happened! I even carried a gun, which they gave me as part of the watchman job.

When I had worked for around three months, one evening on my way home from work, I met two teenage girls walking down the street selling tickets. One of the girls came up and asked me if I would buy a ticket for the church. Quite naturally I wasn't going to turn her down. I told the girl I would buy a ticket if she let me sit beside her in church. She told me her name was Thelma Brown and, yes, she would let me sit beside her in church. I bought two tickets. Thelma said she was seventeen years old. To me she looked much younger and smaller for her age. We sat next to each other in church that night. In church I met Thelma's grandmother, and Thelma invited me to her home. Thelma lived with her mother and grandmother.

After that night, we started seeing each other regularly. We went to movies and out to dinner on my days off. Soon she started coming to my room at night and would stay until three or four o'clock in the morning. We said we was going to the show, so Thelma's mother thought she was in the movies, since the movies stayed open all night.

One evening we was walking down Central Avenue. A policeman called me aside and asked me to buy some tickets for the police benefit. Thelma looked so young for her age, I thought at first the police was going to question me about her age. Since it was just about the tickets, I bought two tickets.

Thelma's mother and grandmother treated me as one of the family. Sometimes I stayed all night at their house. I slept in the same bed with Thelma and her grandmother. I slept on the outside. Wasn't nothing funny happening there. They liked me, the grandmother and the mother both, and they wanted me to marry Thelma. They thought I was a good man. I treated them with respect. But I wasn't in no marrying mood then.

Every evening I would bring candy home for Thelma. Our romance was doing fine until her grandmother started asking questions about our sex together. I was twenty-two at the time. Thelma and I did have sex but kept it to ourselves because she wasn't of age.

Soon we stopped seeing each other. I don't remember what happened, just a parting of the ways. Maybe it was 'cause they was worried about marriage. The grandmother and the mother wanted us to get married; maybe that was the reason. I saw Thelma on the streets several times after we parted. We spoke to each other in a friendly way.

I had a lot of girlfriends at this time. I liked them, I respected them, but I wasn't wanting to get married. Some of them had husbands in the army or on ships. I never did see the husbands. The women told me that when the husband came back we couldn't be together no more. That's the way it was then.

I met a man named Sidney and his wife, Edna. They lived at the hotel at 1217 South Central. We became good friends. His wife worked in Los

Angeles in a restaurant. Sidney worked in Hollywood. We all drank together on our days off.

Unbeknownst to his wife, Sidney also had a girlfriend named Bertha. One night Sidney was driving around town in his car. His wife was sitting in the front seat with him and his girlfriend, Bertha, was sitting in the backseat with me. Sidney had Bertha sit with me so that his wife would think she was my girlfriend. We stopped off at some friends' house for a few drinks. Now Bertha was a nice-looking woman. I didn't want to just let that get by. And Sidney was already married. On our way back to the hotel, I asked Bertha if she would come up to my room. When she agreed, Sidney didn't want to let us out of the car. He got mad but couldn't say anything because his wife was in the car. I had him then, brother, I had him between the devil and the deep blue sea. When we got out of the car, Bertha came to my room and stayed.

The next morning Sidney had got over his anger. He didn't know what we did. I just told him Bertha and I went to my room and had a couple of drinks. We had a great laugh about the whole thing and remained good friends. That's the way it was then. I was young and I liked good-looking women.

For a time I went to work in the cafeteria at the RKO Studio in Hollywood. This was where all the actors ate. I had a combination job—dishwasher and busboy. After I was working on this job for a while I was told it was a union job. A white union man came and told me, "this is a union job," and he brought a white union man to replace me. Now I was in a union but not that union. If I had been told before this happened, I would have joined the union. Well, it became clear to me that it wasn't just a union job—it was another one of those prejudiced jobs! They had it hooked up; they didn't want a black man in that job. I was the only black in the cafeteria. I guess they figured that if they let one in, others might come. It made me realize that some union reps could be prejudiced. They don't want black folks to have a chance. They block you, and that gives the boss and the owner more power to keep the workers divided. It weakens the unions and the bosses can make inroads. You get bad contracts when they keep the black and white or any other workers fighting each other.

In less than a week I was working for Hills Brothers Chemical Company on a machine for packing and tying bags. This was when I joined the Youth Movement of the NAACP—and after a while I even got the president and superintendent of the company to join the NAACP.

I was already in the NAACP from my time in Texas. I found out that they was having meetings at the YMCA on 28th and Central, so I decided to go to join in the struggle. I met a lady named Mrs. Charlotta Bass who was the editor of the *California Eagle* newspaper and the director of the Youth Movement of the NAACP. The Youth NAACP had two hundred members, including some actors and actresses. I learned a lot about movies. Sometimes we went to the Lincoln Theater to see stage shows and movies. On Wednesdays they would let the Youth NAACP members in free.

One night we met at the YMCA with actors and actresses to discuss getting better acting parts for black people in movies. Some black actors and actresses came that night and told the NAACP that they wouldn't play any more Uncle Tom parts in the movies. Lena Horne and Hattie McDaniel couldn't come that night but sent a telegram. Uncle Tom parts for black actors and actresses was encouraged by film producers in Hollywood. This was one reason black actors and actresses wasn't able to show how truly great or excellent they were in their performances. The great talent they had to offer to the public was denied; Uncle Tom parts was the only ones they could get. This is why the Youth NAACP had to step in to fight for better parts in movies and on stage for blacks. Mantan Moreland and Willie Best was well-known for playing these Uncle Tom parts in movies.

I got a chance to meet quite a few movie stars—Louise Beavers, Ruby Dandridge, Dorothy's mother, Darby Jones, Benny Carter, and Peterson. Mantan Moreland and Willie Best often came to the YMCA and talked about parts that was given to them in pictures. Once they got in an argument, in a friendly way, about whose eyes was the biggest, which one could roll their eyes the best, and who ran the fastest in films. Everyone in the YMCA would start laughing at the way they would act. Darby Jones was progressive. He'd stand up for better parts.

One night I ran into Ruby Dandridge at the Club Alabam'. I heard her laughing. I said, "Hell, that's Ruby." She was the loudest thing in there. I went over and talked to her. Wyoming Harris used to sing at the Club Alabam'. "The King of the Blues" he called himself.

Hollywood was exciting and fascinating, even more so to me because I got acquainted with some of the stars, and I actually took parts in a couple of mob scenes in pictures. Some films called for extras to play in different scenes. When this was available, I usually applied for the parts. Every day I looked on a board to find out if extras was needed.

Old Man Gray was a member of the Screen Actors Guild. He was a tall fellow with gray hair. This was one reason he got to act in a lot of films. He was the one who would hire you and send you out to get jobs as extras in mob scenes, which is what they called scenes that had a lot of extras. They wouldn't use your name in the credits. You might be standing up, sitting down, whatever. They paid $9.50 and a meal a day, which was pretty good. You might get one day, two days.

I actually got extra parts in two pictures: *I Walked with a Zombie,* with Darby Jones, and *My Heart Is in Dixie,* with Clarence Muse. I was in a jungle scene in one and picking cotton in the other.

Old Man Gray told me where to buy clothes on credit. With new clothing and a few dollars in my pocket, I started acting the part of a movie star. I wore only pointed-toe shoes, triple A's. I would often be seen at the Dunbar Hotel, drinking only Tom Collinses. My hair stayed conked back; I only let women barbers fix my hair. I was as sharp as Dick was when his daddy died!

At Ella's Cafe on Central the people gave me a name, Kokomo, because of a jungle scene I got an extra part in. They'd say, "Here comes Kokomo." But this later got to be a problem. I had a girlfriend then named Mildred that I had met on the streetcar. She was married but her husband was in the service. One night I took Mildred to the theater to see *My Heart Is in Dixie.* When she saw me picking cotton, Mildred got real angry with me because she was embarrassed by the movie. She told me, "You should be ashamed to play in scenes that are so degrading to black people because you fight in the NAACP for better parts for black actors." When Mildred said this, I really felt ashamed and discouraged with myself. I thought I was a helluva actor, but I wasn't nothing but a fool.

I stopped right then and didn't try to get any more parts. A director said I could act in a good religious scene, but I didn't try to get the part.

One Saturday night I went to a theater and got a chance to see the heavy-weight champion of the world, Joe Louis. He came into the theater with some friends of his. Joe Louis was dressed in his army uniform. I didn't get a chance to meet him, but I was glad to see him. I was sitting five seats from him in the same row. The movie that was playing was *One Dark Night.* Mantan Moreland and Pigmeat Markham and a few more actors was also there.

Another night I went to a rally at the Shriners Temple in Los Angeles. Darby Jones gave me the tickets. I saw Lena Horne, Edward G. Robinson, Pigmeat Markham, Monty Holly, and many more. Paul Robeson was the guest speaker. This was my first time hearing this proud, brilliant man—foremost in the struggle for peoples' rights. He spoke on freedom for our black people here in America. He said, "Black actors and actresses should quit playing Uncle Tom parts in movies. All black people should fight for better schools, better education, and better jobs." His voice was deep and I felt uplifted. I liked the way he talked. I said to myself, "That's the man!" But I never would've thought that years later I'd get a chance to talk to him and be his bodyguard. Paul Robeson's speech kept my heart and soul together, and it made me want to dedicate my life to the struggle for my people.

They was taking up donations that night and I gave the woman my last five dollars in the basket. I told the woman, just take a dollar out the five. Shit, she went to stepping on and I was hollering, "Hey, sister. Hold it! Hold it!" I put on a bigger act than they had up on the stage. People around me went to laughing. Hell, I wanted to keep the four to get me some beer later on!

On 12th and Central Avenue I had met Old Man Johnson. He worked with the choir in Hollywood. He used to work with Bing Crosby singing in the choir. They had a little newsstand at the corner and we used to meet there and talk. He talked about the conditions black people was facing. It hit me that it seemed like a lot of the black people I met was talking about the hard struggle black people was fighting against here in America.

So I started buying books of all kinds. I went to different kinds of book-stores. I bought *The Master Keys of King Solomon* and other books, secondhand books. *The Master Keys* taught how to take care of yourself, how to have faith and courage, and face reality. How to meet people and to be cautious at all times. It told about the three Grand Masters and the 3,600 Master Masons. I didn't know exactly what I was looking for, but I had it in mind that I could look at it and see what I wanted. I studied these books and started educating myself on different subjects, important persons, places, and things. I read books on labor, some political books, some black history, religious books. I was just starting. I wouldn't get deep into books until I went back South.

One day at the hotel I met a schoolteacher who saw how interested I was in learning. Her name was Catherine. She started coming to my room to help me to improve my reading. My grandfather was my first teacher, and I remembered an old white professor I met in Texas had told me, "If you learn how to read you can educate yourself." That's what she was helping me to do. She'd give me a book to read, tell me to study it, and when she came back she'd want me read it to her. Her husband worked in the post office. One thing about this man, he didn't mind his wife coming to teach me classes. Sometimes he used to stop by too, on his way to work. Mrs. Williams, who ran the hotel, was his aunt.

One morning I went to the bus stop to catch the bus for work. A crowd of people was standing on the streets flagging rides trying to get to work. It was a bus strike. I had no idea how to get to work. I had only learned one way to work. I called the boss on the phone and told him there was a bus strike, and asked if he could get me a ride to work. He gave me the directions to the Red car, which was running a short distance from the hotel where I lived. I walked seven blocks and caught the Red car and arrived at work two hours late. The other workers came to work in cars; some walked. The Hollywood Boulevard car was on strike for one week.

They won the strike. I saw again that if people would stick together they could win. I wasn't so concerned about my inconvenience; I was glad to see them on strike. When they won, they made me feel a whole lot better and gave me strength. I knowed that a part of me was out there struggling too.

I was standing on the sidewalk in front of a bar one evening when a man came out intoxicated. He wanted to fight whoever came close to him. He pulled off his shirt and drew the attention of a crowd of people who was passing by. Suddenly a police patrol car pulled up and stopped. The policemen jumped out of the car and grabbed both arms of the man. After putting handcuffs on the man, the police roughed him up. His shirt was off and the police wouldn't let him put his shirt back on. I went and asked the police to let the man put on his shirt. To me what the police was doing was wrong. I say that was harassing and police brutality, roughing up the man. At least let him put on his shirt.

He told me to mind my business and I said it *was* my business. To my surprise I was arrested, put in the patrol car, and taken off to Newton Station and charged with "interfering with police officers." I was put in this huge jail. The officer led me to a cell and closed the door. I sat on a cot uncertain what would happen in court the next day. I thought to myself, this is my first time being in jail or in any trouble with the law and I shouldn't have been put in jail. I didn't make a phone call that day because I didn't know anyone to call.

The next morning a jail officer took me to the court room. I sat restless, waiting for my name to be called to appear before the judge. Finally one hour later, I stood before the judge with no attorney to defend my case, except myself. The two officers who did the arresting didn't appear in court. However, the judge carried on with the case. I explained to the judge that this was my first time in trouble with the law and the way those policemen was treating that man, it was plain police brutality, happening on the streets. I asked the judge for a suspended sentence. Since the judge didn't have much of a case, with no officers appearing in court to testify against me, the judge then gave me six months' suspended sentence with a lecture about how this interfering could have incited a riot. The judge said, "If you ever see something like you saw happen on the street again, you wait until you get to court and report it to the judge." When the judge got through talking, I started back toward the cell, but the judge called out, "The case is closed; you can leave."

When I was leaving the courthouse, two black detectives driving down Central Avenue offered me a ride, which I accepted. We got to talking and it turned out they were in the NAACP too. They said it wasn't right for the police to mistreat the brother but I should've waited until we got to court to say something. They said sometime you should keep your mouth shut and wait for the proper time. But I was talking about speaking up, about struggle, and they wasn't saying "amen" to that!

When the detectives reached the hotel where I lived and stopped the car, I got out of the car and thanked them for the lift. Our conversation was very interesting. This is when I really started thinking about the poor conditions under which black people are forced to live in this country, especially prejudice and police brutality. The conversation also brought to mind about my grandfather who died because hospitals and medical help for black people wasn't close.

I went to work at the Armour Packing Company, loading and unloading meat on trucks. Meal tickets was given to all employees to eat in the cafeteria. I got to talking with a Spanish fellow who was working there and he told me about the union. I told him I'm a union man; I want to join it. He told me that union members would also get a raise that was coming up. This was Local 12 of the packinghouse workers union.

The Armour Packing Company paid a dollar five cents an hour—the highest wages I received from any of my jobs—and it made me realize the importance of being a member of the union. I felt more independent with sufficient income to live on.

Soon I moved off Central Avenue and got a room, with the use of the kitchen, at Rev. Victor's home. Rev. Victor was a quiet person. In fact, the neighborhood was quiet. Living in this pleasant environment, I got a chance to study without being disturbed.

One evening, a letter came from Aunt Betsy. The letter came from Louisiana. Before I opened the letter, I wondered how Aunt Betsy got my address and what purpose she had in contacting me after all these years. Aunt Betsy was ill and wanted me to come to Louisiana to see her. I thought she probably wanted to talk to me about my grandfather's land. But I still felt the same about her, and I didn't go back. I never heard from her again.

With the different kinds of books I had collected, my room started to look like a library. The more I studied, the more knowledge and information I received from these books about what was really happening in this country and around the world. I was especially interested in the long struggles, suffering, bloodshed, beatings, and jailings of black people here and around the world, and what black people are still enduring at this present time. I made a promise to myself to continue helping my people, to the best of my ability.

It wasn't long before I began thinking about New Orleans, the city where I was born. Maybe it was the letter from Aunt Betsy that got me thinking. I decided to try to find my mother and my half sister and half brother who was supposed to have been living in New Orleans. I left Los Angeles early one morning. I still had my railroad card, which I flashed to get on the train.

When I arrived, after riding three days, I knocked on the door. My father's cousin Doretha answered the door. We called her "Sugar Duck." I told her my name. Sugar Duck embraced and kissed me with happiness and said she thought I was dead because she never heard a word about me since I was a child. Sugar Duck and I had a long conversation about how I had been living through the years. She asked why I came to New Orleans. I told Sugar Duck I came looking for my mother and other relatives on my mother's side of the family. She explained that at one time she knew where my mother lived, but since that was a long time ago, she might have moved. She said she would help me look for my mother.

We went to the Louisiana Insurance Company to inquire. The insurance company representative said that they would try to locate mother and would notify me if I left my address. My visit in New Orleans was brief. Then I returned to Los Angeles.

In three weeks time the insurance representative notified me. They had located my mother and gave me her phone number and address in New Orleans. I hesitated for several days before calling. After all, we hadn't seen one another since I was five years old. When I finally phoned, mother's voice sounded soft and warm. I told mother I was her son, Lee Brown. She sounded so happy and rejoiced to hear my voice. We talked about my past and my future. Mother explained that she was ill and wanted to see me. I told Mother I would come to visit her and meet some of my relatives on her side of the family because I only knew relatives on my father's side. When our conversation was over, I felt a feeling of love and respect. In the meantime, uncertain about when I could leave for New Orleans, I continued working and attending the NAACP meetings. As weeks passed my mind stayed on my mother. Not really sure how ill she was, I decided to start preparing to leave for New Orleans. Before I left my job, I told the superintendent I was going to visit my mother because she was ill and I hadn't seen her since I was five years old. I didn't know how long I would be gone. The superintendent said that if I ever came back to Los Angeles and wanted to work, a job would be waiting. I had my union membership set up to be transferred from Local 12 to any union in New Orleans, when the time came for me to look for work. I had one sad task left to do: to be separated from my books! These books was valuable to me and important, but I sold my books to used book stores and left Los Angeles.

Black Workers
on the New Orleans
Waterfront

ROBERT L. ALLEN

Early History

Even before the Civil War, black workers had a significant presence on the docks of New Orleans. Slaves were often hired out by their masters as stevedores, and free blacks also worked on the waterfront. Many white immigrants, especially Irish peasants fleeing the potato famine, worked on the docks as well. Race relations on the waterfront were sometimes tense as men competed for jobs and employers sought to use black workers to break strikes by whites. But working-class solidarity emerged, albeit fitfully, as unions struggled to gain a foothold in the Reconstruction period. In 1865 black and white levee workers struck together for higher wages, although blacks were excluded from membership in many New Orleans trade unions at the time. The New Orleans *Tribune*, the first daily black newspaper in the United States, supported the levee workers' joint action. During a subsequent strike by white bricklayers during which black bricklayers, who were excluded from the union, continued to work, the *Tribune* criticized the racial exclusivity of the white union, urging that it admit black workers to membership to promote labor solidarity. "As peers, they may all come to an understanding and act in common," the *Tribune* wrote. The white union refused to open its ranks and lost the strike.

Excluded from white unions, black workers acted independently and they formed their own labor organizations. In May 1867, 500 black longshoremen went on strike when contractors refused to pay them the agreed-upon wages.

Another strike by black dockworkers occurred in 1872. By 1880 black steve-dores in New Orleans had organized four longshoremen's unions, the largest of which had 450 members. In addition to their watchfulness over wages and working conditions, the black unions established funds to help the sick and bury the dead, as well as sometimes set up small businesses, and provided community social activities.

The heyday of the Knights of Labor in the South in the 1880s brought a pe-riod of interracial labor solidarity in New Orleans. The Knights recognized the dangers posed by racial disunity and they officially welcomed all workers into the fold. Cooperation between black and white trade unionists expanded. The newly formed American Federation of Labor, although espousing segregated locals, at least advocated that black workers should be organized.

As early as 1875 black and white dockworkers in New Orleans agreed to share the work and to demand equal wages. Initially white workers saw this as a way to prevent the use of blacks by employers as strikebreakers. In 1886 this agreement was expanded to also require *equal* sharing of waterfront work. It became known as the "half-and-half" agreement and would become the gov-erning principle, not without setbacks, of work and labor relations on the docks. Ultimately, the agreement was expanded to require joint negotiating teams (half black, half white), joint demands, racial alternation of speakers at meetings, and in general interracial agreement on any issue affecting dock-workers. Half-and-half was anathema to employers and city officials, who saw it as undermining employer control over work and New Orleans's competi-tiveness with other ports.

In October 1892 New Orleans workers launched a massive general strike. Three unions, including an all-black teamsters' union, formed a Triple Al-liance to demand a ten-hour workday, higher wages and overtime pay, and the closed union shop. Employers said they would negotiate but only with the white unions. Despite press attempts to foment racial dissension, the Triple Al-liance unions refused to be divided and instead walked out. By early Novem-ber the strike had gained the support of other unions. Led by a Committee of Five that included black longshoreman James E. Porter, some 30,000 workers were on strike. The city was in crisis. As employers prepared to bring in thou-sands of strikebreakers from other areas, the governor banned street gatherings and declared that he would send in the militia. After three days the strike was called off and a settlement was reached granting the ten-hour day, higher wages, and overtime pay, but not the closed shop. Although some observers accused the strike leaders of retreating in the face of employer and government threats, others viewed the general strike as a high point of black–white labor solidarity in New Orleans.

On the waterfront the depression of 1893 undermined interracial solidarity as wages plummeted and dockworkers fought—several black workers were killed—over distribution of available jobs.

By 1902 the International Longshoremen's Association (ILA), which was organized in 1894, had gained a major place among waterfront unions in New Orleans. The ILA was one of the few AFL affiliates that admitted black workers, although to separate locals, and elected blacks to leadership positions. Joint meetings were held and James Porter served as a national vice president. The ILA maintained the half-and-half policy in New Orleans and other southern ports, but the ILA's practice of racial segregation fueled resentment among many black dockworkers. Years later in 1937, the ILA would be challenged by a radical new union, Local 207 of the International Longshore and Warehouse Union, under the leadership of Andrew Steve Nelson and Lee Brown.

With the South increasingly in the grip of the system of Jim Crow segregation as the new century unfolded, employers in New Orleans were determined to undermine the interracial solidarity that was the basis of the power of the waterfront unions. The economy of New Orleans depended heavily on shipping cotton through the port. Some thirty-six waterfront unions representing 11,000 dockworkers had organized the Dock and Cotton Council to coordinate actions of the unions. The council was composed of seventy-two representatives—thirty-six black and thirty-six white—drawn from constituent unions on the principle of half-and-half. The officers of the council were divided equally between white and black, and each year the offices were rotated to ensure that each office was filled by alternating black and white incumbents.

Seizing their opportunity, employers refused to renew a key union contract and locked out workers in the fall of 1907. The employers had hoped to split the unions, but the lockout precipitated a general strike on the waterfront. The strike severely crippled the operation of the port for nearly three weeks. Finally the employers capitulated and agreed to negotiate, but the business leaders declared that they would never negotiate with black representatives. In accordance with the principle of half-and-half, however, the strikers selected two white and two black delegates to represent them. The employers and the white press were outraged. Invoking white supremacist ideology, they accused black unionists of using the strike to promote social equality. The mayor of New Orleans hastened to a meeting of the Dock and Cotton Council to urge reconsideration, but the workers held firm. A black unionist noted that white employers had negotiated with black representatives in the past; what was the problem now? In the end the employers were compelled to choose representatives who, willingly or not, would meet with an interracial union negotiating team. The general levee strike of 1907 was a great victory for black and white waterfront workers, and a high-water mark of the tide of dock unionism in New Orleans.

The years that followed were marked by occasional small victories, but the strength of the waterfront unions slowly diminished until the Great

Depression and the CIO era. This process was related to other changes that were occurring in New Orleans and the larger society. The continued entrenchment of segregation worsened conditions for black people in New Orleans and led to increasing marginalization. At the same time more blacks were seeking work on the docks during a period when whites were moving to other jobs. At the turn of the century black and white workers had about equal numbers on the waterfront, but by the early 1920s black dockworkers far outnumbered white. In this context the half-and-half division of jobs worked to the disadvantage of a growing black labor force and weakened interracial cooperation. Moreover, even with a black majority workforce, black unions had never achieved parity with regard to foremen's jobs. In addition, the emergence of new technologies in shipbuilding and cotton compressing eliminated skilled job categories and entire unions, such as the screwmen (skilled cotton stowers), who had been at the forefront of important union struggles, including the 1907 general levee strike. By the end of World War I most of the remaining dock locals, black and white, were affiliated with the ILA. Finally, intervention by government agencies, especially during and after World War I, sought to promote cooperation between labor and management on the waterfront and reduce labor strife in the interest of national security. In practice this weakened unions and fostered conservative labor politics.

These factors combined in September 1923 to mortally wound unionism on the New Orleans waterfront. When contracts for the longshoremen and screwmen expired, their locals demanded increased pay and the hiring of additional workers. Although black dock locals and some whites opposed it, a strike was called. The employers brought in strikebreakers and moved to crush the screwmen's union. When violence broke out between strikers and scabs on the docks, the employers secured an unprecedented federal court injunction barring strikers from the docks. The employers moved to make the strikebreakers permanent workers and to impose an open shop on the docks. In October the U.S. Shipping Board, a wartime government agency that operated some port facilities, accepted the strikers' demands at its piers, but the private employers continued to refuse a settlement, leaving the strikers with no option but to contract with the Shipping Board, which controlled only 30 percent of port commerce. Thus 5,000 union workers found themselves excluded from most waterfront jobs. The subsequent decision of the Shipping Board to lease its operations to private employers further sealed the fate of militant unionism. The employers announced that they did not oppose the right to organize. "What we objected to was the arbitrary, intolerable aggressions of the leaders of the unions that walked out," the employers gloatingly proclaimed. "We do not mind dealing with any sort of association reasonably managed."

This left company unions and a "reasonably managed" International Longshoremen's Association as the main vessels for union activism on the waterfront until 1937. (A small IWW-organized union, the Marine Transport Workers Industrial Union, continued to carry the banner of racial solidarity and led a strike by several hundred black and white New Orleans dockworkers in 1930.)

History of Local 207

The hardships of the Great Depression inspired a new wave of union organizing spearheaded by militant industrial unions in the AFL. The radical unionists advocated organization of all workers in the same industries—black and white—into the same unions; they opposed the AFL concept of racially segregated locals. The radicals were opposed by the craft union leaders of the AFL, and in 1937 the industrial unions were expelled from the AFL. They formed the Congress of Industrial Organizations (CIO). The CIO launched a national organizing drive that took one of its unions, the International Longshore and Warehouse Union (ILWU), into New Orleans to challenge the ILA as the bargaining agent for dockworkers. Just a short time earlier, ILA members on the Pacific Coast had broken away from the ILA and formed the ILWU under the leadership of Harry Bridges, an Australian-born political radical who was a militant waterfront leader at the time of the great strike in San Francisco in 1934.

The situation in New Orleans, the nation's second largest port, seemed ripe for a new organizing drive. According to historian David Lee Wells (in a master's thesis entitled "The ILWU in New Orleans: CIO Radicalism in the Crescent City, 1937–1957," on which my account of the history of Local 207 is largely based),

> Longshoremen in the Crescent City were organized by the ILA into segregated locals, both descendants of the company unions formed by the New Orleans Steamship Association [employers] during the open shop days of the 1920s. Rank and file dockworkers resented the "shape-up" hiring system [a discriminatory and corrupt system by which workers were selected each day by employers for work on the docks] endorsed by the ILA, which also required its members to pay five percent of their weekly wages back into the union. Of the 10,000 or so warehousemen in New Orleans, few belonged to any union at all and none were protected by collective bargaining agreements. Longshoremen at that time earned wages of 75 cents per hour; warehousemen rarely earned more than 35 cents. The great majority of these workers were unskilled, uneducated blacks, toiling long hours under the poorest conditions. Stricken by a succession of misfortunes—first, company unionism followed by racial strife, strike-breaking, corruption and double-dealing by AFL officials—many New Orleans workers secretly longed for a new Moses to lead them out of the bondage of the depression-ravaged South.

The struggle between the ILWU and ILA in New Orleans was bitter. The ILWU sent its best organizer, Bob Robertson, a veteran of the San Francisco struggles. Willie Dorsey, a black longshoreman and former Baptist preacher with twenty years' experience on the riverfront in New Orleans as a member of the ILA, was recruited as an organizer. Through 1937 and into 1938 Robertson, Dorsey, and other organizers signed up enough workers to petition the National Labor Relations Board for a representation election, which was scheduled for October. Harry Bridges came to New Orleans in April and spoke to a mostly black gathering of several thousand maritime workers. Bridges, who was already being hounded by the government as a "red," and other ILWU organizers stressed the theme of interracial unity and union democracy. They denounced the corrupt shape-up system and proposed replacing it with a union hiring hall.

The AFL, along with the police and local and state officials, went all-out to stop the CIO/ILWU drive. Violent clashes between AFL and CIO supporters became common, and it was estimated that the AFL spent over $100,000 to stop the CIO organizing drive. City police raided the CIO headquarters in June, arresting eighty-four people. The police also picked up Bob Robertson and told him to get out of town or else. When Robertson refused to depart, he was beaten by police and sustained two broken vertebrae. Many other CIO supporters were beaten and arrested, and union records and membership cards were seized by the police. In July, the Louisiana legislature unanimously adopted a resolution condemning communism and directing local and state officials to stamp it out. The resolution deplored the "organization of negroes" that had "unfortunately taken root" in New Orleans and now "endanger[ed] white supremacy." In an apparent reference to Harry Bridges it denounced the ideas of "alien emissaries and agitators" and "imported alien radicals."

When the representation election was held in October, the ILA received 2,701 votes to only 874 for the ILWU. The outcome surprised CIO organizers who counted on the support of some 3,000 members among the dockworkers. But the anti-Communist hysteria along with police violence and intimidation had taken a toll among ILWU supporters. No doubt the ILA's vote buying and its access to jobs contributed to the CIO defeat. ILA president Joseph Ryan was also smart enough to choose a black man, "Big Paul" Hortman, to head up the struggle against the ILWU. Finally, local church leaders, with the exception of a few Catholic priests, publicly opposed the CIO.

After this defeat the ILWU leaders returned to California, leaving Dorsey to run the small ILWU unit in New Orleans. Over the next four years Dorsey, with a white organizer named Caleb Green who worked as international representative, signed up 300 warehouse workers and established a new local that was chartered as Warehouse and Distribution Workers Union, Local 207, ILWU–CIO. The local was one of the few ILWU units in the eastern half of the country, and its distance from San Francisco did not help communications. Local 207 focused on workers who loaded river barges, leaving the seagoing ships to the ILA. Soon Local 207 became involved in several unsuccessful strikes, but a chronic problem emerged between the local and the international union. Starting in 1940 the local began falling behind in its payments of "per capita tax" (a share of dues payments) to the International. This may have been caused by the drain of the unsuccessful strikes and the lack of a dues checkoff system, but the problem persisted over the next two years.

Eventually in 1942 the International intervened and appointed another international representative, Howard Goddard, who replaced Green after he resigned. A young black man named William Spooner was also brought in as an organizer. Financial practices were to be reorganized, but escalating disagreements between Dorsey and the two new men only made matters worse. Dorsey accused Goddard and Spooner of attempting to bring the programs and policies of the Communist Party into the union. Goddard replied by accusing Dorsey of corruption and of being "a stool pigeon and a rat to boot." Then in early 1943 Bob Robertson was sent back to New Orleans to deal with the situation. After a tumultuous meeting Robertson, with Bridges's approval, placed the local in receivership and suspended Dorsey and four other local officials on charges of misappropriating union funds. Goddard and Spooner were placed in charge of the local.

Dorsey accused the International of racism and sought to mobilize support among anti-Communists in the labor movement and the Catholic Church. Dorsey also sued the union—twice—but his request for an injunction was denied. In the course of these events Dorsey's attorney reportedly said that Dorsey had been getting money from the House Un-American Activities Committee for reporting on "reds" in the CIO. Dorsey was expelled from the ILWU and went to work for a rival union, Local 389 of the United Retail, Wholesale, and Department Store Employees of America.

Meanwhile, the International hired Andrew Steve Nelson, a young black Communist, to work on a temporary basis as business agent for Local 207. Nelson began working with Spooner to rebuild the local. Nelson soon established a reputation as a tough negotiator in dealing with employers. In 1944, when the receivership expired, Andrew Nelson was elected president of Local 207. By then William Spooner had been drafted and Howard Goddard had moved on to Texas to become the ILWU's chief organizer in that state. Chester Meske was sent from California to replace Goddard as international representative, and August Harris replaced Nelson as business agent. Both Meske and Harris were also Communists. In 1944 Lee Brown moved to New Orleans, got a job on the waterfront, and joined Local 207. Brown would also join the Communist Party. Nelson and his organizers launched an aggressive campaign to consolidate and expand the union. Their first big victory was at the Flintkote

Tar Paper Mill, where white workers at first resisted joining a union with a black president. But once the certification election was won, more and more workers signed up with the union. By 1946 the union's membership had grown to 850 and was fully integrated.

The years 1946 to 1957 witnessed the ascent and decline of Local 207. In its first year under Nelson's leadership the union launched eleven strikes. By April 1947 it represented over 1,700 workers at fourteen companies. But the clouds of Cold War anticommunism were lurking on the horizon and would eventually gather into a furious storm against the feisty interracial union. The Taft-Hartley Act was passed to curb labor militancy by requiring union officials to sign affidavits swearing that they were not members of the Communist Party. Some CIO leaders, such as Mike Quill of the Transport Workers, Joe Curran of the National Maritime Union, and Walter Reuther of the United Auto Workers, were also swinging to the right and denouncing alleged Communists in their unions. The CIO would soon act to purge itself of those identified as Communists. Not surprisingly, the AFL seized the opportunity to intensify its long-standing drive against communism and political radicals in the trade union movement.

In New Orleans Local 207 struggled not only for workers' rights but also for civil rights for African Americans. In coalition with the Communist Party and local civil rights organizations it also actively promoted black voter registration. The union played a part in supporting the Progressive Party presidential campaign of Henry Wallace in 1948.

Harry Bridges's 1950 perjury conviction for denying he was a Communist in his 1945 citizenship application fueled the anticommunist drive against the ILWU. The International was on the verge of being expelled from the CIO, and in New Orleans Local 207 was being red-baited and was facing a challenge from another CIO union for representation of the workers at the Flintkote plant.

Initially ILWU officials had refused to sign the anti-Communist affidavits demanded by the Taft-Hartley Act. This stance cost Local 207 an election among workers at the Flintkote plant in 1948. The company would not allow Local 207 to participate in the election because its officers had not signed the affidavits. But Local 207 still claimed jurisdiction. By 1949 Harry Bridges realized that the ILWU would continue to lose shops without access to the NLRB-sanctioned election machinery. Word went out to ILWU local officials to sign the affidavits.

The change did not help Local 207 in its struggle at the Flintkote plant. Fierce red-baiting and the defection of a shop steward to the rival CIO union led to a defeat for Local 207 in the election.

Over the following years more attempted raids ensued, but Local 207 hung on and even won occasional victories. Ironically, the local was beset by the problem of delinquent per capita taxes owed to the International, which had led to Dorsey's downfall. The International investigated and determined that there was no malfeasance or financial incompetence. Warehouse work was seasonal, and consequently the local's membership swung dramatically over the course of a year, reaching a high of eight hundred and then dropping to four hundred during off periods. Nelson sent the International an installment on the dues owed and tried to develop a plan to stabilize the local's finances.

Along with its financial woes, Local 207 faced mounting anti-Communist attacks from the AFL. In 1953, in the midst of a struggle between Local 207 and the Teamsters Union for representation of workers at the Gulf Shipside Storage Corporation, the AFL circulated a scurrilous leaflet in the style of an FBI Wanted poster bearing a photograph of Andrew Nelson and a boldface headline asking, "Do you know this Communist?" Answering its own question, the leaflet continued, "his name is Andrew Steve Nelson—he is a representative of COM-RAT HARRY BRIDGES' organization—he has been a member of the Communist Party since 1939 and still takes his orders from the Communist Party." The leaflet urged the federal government to go after Nelson: "If Nelson signed a NON-Communist Affidavit then the Federal Government should take action against Nelson." As if that weren't enough, the leaflet suggested physical attacks: "As a loyal American, you do not want anything to do with men like Andrew Steve Nelson, when he comes around your place of employment, run the HELL OUT OF HIM." The leaflet was signed "Organization Committee, American Federation of Labor, New Orleans, La."

The 1954 U.S. Supreme Court decision declaring segregation in the public schools unconstitutional was a major step forward in the struggle against racism. But in the McCarthyite climate of the times, the decision inflamed segregationists and opened the door for more anti-Communist attacks. An upsurge of white racism throughout the South and political reaction throughout the nation combined in a hellish assault on progressives, especially south of the Mason-Dixon line. In the years after 1954 a host of reactionaries in Congress traveled to New Orleans to "investigate" individuals and organizations that advocated social change and racial justice. The House Un-American Activities Committee held hearings on groups suspected of subversion. Led by ultrareactionary Senator James Eastland, the Senate Internal Security Committee made a foray to the city to interrogate leftists about their political activities, particularly their membership in the Communist Party. Those who refused to cooperate lost their jobs. HUAC returned in February 1957 to query Lee Brown about whether he was a Communist Party member. He refused to answer. A year later he was on trial in federal court.

Louisiana state legislators also joined the anti-Communist bandwagon, holding their own hearings and investigations. At one such hearing held in

Baton Rouge in 1957, Hubert Badeaux, head of the "red squad" in the New Orleans police department, claimed to have obtained the minutes to more than one hundred meetings chaired by Andrew Nelson. Badeaux said these records showed that Nelson regularly preached the Communist Party line to the members of Local 207. (Presumably these were the minutes Lee Brown said were stolen from the union hall. See chapter 4.)

The anti-Communists virtually hounded Andrew Steve Nelson to death. In 1956 Andrew Nelson was indicted by the federal government on charges of falsifying Taft-Hartley non-Communist affidavits that he had signed in 1952 and 1953 stating that he was not a member of the Communist Party at that time. The ILWU leadership, which came to Nelson's defense, denounced the indictment as an outgrowth of the racist and anti-Communist hysteria of the times. The trial was held in September 1956 before an all-white jury. The most damaging testimony was by Arthur Eugene—a black former Communist Party member who was a paid FBI informer—who testified that Nelson told him in 1952 that he intended to stay in the party. Nelson's health was failing (he suffered from kidney inflammation—chronic nephritis—and high blood pressure) and he did not testify at his trial, although he did issue a statement saying that he had not been a member of the Communist Party "at any time since the early part of 1948."

Nelson was found guilty and sentenced to five years in federal prison. His attorney, James McCain, filed notice of appeal. Free on $7,500 bail, Nelson, despite his declining health, gamely sought to raise funds for his defense. He did not live to appeal the conviction. Andrew Steve Nelson died on January 12, 1957.

With the death of Nelson and with Lee Brown soon under legal attack, Local 207 was rudderless, and its rank-and-file members became confused and disillusioned. Thomas West, who had never been a member of the Communist Party, was elected president. Bob Robertson came from San Francisco in the summer of 1957 to meet with West. It was agreed that Local 207 should cast off from the ILWU, as much for reasons of geography as politics. ILWU Local 208 in Chicago had recently dissolved and merged with the United Packinghouse Workers of America. The UPWA was a militant union with a democratic tradition similar to that of the ILWU. Robertson recommended that Local 207 also merge with the Packinghouse Workers, which it did on July 23, 1957.

With the merger an era in the history of New Orleans labor came to a close. For twenty years Local 207 had carried the banner of labor militancy based on interracial solidarity. An integrated union with black leadership, it presented a model—especially during the Nelson years—of what was possible for a progressive working-class organization and, at the same time, it represented a threat to entrenched white supremacist power based on racial division. It was inevitable that the white powers that be, at the local as well as national level, would go all out to destroy this beacon that illuminated a path towards a new, egalitarian, and democratic America.

Over its history thousands of workers, black and white, learned lessons in the school of labor militancy that Local 207 constituted. In the pages that follow, one of those workers, Lee Brown, recounts a remarkable journey as a person whose life was shaped by the struggles of black workers, and especially the struggles, triumphs, and tribulations of Local 207.

CHAPTER FOUR

New Orleans and Local 207

After packing my suitcase, I bought a ticket on the All American Bus Line and left for New Orleans one foggy morning in 1944. I changed buses four times; the last change was in Dallas, Texas. Then I caught a Trailways bus that was already waiting in the bus station, and it rolled into New Orleans at three o'clock in the morning.

When I stepped off the bus, a lady acquaintance that I had met on the bus was with me. This lady was looking for a friend to meet her, but no one came. With great disappointment, she came along with me to the address of Mother's house that had been given me.

As we came near the house, I was trying to imagine what my mother would be like and if I should call her Janie or Mother. I hadn't seen her since I was five or six years old and she brought me back to grandfather's farm after taking me to the boardinghouse she was living at in New Orleans.

In a few more seconds, I was knocking on the door. A smiling, dark-skinned lady came to the door. When she saw who I was, she spoke with a soft voice, "Lee Brown, I am your mother." As my mother embraced me, I felt good. I was very glad to see her. Even though we had been separated for so long, I still had that mother feeling, you know, love for my mother. That's why I can't understand people who was raised up by their mother but don't have feeling for her. I was separated but I still had love for my mother.

Suddenly Jeanette, my half sister, ran from a room and started hugging and kissing me. The last time I saw Jeanette we was children. She was three years

old then. Now she had grown up to be a beautiful young lady. When I first arrived at Janie's house, I didn't know my half brother, Pete, who I hadn't met
yet. He hadn't been raised by Janie either. Pete was married and living some
other place in New Orleans. Only my half sister stayed with Janie. (By the
way, I decided to call my mother by her first name, which was Janie. Pete also
called her Janie.)

Despite all the excitement, the lady who came along was eventually introduced. It was about 3:30 in the morning. With all the talking and getting acquainted all over again, before we knew it, it was daybreak.

Janie wasn't so ill as I expected she would be when I arrived in New Orleans. At seven o'clock Janie left the house, went to the store, and brought
back some food she fixed for breakfast. Jeanette got dressed and went to work.

After breakfast the lady acquaintance and I left the house to find her
friend. We walked down Rampart Street, in and out of bars. We continued
walking for hours. Finally at the last bar on the street, we found her friend.
The lady thanked me for helping. Then we parted. Although this was my
first time getting around in New Orleans, it wasn't difficult finding my way
back to Janie's house.

During all the first conversations I had with my mother, I wanted to ask her
why she hadn't come to get me to live with her when grandfather died. Did she
ever try to find out who I stayed on the farm with or what I was doing? So
many questions I wanted to ask Janie, but I only felt gratitude being in her
presence. Without complaining about things that happened in the past, I settled down to make New Orleans my home for the time being.

I rested around the house for a day or so and then started inquiring about a
job. Janie thought about a man named Walter, who was a member of a union.
She said, "Walter lives three blocks from the house and he might be able to tell
you where to find work." I thought Walter might be at work in the morning, so
I waited until the evening before going to his house.

Walter had just come in from work. I introduced myself and told Walter
that I was Janie's son, who had just arrived from Los Angeles, California. I
also asked Walter what union he was a member of. Walter said he was a
member of Local 207 ILWU, the warehouse and distribution workers' union
located at 420 Gravier Street. He said the president's name was Andrew
Steve Nelson. He told me about the union and the work. With directions
from Walter on how to find the union hall, at 10:30 the next morning I arrived at the union hall. I waited twenty minutes before the president, a black
man, came through the door. Inside his office, I introduced myself and
showed him my traveling card from Local 12. He was a tall, dark fellow,
and he seemed very friendly. We sat down and talked and he asked different questions about my experience. I told him I was looking for work. I
asked if he had a job open. He answered, "We can get you a job." I told the
him, "Since you have a job open, I'd like to transfer to your union." He ac-

cepted that. Then he wrote out a worksheet for me to take to the Federal Barge Lines to give to Orange Dickie, who was the shop steward.

Later on, when I got to know Nelson better, I found out that he had been in the union for a couple of years and that the president before him, a man named Spooner, was also black. Nelson was an organizer, something like a business agent. Nelson had worked with Spooner at the union hall, and when Spooner left, Nelson became the president.

The Federal Barge Lines was located at the Galvez Street wharf in New Orleans. Nelson had written down the directions. I caught a streetcar, transferred to Canal and Galvez, and stayed on the Galvez bus until it came to the end of the line. When I got down to the Federal Barge Lines I asked some men, "Anyone know Orange Dickie?" They said, "Oh, yeah. See that big man driving that tractor? That's Dickie." I stopped him and told him brother Andrew Nelson from Local 207 sent me there to see him. I gave him my worksheet and he taken me upstairs to see the personnel manager. The personnel manager signed me up and told me to come to work the next morning.

Feeling great about getting this job, I couldn't wait to get home to tell Janie, who was sitting in the front room when I got home. I told her about getting the job. She said, "You're lucky to get a job so soon." I explained to Janie, "It's not luck when you belong to a union and you're determined to work. Members of the union often look out for each other. I didn't have trouble because I had my traveling card from Local 12."

The next morning when I went to the union hall, I was given a number to check in. Local 207 had a few rooms in the same building with the transport workers union. Mrs. Jessie Sims was the office secretary. She kept the office organized, and when I got to be an officer later she helped me with reading and writing letters and reports.

One thing I liked about this new job was the wages—$1.25 an hour. In addition, the other workers helped me get started. This work was almost the same as when I worked in the warehouse in Los Angeles, except this time it was on the dock loading and unloading boxcars and barges. We were loading things like ground-up oyster shells in fifty-pound bags, canned goods, raw sugar, cases of beer, all kinds of different things that came down the river.

Inasmuch as I had gotten a job, I was now anxious to look New Orleans over and get acquainted with some people. I soon found out it was a fact: New Orleans had the most beautiful black women in the world. Black women every color of the rainbow! I also went to the French Quarter, where most of the mulattoes live. Bars stayed open all night. Each bar had a dance floor. Unlike most bars in California, you could bring your own bottle and put it on the table.

A week passed before I had got to meet Pete, my half brother, and his wife, Henriette. They came over to the house and we got acquainted. We talked a long time about the many years we had been separated from each other. Pete was the oldest in the family. His grandparents raised him. Now it was obvious: Jeanette, Pete, and I had different fathers. Under those circumstances, I could easily see why our family members was so separated. But as time passed, we became a close family and the differences between us seemed very unimportant.

After I had worked on the dock a few weeks, Walter Green and Chester Langley took me to the union meeting. We had gotten to know each other at work. They came by to get me and took me to an executive board meeting. There was both men and women there, black and white. I remember Albert J. Taylor was the recording secretary. I got to know him. He was the one who took the minutes. He was a heavy drinker but he kept good minutes. It was his minutes book that was stolen from the union hall later. I always thought the government stole the minutes.

At the meeting they talked about improving the organizing at the cotton compress, the feed mills, the barge lines, and the packing company. Attending this meeting for the first time gave me more confidence toward helping my people. I started attending meetings and speaking at them.

On the job the men liked the way I talked and elected me shop steward at the Federal Barge Lines; I was also placed on the union's executive board. I was constantly involved in fighting for better working conditions for union members. The workers on the dock had one hour for lunch. Whenever I called for a noon meeting, nearly half an hour would be spent on discussing working conditions and the trade union movement with the workers. I could see that they didn't have no upgrading for black workers on the dock. The only thing the brothers could do was common labor. So I talked with Nelson about getting upgrading. They should put the jobs on the bulletin board so black workers could fill other positions, like cooper or watchman or crane operator. There was both black and white workers in Local 207, but most of the white workers worked at what they called the Lower Fleet cleaning and painting barges, which was a better job because you didn't have to do no heavy lifting. White workers could get the better jobs. I proposed putting the jobs on the bulletin board and giving a person forty hours to see if he was qualified for different jobs like crane operator. Nelson and I worked together on this in the union.

Nelson and I started talking more about the trade union movement and political issues and conditions that existed in the black community. We became good friends. He used to invite me over to his house on Sundays. His wife's name was Susan and they had five children. They treated me like part of the family. He would make a salad . . . I used to know how to make that salad. I should have put down the recipe. Now I don't remember what goes in it, but it was a good salad!

One time I fell down on the street and sprained my back. Nelson came over in his car from the union hall to take me to the doctor. He was like a brother. He practiced what he preached, and he preached what he practiced.

On Fridays we used to go to the oyster bar or to the Snow White restaurant or Dookie Chase's to have lunch or dinner. We talked all the time about mobilizing the trade union movement and building unity and improving conditions on the job. We talked about strategy and tactics for organizing at the cotton compress or the fertilizer plant or the feed mills.

I was concerned, and Nelson was concerned, to try to help our people. We knowed that they was getting mistreated with low-paid jobs, bad housing, bad health, no seniority, things like that. So we discussed conditions that existed in the black community.

One night Nelson invited me to attend a political meeting in the Godchaux Building on Canal Street. I had been talking about things we needed to do and he said he could take me to a Communist Party meeting where they would train you how to work and organize people. I didn't know too much about the party. In Los Angeles at the Armour Packing Company there was this Spanish fellow who used to talk to me about the party, and it sounded very good to me. I was interested in anything that would help me do something in unions and for black folks.

At the meeting Nelson introduced me as a member of his union who had just come in from Local 12 in California. I said a few words to let them know that I was glad to be there. I knowed that I wanted to get involved in a program for better conditions for workers. To me my main aim was to upgrade and help black workers. My main thing was to get rid of Jim Crowism—to bury Jim Crow.

This was my first time to attend such a meeting. I listened to them talk and I looked at their program, and to me it was a damn good program. I could see that capitalism was not gonna solve the problems of working people; it only helps a few people. I wanted to help black folks and I figured that the party could help black folks 'cause capitalism was not gonna solve the problems of black people. It's only a few that's gonna get the crumbs from the table. You must have a socialist country.

I attended every time the Communists had a meeting. Nelson would let me know when a meeting was scheduled. After attending these meetings for a while, I joined the Communist Party. They wasn't so anti-Communist then, so I was out in the open about being in the party.

Nelson was doing a lot of the party work. He was on some kind of national committee of the party and he went to its meetings. When he came back, he would relate things to me. We talked about political issues affecting black people and the whole country. There was only four black people in the party at that time—Wright, Johnson, Edwards, and a nurse who was bad news 'cause she turned out to be an informer. Later we got more brothers to join the party. I had a lot of confidence in the white people in the party 'cause they acted like human beings. The district organizer, Emanuel Levin, who was white, he and his wife bought me some books. C. J. Meske came from the International and he and I would go around selling *Political Affairs* and books. (One time Nelson told us we was supposed to be organizing for the union, not selling books!)

Meanwhile, I started studying. I read books on Marxism, V. I. Lenin's philosophy, African history, and black history in America. With knowledge from these books, I was better able to struggle around political issues in the community and on the job.

I attended party meetings and special meetings of the party to get accustomed to fighting around issues, staying active, and getting acquainted with other party members. I learned how to run meetings and set up committees. Sometimes we had all-day meetings on how to organize people, how to get them to register to vote by educating them, how to work with politicians, and how to fight Jim Crow. I liked the party because the program opposed capitalism and advocated socialism for the working class. The party also fought against Jim Crowism, for better education, decent homes, health institutions, and the necessities of life like food and clothing.

Every child should get a high school education or special trade school training to be able to earn a living, and this should be paid for by the federal government; also, four years of college. In this way a child won't have to drop out of school to help his parents earn a living. With the highest possible degree of education, a child would be able to earn his own living. Special trades like lawyers, doctors, nurses, any jobs that call for special education should be paid for by the federal government, regardless of race, color, creed. I learned this should be done at the Communist Party meetings.

In a short while I fell in love with New Orleans. The people there was more friendly toward each other, at least more so than in California. Neighbors wouldn't pass you without speaking, and sometimes they would stop and have a long conversation with you. The people seemed so concerned about your well-being and they would often invite you over to dinner and make you welcome in their home. I enjoyed the Creole food that was served in restaurants and in homes. Actually this Creole food is the best you can eat anywhere. One of my favorite dishes is gumbo and oyster loaf, which I ate all the time. These are some of the reasons I fell in love with New Orleans so quickly.

In 1945, one Sunday at a general membership meeting of Local 207, I noticed a beautiful brown-skinned lady in the meeting. I didn't get a chance to meet her that day. In the meeting that day a union member nominated me to a convention, which was to be held in Detroit. I declined the nomination. Then the union member spoke on my declining. He said, "I nominated Brother Brown to go to the convention because Brother Brown doesn't have a wife and I figured he was the best qualified man to go to the convention." Anyway as it turned out I didn't go to the convention. This was the day this beautiful lady started paying attention to me.

One Friday night I met her at our Local 207 executive meeting. She was sitting about three seats in front of me in the meeting. She kept looking back at me and smiling. Shortly afterward, I got up, stood on the floor, and spoke about the need for unity and about how we needed to organize other jobs besides just the barge lines. I talked about how we had to work together, workers at the barge lines, the feed mills, and the fertilizer plant. After the meeting had adjourned, the lady came over and shook my hand and told me, "I liked your talk. It was very good and you shook up the union reps." I told her I didn't have anything personal against any of the union officers. I was only trying to get them involved in building a strong rank-and-file local. I went on to tell her that a strong rank-and-file local means better working conditions on jobs, welfare, and pension plans with job security.

As our conversation continued, she told me her name was Rose Robinson. Rose said that she heard the union member say in the last general membership meeting that I didn't have a wife. Then I asked Rose where she lived and if she had come to the meeting alone. She told me, she said she came to the meeting alone. I asked her if I could see her home. She said yes.

My intention was to build a better relationship with Rose and to get her more involved in union affairs. She seemed to be very interested in my talk at the meeting and in the union. Rose was shop steward on her job, working in the feed mill in the city. Rose and I left the union hall and took a bus to her home. Before we reached her home, we stopped at a bar about a half block from her house. Rose asked me if I drank. I told her yes. We ordered two glasses of draft beer and sat for about an hour or longer, talking and getting acquainted. Rose and I talked on different subjects. I talked a little about myself and my activities in the union. I didn't tell her at that time that I was a member of the Communist Party. (Later Rose found out I was in the party when we got arrested at a Progressive Party meeting, but she never expressed interest in joining the Communist Party.)

When Rose and I finished our drinks, we went to her home. Rose asked me in. Once inside, we talked some more, until it became late at night. I stood up and said, "I believe I better go." Then Rose said, "It's getting so late and the buses run slow. I don't think you should go back across the Industrial Canal at night because it's very far. While you are standing waiting on a bus, someone might try to rob or hurt you. I suggest you stay here."

Without any hesitation, I accepted her invitation. To me, Rose was quite impressive and desirable. I told Rose I didn't have to work the next day, which was a Saturday. All I had to do was to go pick up my paycheck Saturday afternoon. At the time I was working on Galvez Street wharf, loading and unloading boxcars and barges.

Next morning Rose went to the grocery store and bought some food for breakfast. Not only was Rose beautiful, but she was a real good cook!

At that time, I was still living with my mother and sister across from the Industrial Canal in a two-room apartment. There wasn't much room for the three of us. I discussed this problem with Rose. She told me, if I would like to,

I could stay with her because she had plenty of room and only her sister's son lived with her.

I agreed to live with Rose. So I went to pick up my paycheck that evening and went by my mother's house. I gave Janie some money and told her I was going to live with a lady who was a member of my union. I told Janie I was doing this so it wouldn't be so crowded and I would always come by to see her. She agreed with me; my sister didn't have any comment on the subject. I took some of my clothes and went back to Rose's house to live.

As time passed, Rose and I grew very close to each other and we was able to help each other in the labor movement. However, this was only half the picture. Rose was separated from her husband. She hadn't mentioned that she had any children until we had been living together for a while. Then Rose sent for her children, who was living in the Mississippi Delta with their grandmother. Rose had five children, three girls and two boys, including the boy who was living with her when we first met. This was not her sister's son but one of her own. Actually, it didn't matter to me that she had children. I liked the companionship. All Rose's children accepted me and I accepted them. Before long we was living together as a family. Her children called me their father.

Several years later, Rose had a son for me. He weighed twelve pounds and we named him Lee Brown Jr.—Brownie for short. As we continued living together, Rose, under the law in the state of Louisiana, became my common-law wife. With my family and beautiful common-law wife and my trade union activities I had a full life.

By this time I was a shop steward at Galvez Street wharf and was on the negotiation committee. I was also executive board member, member of the political action committee of my local, member of the trustee committee, and one of the advisers on the three-man committee that advised our union president.

As a member of the Communist Party in 1946, I was active in my club, which was known as the French Quarter Club. Later I was transferred to the Trade Union Club. I worked very closely with the district organizer. I gained much knowledge about the labor movement. Also, I learned how to get involved in issues that was facing black workers in the South.

I was gaining knowledge from reading a lot of literature about the union and the party. C. J. Meske, an old-time trade unionist and party member, kept me up with the literature and kept me well-informed on issues that we was facing and had to get involved around: Jim Crowism, segregation, discrimination. He pointed out to me that these was the reasons for our low wages and bad working conditions. The majority of the workers wasn't organized in a union. The Jim Crow system kept the workers divided, especially in the South. That is one of the bosses' main weapons that they use against the workers to keep them divided, which meant that we would always have problems facing the black workers and poor people in the South.

This also meant the black workers would be denied the right to the vote, education, health institutions, and adequate housing. Conditions would remain the same in the ghettos, especially in the South. Millions of black children would go to bed hungry unless the unions could organize the workers in the South, both black and white.

To change this would mean that black workers would have to fight to register and vote as first-class citizens of the United States of America. Also, they would have to fight for decent wages on jobs, as well as job security, seniority rights, health and welfare plans, and pension plans—all of which should be open for all workers!

A union means black and white workers working together. In doing this we can destroy our main enemy—Jim Crowism and discrimination. As long as these exist, problems will always confront the workers in the South and in the whole nation.

C. J. Meske and I discussed all of these issues frequently while we was having lunch. Years have passed and gone, and I don't know, at this time, if Meske is living or dead.

I got myself involved in a lot of these problems that was confronting black and poor workers in the South. I fought for the right to register and vote.

One December Rose and the children was away in the Mississippi Delta visiting her parents for the holidays. With nothing to do one night, I went walking the streets about twelve o'clock, as was usual for me, just to observe people. For a while I was standing on the corner, just watching people's behavior. Then I walked down a poorly lit street going to a bar on that street. I noticed three youngsters coming toward me.

When they got close to me, one of the youngsters asked me if I had a match. Not realizing what the youngsters had in mind, I ran my hand into my pocket. With one hand in my pocket, one of the boys hit me over the head with a garbage can top. Then they took my leather gloves, my wallet, and my overcoat. (It so happened that I didn't have much money in my wallet, only three dollars.) If I had known in advance what they planned to do, I would have protected myself better. During the robbery, the youngsters seemed so frightened! They seemed like they hadn't been in the business of robbing too long.

As soon as I recovered, I went to the 12th precinct and reported the robbery. I made a statement to a policeman describing what had happened and what had been taken. The policeman told me, "Nigger, you didn't have a damn thing!" I explained that I could have gotten hurt or killed with people robbing on the streets and no protection. I told the police, "You people are not concerned for black people, robbing and beating each other up in this city."

Then the policeman told me, "Run, nigger!" I told the policeman I didn't have no reason to run—I was the victim, not the robber! He probably wanted to shoot me in the back, the son of a bitch! I told him, "I see now black people have no protection in this city from you white, racist, segregationist policemen!" I've always spoken up for myself. My grandfather taught me to speak up for myself when I was being attacked by the unjust. That was the reason I wasn't afraid to speak up to these so-called peacemakers. This was all amusing to the policemen. They was laughing about the whole thing. I told the policemen, "That's all right. Forget it!" See, that's the kind of thing that provokes you and motivates you to fight, 'cause you know what kind of shit you're living with.

Then I left the station. Since Rose and the children wasn't at home, I went and spent the night with my cousin. Early the next morning, walking down the streets, I met a friend. He went back with me to the scene of the robbery. We looked around trying to find out if one of the youngsters had dropped my wallet. With no such luck, we went in and out of bars to see if I recognized any of the youngsters. My friend and I soon gave up. Then we went to the office of the *Pittsburgh Courier,* a national black newspaper. The young news reporter of the *Pittsburgh Courier* took my statement. I told him what had happened, about the robbery and the bad attitude of the police at the 12th precinct. I asked the reporter to go to the superintendent's office with my friend and myself. The superintendent was like the chief of police. The three of us went to the superintendent's office.

Seemingly we was well received by the superintendent, A. A. Wallace. I made the same statement to him that I had made to the reporter. When the superintendent finished hearing my complaint, he said, "This is the first time anyone has come in this office and made a complaint about the police." He went on to say, "I had been hearing rumors about the policemen for a long time—in the black communities. But no one had the guts to come forward and make a complaint until now." The superintendent asked me, "Could you recognize any of the policemen again?" I told him yes. Then the superintendent asked me, "Did you get the policeman's badge number?" I said I hadn't. Then the superintendent said, "The officers are on the night shift. Can you come back at night and identify them?"

The newspaper reporter who came with us was concerned about what happened to black people in the South. The reporter began talking with the superintendent about what had happened and took notes while he was talking. Then the superintendent asked me, "What action do you want me to take to clear up these problems?" I said, "As a first step, you should hire black policemen, because I feel that black people need some protection against crime in the black communities." Then Wallace had nerve enough to ask me, " Do you want to be a policeman?" I said, "No! My job is to fight for the rights of my people here in the South."

The superintendent didn't give us any direct resolution to this problem, except that he wanted me to come at night to the 12th precinct to identify the policemen. We talked awhile in the superintendent's office and left. Once outside the reporter advised me not to go back to the police precinct at night alone because all the policemen stuck together and they wouldn't tell you which one was on that Friday night anyhow. Added to this, some friends told me not to go at night 'cause I would be leaving myself open to get hurt or framed by the police. August Harris, the union's white business agent, said don't make that mistake, going back to the police station at night. I still was angry about the behavior of the policemen when I reported the robbery, but I didn't go back that night or any time.

Two black newspapers supported me—the *Pittsburgh Courier* and the *Louisiana Weekly*. They put in their papers that Lee Brown was asking for black policemen to be put on the police force in New Orleans. This was the first beginning of getting better security for the black communities in New Orleans. Later on, two black policemen was put on the force. The black communities felt a little safer. White police couldn't relate to the black people. Black people was more afraid of the police than they was of the criminals. White police at that time was racist and deadly against the black workers in the South.

These are some of the things I faced in the South. The white police department was antilabor and antiblack. It was the same as fascism in Germany. The police could be worse than the criminals against the black workers and the poor people.

CHAPTER FIVE

Organizer at Work

The Progressive Party was nationally known for running Henry A. Wallace for president of the United States in 1948. We discussed the Wallace campaign in Communist Party meetings. Wallace had been vice president during Roosevelt's administration and we felt that he was the best candidate for the working people, particularly in the Deep South. He was against racism and prejudice and Jim Crowism. Members of the Progressive Party was very active in the struggle for the working class and poor people. The party decided to support Wallace, and Andrew Nelson and I brought up the Wallace campaign in the union. Our union, Local 207, organized the Wallace for President Labor Committee, and I was on it.

The labor committee sent us into rural areas teaching people how to register so that they could vote for Henry Wallace for president. We also explained to people why we thought he would be the right man for president. One thing for sure, we explained that he was for small farmers and sharecroppers and the working people as a whole. He was for labor and supported organized labor; that was why we thought it was very important to become registered voters, particularly all the poor people. Registering voters would become one of the main weapons to achieve some of the things we wanted and needed to improve our living condition.

With deep concern for poor black people, I told them to tell all their neighbors and friends, whatever they do, try and get out to register, so they can vote! It is known through experience that voting power is poor peoples' power. In my opinion, poor people should be educated politically and become trade union conscious from the grassroots level. I believed that we as trade unionists should be interested in organizing the unorganized throughout the country.

Millions of black people in the southern states wasn't registered to vote. Some white people didn't want black people to vote. So it was hard to get them registered. Our union went to the country to teach black farmhands politics and how important casting votes was. If you are not registered, we said, go and try to get registered. If you vote for an independent candidate, he can get some things you want and need, or he can work some issue for you to help your family and the community.

We had meetings at churches and lots of the country people came. We had a good response. The churches would be packed at night in the countryside. They were concerned about learning. All they needed was some leadership to get mobilized. We talked to them about freedom and justice and equality, and jobs and health and schools, and they responded. We just had to bring it to them. When we finished trying to teach politics to the farm people, some church ministers would take a group of black people to try and register so they could vote. But they was often turned back.

I had trouble getting registered myself. I was living in New Orleans Parish but had to go back and forth sixteen times before I was registered. The fact was, white people didn't want black people registering to vote. I filled out a registration card and I presented it to the white man who was in charge. He looked at the card, tore it up, and said, "You are not qualified." I asked him, "What rules and regulations make me eligible?" He answered, "I am the one who decides who is qualified to vote or not to vote." I wouldn't quarrel, knowing this would have been a good chance for him to call the police and have me arrested. Instead I told him, "I will be back tomorrow, and I'm gonna bring my lunch." I decided to worry him down. I was determined to register 'cause I was voting in Los Angeles during the Roosevelt administration. Why couldn't I vote here? So I kept coming back. This went on day after day for sixteen days!

This man saw how determined I was in getting registered. I was about to wear him out. Then one day he looked at the card and went back and got this huge registration book. When I signed my name, I knew I was a registered voter.

In small cities, towns, and throughout the rural areas, it was even harder for black people to register. I along with the other union representatives continued teaching farmhands politics.

Sometimes this turned out to be dangerous for us, since white people opposed the idea. In particular, I remember one night when four union representatives went with me to a church in the countryside. This church was crowded with black people. Some were registered to vote and some wasn't. Each one of us made a talk about the importance of votes. When the meeting was over, the four of us left together in our car to drive back to New Orleans. A white union rep named Red O'Brien, with the food and tobacco workers union, was driving the car. Suddenly we heard shots: somebody was shooting at us! We looked back and saw a car trying to overtake us. Red started driving faster. Then he said, "Hell, I got a gun in my glove compartment." He reached into the glove compartment, pulled out a gun, and started shooting back. Them bastards turned off. Scared their asses! We wasn't sure if it was the Klan or the sheriff. No doubt, white people in the southern states hated the idea so much they was willing to try to kill anyone who tried to teach black people about politics and voting. After the shooting Red drove at a steady speed back to New Orleans. No one was hurt, just shook up.

Things wasn't always this exciting. I gained knowledge from taking part in many political activities. Aside from attending union meetings, getting elected to different committees, being a shop steward, being a member of the trustee board, executive board, and the political action committee, I also carried a press card for the *Dispatcher,* which was the longshoremen's newspaper. But the most important thing to me was the organizing work.

One afternoon in February 1948 I went to see the manager of the Palace Theater in New Orleans with a letter from Local 207. The letter said: "Dear Sir: This will introduce Mr. Lee Brown, member of the political action committee of our local. The membership at their February 1 meeting instructed Mr. Brown through resolution, passed by overwhelming majority, that he pay you a visit and hold a conference with you concerning a very important matter. The membership as well as the undersigned will deeply appreciate your honoring Mr. Brown with such a conference." The letter was signed by August Harris, who was then our vice president.

When the manager finished reading the letter, I asked, "Would you agree to show a picture at your theater? The name of the film is *The Roosevelt Story.*" I said, "Our local is campaigning for Henry A. Wallace to become the president of the United States."

By showing this picture, we hoped to bring in more votes. Mostly, all the poor people wanted Henry A. Wallace because they remembered he used to be vice president under President Roosevelt. Wallace said he would get 60 million jobs for people, better houses for low-income families, better education, and better health institutions. When I finished explaining the reasons, the manager agreed to run the picture for two days.

Black people and poor people wanted Henry A. Wallace for president but the ruling class and the middle class was afraid of him because he claimed to be a progressive capitalist with socialist ideals.

Meanwhile, Paul Robeson came to New Orleans during the 1948 campaign. He was campaigning for Wallace. He came to our local and we had a discussion about Wallace's campaign. I was glad to see Paul Robeson and honored to be in his presence. The last time I saw him, he was on stage in the Shakespeare play *Othello* in Los Angeles.

Paul Robeson was loved by everyone who met him. Despite his fame and stardom, his speech and actions showed him to be down-to-earth. In fact, at our committee meetings he would often sit on the floor, and we would sit with him on the floor at the union hall to discuss the condition of black people. (That's what Harry Bridges used to do too, when he came—sit on the floor.) Paul Robeson had all the black workers at heart, and he spoke very plainly so everyone could understand what he was talking about.

Paul Robeson was at that time the chair of the Council on African Affairs and a member of the executive committee of the World Peace Congress, and a national leader of the Progressive Party. And he was a concert singer and actor of world renown. I was with him for fourteen days in New Orleans.

During the time Paul Robeson was in New Orleans the unions took every means of precaution for his safety. Nelson appointed me to be security, so I was Paul Robeson's bodyguard every place he went in New Orleans. We had two more guys from the transport workers union who was also bodyguards.

First I took Paul Robeson to a good place to eat, Dookie Chase's restaurant on Orleans and Galveston Streets. He could eat too. He liked to eat plank steaks, two large planks and two large glasses of lemonade. I told him, I said, "No wonder they call you 'big fella'!" He had to laugh. Him and I got down tight. He used to call me "Brownie" and he called Nelson "Andy."

We had tight security. When he went to eat in the restaurant, sometimes I would stand up over him, sometimes I would sit down. So many people when they realized that was Paul Robeson they wanted to get to him, so I had to stand by and not let them crowd him. When he wanted to go to the bathroom, I would go in first to check it out and see if there was anybody in there. Then I wouldn't let nobody else in while he was in there. He stayed at a friend's home while he was in New Orleans. At meetings I stood with him and the other two guys was in the audience. In case I needed them I had a sign I would make.

I learned something about Robeson. I wondered why he didn't carry a lot of clothes, just his little briefcase and one suit. I used to take him to get his suit pressed at the cleaners. If he had to move fast, he didn't have to worry about packing clothes! He traveled light.

I would take him around to different meetings. One day we had a meeting with the editors of the *Louisiana Weekly* newspaper and other business and professional black people. Then there was community meetings at churches. Another time Paul Robeson came to our union meeting and made a talk to members of our local. He met with other unions too. He also sang at the Coliseum before leaving New Orleans. Everyone was so glad to see him. When he left, black and white people shook his hand and told him, "You are welcome in New Orleans whenever you come back."

One time I asked him about his films. He said there was one film he didn't like and that was *Emperor Jones*. "I didn't like to kill my people," he said. I told him I saw him in Los Angeles in *Othello*. "You liked that?" he said. I said I did. "That was great acting," I said. I didn't know he was a football player 'til later.

I also talked with Paul Robeson about issues facing black workers and their problems in this country. I asked him, "Would socialism help some of the workers' problems?" He answered, "We need socialism in this country. Socialism would solve the workers' problems as a whole here in America. In order to fight racism, we have to fight imperialism and capitalism. We're not going to get freedom under capitalism. Only a very few black people are going to get the crumbs that fall through the cracks—the intellectuals, professionals, middle class, bourgeoisie. The masses of black working people, or any other working people, are not going to achieve complete freedom as long as we have capitalism. Who's going to profit? Big business—and those who support the capitalist system and help hold back the masses of the people to keep them from organizing. Movements have to organize to change things. A new labor movement, new unity, new struggle." He said the Communist Party was a political party just like any other and that you had a right to join any political party. Paul Robeson had very progressive ideas for the advance of the working class. He understood the struggle.

We talked about Africa, and Paul Robeson said the same thing as Kwame Nkrumah—that Africa must unite. Africa is gonna have to get together, he said. I agreed with what he said. Black people throughout the world must get together. That don't mean that we should be fighting against other people, but we have to get ourselves together and work with other people to set the working people free. We got too many people that's suffering in Africa and Latin America, dying from starvation. No child should go to bed hungry. And they got people fooled, talking about this is God's will. That's a lie. It's a system causing people to starve, suffer, and die. Tell me people can't see that? That's bullshit!

Another thing Paul Robeson and I talked about was books about Africa. He recommended some books to me, and over the years I've added more books to the list, including some books on Paul Robeson himself. Here is my list:

1. *Africa's Gift to America,* by J. A. Rogers
2. *The Whole World in His Hands,* by Susan Robeson
3. *Apartheid: The Facts,* International Defense and Aid Fund for Southern Africa
4. *How Europe Underdeveloped Africa,* by Walter Rodney
5. *Southern Africa/Black America: Same Struggle/Same Fight,* by Bill Sales
6. *Organize or Starve,* by Ken Luckhardt and Brenda Hall
7. *African Socialism,* edited by William Friedland and Carl Rosberg
8. *The Real Facts about Ethiopia,* by J. A. Rogers

9.   *Ethiopia: Population, Resources, Economy,* by Georgi Galperin
10. *The Challenge of Nationhood,* by Tom Mboya
11. *A Guide to African History,* by Basil Davidson
12. *A Glorious Age in Africa,* by Daniel Chu and Elliott Skinner
13. *Great Rulers of the African Past,* by Lavinia Dobler and William Brown
14. *Here I Stand,* by Paul Robeson
15. *The World and Africa,* by W. E. B. Du Bois
16. *Inside Africa,* by John Gunther
17. *South Africa: Foreign Investment and Apartheid,* by Lawrence Litvak, Robert DeGrasse, and Kathleen McTigue
18. *Philosophy and Class Struggle,* by Dialego
19. "What Africa Thinks of Karl Marx," from *African Communist,* 94 (Third Quarter, 1983)
20. *Apartheid,* by Alex La Guma
21. *The Apartheid Handbook,* by Roger Omond
22. *Axioms of Kwame Nkrumah,* Freedom Fighter's edition
23. *Zed Pan Africa,* by Henry Freedman and R. Molteno
24. *Class Struggle in Africa,* by Kwame Nkrumah
25. *Africa Must Unite,* by Kwame Nkrumah
26. *The Suppression of the African Slave Trade,* by W. E. B. Du Bois
27. *Ghana: The Autobiography of Kwame Nkrumah*
28. *No Easy Walk to Freedom,* by Nelson Mandela
29. *Handbook of Revolutionary Warfare,* by Kwame Nkrumah
30. *U.S.S.R. and Countries of Africa,* E. A. Tarabrin, general editor
31. *Resistance against Fascist Enslavement in South Africa,* New Century Publishers
32. *Great African Thinkers,* by Cheikh Anta Diop

Paul Robeson and I also talked about the people in China under Mao Tse-tung fighting for freedom. I had a lot of faith in Mao Tse-tung. Later, at the National Democratic Committee meeting in New Orleans I raised the issue of international trade with the people of China. I was the only black man in the crowd who shot that question. Oh, brother! I was sent there by the local. Nelson called me his troubleshooter. And I was shooting! I think he sometimes sent me places where he was afraid to go. But I didn't have no fear 'cause I believed that everybody had the right to talk about what they wanted. Freedom of speech. And I was right! Shit, I'm a citizen just like anybody else, and if they try to deny that to me then something is wrong with the system. They ain't living up to the Constitution. Why tell me all this shit about the Constitution and then try to stop me, which I did get some time. When they sent me to the penitentiary in the 1950s, that was as fake as a three-dollar bill. They ain't had no more business sending me to the penitentiary than they would have had sending the pope!

Henry Wallace lost the election, but we continued teaching politics in our union and whenever we was in any large gathering.

Whenever we could, we tried to have relationships with other unions. In New Orleans the International Longshoremen's Association was strong among the deep water dockworkers. (In Local 207 we handled the inland river barges.) The ILA locals was segregated, one black and one white. We had a good relationship with some of the members of the black local. There was a guy named Smitty who ran for president of the black local. I used to go to him and talk to him, tell him about how to raise issues for his members, like upgrading, vacations, and so on. I used to give him the *Dispatcher* to read.

We worked with other unions too, but we had trouble with the Teamsters. They used to red-bait us all the time. One time a party leader came to New Orleans and the Teamsters came out and threw tomatoes at him. Ernest J. Wright was a black Teamster, and him and I had a good relationship. Wright had a group called the Peoples Defense League, and I used to speak at their meetings at Shakespeare Park.

Strikes were going on in the Henderson sugar refineries in the towns of Gramercy and Reserve, with United Packinghouse and Food Allied Workers Local 591. The workers was demanding higher wages. The local representative asked for help to try to settle the strikes in the two sugar refineries. Nelson decided to send his troubleshooter. I started going there and talking to the workers. Three or four other union reps came along to watch my back 'cause I was raising hell. Every day I made a speech at Gramercy at twelve o'clock and another one at Reserve at three p.m. My speech was about unity, working conditions, and what unity would mean in helping to win strikes. White workers and black workers in both places was in unions, but they wasn't as united as they needed to be to win. When I arrived, all the workers met in the union hall, but they were separated, blacks on one side and whites on the other.

My speech went like this: "Workers suffer because they are kept separated. We must get rid of Jim Crowism and white supremacy and racism throughout the nation. To achieve this, all workers, regardless of race, color, creed, must organize together. Those responsible for these evil things are the bosses in the nation—bankers, industrial firms, plantation owners, factory owners, landlords. Any considerable business is capitalism. These facts remain the real enemy of the people in America, and all workers must fight."

My speeches to the workers went on for eight months. Slowly the black and white workers began to change toward one another. One day I came in and for the first time black and white workers was sitting together in the union hall. They took down the signs that said "white" and "colored." They even started using the same bathrooms and water fountains. The workers began to realize this was a bread-and-butter issue. If you are starving together, you'll fight together.

As time went on all the workers would applaud every time I walked into the union hall, even the deputy sheriff of Gramercy and his detective. They came to the union meetings to "keep peace" if trouble arose. The deputy sheriff stayed on the outside of the hall; he told me to speak loudly so he could hear me because he said he liked the things I was saying. Every day I spoke to the workers on different subjects: better wages, better working conditions, decent houses, and better schools.

At the beginning of both strikes much violence occurred, and some people got hurt. Some was thrown into the river and drowned. All the bloodshed happened in these strikes because nonunion members was trying to take the union members' jobs when the strikes first started. I continued every day with one main subject—unity—so we could win the demands against the bosses. I was calling for trade union democracy among the workers.

I went out there for eight months. By the time both strikes were won, the whole environment had changed. One Sunday morning, the officers asked me to be the guest speaker at a church in a rural area. The church was packed with black and white workers. Later the workers and union officers took me to a community hall where refreshments was being served. Everyone was enjoying eating crabs and crawfish. I in particular enjoyed this event; just to be able to stand back and actually see black and white workers united against the bosses . . . realizing the power isn't in the power structure but lies in the hands of the working class.

I shook hands with all the people and got comments about the victory we had accomplished with black and white workers in the South. Before I left, the workers said, "Brother Brown, you encouraged us to win this victory. We got rid of Jim Crowism on the jobs and we have better understanding." All the officers, the director of District 5, among others, congratulated me on the victory that was won.

I had a feeling of joy, being able to help win those strikes, meeting new friends, and talking among all the workers. This gave me courage to fight more in my local and in the community for things the workers wanted and needed for survival. I was determined to continue my efforts among workers in other places in the Deep South.

Sometimes the struggle took unexpected turns. One night in New Orleans we had an integrated party: black and white workers together. We didn't believe in segregation. We believed in relating with each other and working together toward accomplishing our cause. All of us knew that Jim Crowism was one of the bosses' main weapons for lower wages, bad housing, bad schooling, bad health institutions, and so on, while they get richer and richer and we get poorer and poorer. They was exploiting workers in the South, pitching one worker against the other workers. That night there was a big group of us partying in a white friend's home in the French Quarter. Some of the white people had come down from the North to help break up Jim Crow. The lady who owned the house was a member of the Progressive Party. We had plenty of food, drinks, and good music playing. They had a lady playing the guitar. Said she was from Paris or someplace. Black people and white people was dancing together and raising sand. Rose was there with me. Nelson didn't come; he never did come to the parties we had. I reckon because of his health; he had asthma real bad.

I had me a fifth of liquor that I kept under the sofa. Every now and then I'd get me a little sip. I didn't want to go in the kitchen where everybody else was drinking, 'cause I didn't want them to know I was drinking. I was supposed to be a labor leader; I didn't want to get too far out there.

About eleven o'clock, the party was getting off to a good start. Rose was dancing with somebody and we was having a good time. All of a sudden we heard loud knocking on the door. It was the next-door neighbor who came to complain to the lady of the house about the loud noise we was making. When the lady of the house opened her door and her neighbor saw all the black and white workers dancing and drinking together, it must have made her so upset that she went home and called the police. No doubt she told the police that black and white people was mixing at a party next door because two cars loaded with police, plus the police sergeant, came to the house.

When the sergeant knocked on the door, the lady of the house opened the door. Of course, the police sergeant noticed this was a mixed party with black and white dancing together. The police couldn't stand to see black men dancing with white girls. The sergeant said, "I got a complaint that you are disturbing the peace—and all the niggers have to leave!"

The lady of the house replied, "All my guests are welcome in my home. No one has to leave. We have no discrimination here. They are all my friends." At that point, the police sergeant took his two cars full of police and left the house.

About this time the party was in high gear. An hour later the police sergeant returned with four patrol wagons. When the lady of the house opened the door, the police sergeant announced, "All of you are under arrest. You are violating Louisiana state law. It's against the law to have mixing of races in this state."

By this time I was well known in New Orleans. The police sergeant singled me out and grabbed me out of the crowd. I was arrested first. He told me to put my hands up over my head and lean against the wall and spread my legs. I knew he was trying to harass me because I was the only one out of the whole group he told to do this.

While this was happening, some of the people ran from the house and got away. The rest of us, sixty-four in number, was put in the patrol car and taken to the 12th precinct and booked for "disturbing the peace." Shit, I even forgot my damn whiskey!

Later a friend was contacted by someone in the group. During the night we got an answer from our contact. We was told that someone would be coming down to the precinct to bail us out right away. Our contact didn't want any of the blacks staying in jail overnight because they was afraid some harm would come to us. Interestingly, a judge's daughter, who was white, and one of our attorney's sons, also white, was arrested with the group.

This happened on a Saturday night. Bail money was hard to get on weekends. Bail for all sixty-four was set at $75,000. In the meantime, we was put in separate cells, black women in one cell, white women in another cell. The same arrangement was done with the black men and white men. Rose was scared. This was the first time she was arrested. I told her to take it easy, that everything would be okay.

When the black men was being led to their separate cells, the police was standing all around. From the expression on their faces, they were glad to see so many black men in jail at one time. They tried to provoke us by pushing each individual into the cell. When a policeman pushed me, I turned around to make a remark on the harassment, but a black schoolteacher advised me not to utter one word—just walk on in to the cell—because the police was waiting for an excuse to beat or kill one of us in jail and nothing would ever be done about their act of violence. The policemen in New Orleans was known for their terrorizing, harassment, and brutality toward black people in jails, as well as in black communities. So, all the black men went quietly into their cells with no trouble from any one of us.

Early that Sunday morning we was released from jail. Dr. Oakley Johnson, who used to teach at Dillard University, got the money for bail. We was all happy to be out. Our hearing was set for Monday at noon. Our defense attorneys said they wanted to rush the hearing and be as brief as possible so that it wouldn't be going on into the night, for safety reasons. Our attorneys worried that some trouble would occur when we left the court. They had heard that some Ku Klux Klansmen would be waiting outside when court dismissed.

At the hearing on Monday we had five defense attorneys. Instead of the judge putting all of us on trial at the same time, he called each one up to stand trial individually. We found out why they couldn't charge us with anything except "disturbing the peace." The reason was that we was in Orleans Parish within the city limits and there was no laws against race mixing. All sixty-four, black and white, was found guilty of disturbing the peace. The judge fined us $5 each. I never did see any Klansmen.

We was displeased with the judge's decision and called a meeting with our attorneys outside the court to instruct them that we didn't like paying the fines. After all, our opinion was that if white workers wanted to associate with black workers in the state of Louisiana or any other state, it shouldn't have been any crime. We wasn't going to let the reactionaries take away our rights as human beings, particularly black workers who have suffered so long to make the South a better place for all human beings to live.

Later, the case of the sixty-four was appealed before a high court and we were found not guilty. We helped establish the right to associate and visit each other's homes and attend meetings or demonstrate together regardless of race, color, or creed. To me this was a victory for the working class in the South—not just black workers or white workers. It was the working people as a whole that won. We put a nail in the coffin of Jim Crowism!

One evening I was sitting alone in the Elite restaurant located on Rampart Street in New Orleans. The Elite restaurant was where I usually enjoyed eating. I sat down and ordered fried chicken and Miller High Life beer. Suddenly a man came over to the table and asked me, "Is anyone sitting at the table with you?" I told him, "No, you're welcome to sit down." When the man sat down, I noticed he had a sad, worried look in his eyes. He started to talk on different subjects. He told me his name was Brown, that he had been working in Empire, Louisiana, on a fishing boat, but he had quit his job and come to New Orleans looking for a better job.

Then Brown began telling me this story: "All the black men in Empire worked on the boats. We went out to sea to catch big fish to bring back to make fishmeal fertilizer. Men would stay five to six months at a time on the water. Conditions on the boats was bad. Men had to sleep on bunks stuffed with hay. Food wasn't worth eating. Working conditions was bad. If the men caught a large number of fish, they only made only a few cents a thousand pounds, and they had to pay for room and board on payday, when they came back to Empire."

After a short pause, he continued with his story: "When the captain of the boat paid off the men, he waited until night. Then he sent to town and got the sheriff and detective. The captain paid off the men by candlelight. A candle was placed on the table, and he threw the money on the floor. When the men went to pick up their money, it was hard to see. While doing this, the captain also kept some of the money. If one of the men complained to the captain about his money, he called in the sheriff or the detective and said the man was causing trouble. Then the sheriff would arrest him and put him in jail overnight. Mostly the men wouldn't say anything to the captain. They took his treatment only because they didn't have nobody to back them up. Sometimes a few men from the boats would leave and go looking for other work. But usually they had no luck, and they soon returned to the boats."

Being a union representative, I told Brown that maybe I could help. I discussed the whole thing with Brother Nelson. He thought we should do something. I asked Brown if Nelson and I went to Empire would he be afraid to go back and show us the way? Brown said no.

The three of us drove down to Empire. When we arrived, the workers happened to be back from the river, sitting in a bar and drinking beer with the little money they had. Beer was all the fish workers could afford to drink. This bar was owned by a black lady. The president and I started talking to some workers, but we only told one man what business we had in Empire.

This man told the other workers, "These brothers are here to help us. Come on the outside and listen to them talk." The lady owner of the bar hollered out loud, "You don't have to go on the outside and talk. Cut off the juke box! No more playing music until this meeting is over."

Brother Nelson spoke first, telling the workers, "We are here to organize a union on all boats, but we have to contact other unions so funds can be raised to set up an organizing committee in different areas where boats are going out to catch fish." Then I spoke to the workers. "Conditions would be improved by forming a union. A union means better working conditions, increase in pay, seniority, vacation pay, and health and welfare plans. A union means better schools for children, better health institutions. A union means that we are in a fighting position for the right to vote and to fight against Jim Crowism. A union can put pressure on our local, state, and national representatives in Washington, D.C., so we can get things we want and need. All workers should register so that they can get political power to get the necessities of life to survive. This is very plainly a bread-and-butter issue."

Brown talked to the workers also. Then I asked the fishermen to tell their stories about the job. They told us pretty much the same stories that Brown told me in New Orleans.

Then Brother Nelson and I told the fishermen that we had to contact other unions. If successful, next time we would bring some pledge cards. After talking to all the workers present, Brother Nelson, Brown, and I left Empire and returned to New Orleans. Brother Nelson phoned representatives from a few unions to discuss the problems that the fishermen was facing. He explained to the union representatives that all the men working on the fishing boats was black men. The union representatives said, "We are willing to help organize, but we have to contact our international representative to get permission and pledges for funds to organize." In a few days Nelson got a phone call from the union representatives. They said for him to start the ball rolling. Our union, Local 207, was sent pledge cards.

Brother Nelson, four union representatives, and myself went to Empire. When we arrived, some fishermen was out fishing and some was still on shore. One fisherman was put in charge of getting pledge cards to those who was out fishing. The fishermen on shore signed pledge cards. News of this spread like wildfire throughout several other areas where fishmeal for fertilizer was being made.

After all pledge cards was signed, all the fishermen was organized. Later, we sent in union representatives to help draft a working agreement. This agreement was sent to all companies. Of course, the companies refused to talk with the negotiating committee in some locations. The negotiating committee had to call strikes. Then some unions started calling other unions for support. Nelson contacted the food and tobacco workers, the fur and leather workers, the packinghouse workers, and some others. People started sending in money, food, and clothing. Communities from many different areas gave support.

Lee Brown carrying a placard at a senior citizens demonstration at Republication Party headquarters in the fall of 1995. After his retirement Brown became active in the movement for senior citizens' rights.

Early years of Local 207, International Longshore and Warehouse Union: Gathering signatures on a petition initiated by the ILWU to grant U.S. soldiers in World War II the right to vote. Standing in the rear are (right to left) William Spooner, acting president of Local 207, and Howard Goddard, ILWU regional director. Courtesy of ILWU Library.

The Local 207 picket line in 1946 demanding better wages. Courtesy of ILWU Library.

Black and white members of Local 207 on strike against Swift & Co., 1946. Courtesy of ILWU Library.

Elected officials of Local 207 in 1947. Seated at the right is Lee Brown, who then served on the trustee board. Other officers are (standing left to right) Andrew Nelson, president; August Harris, first vice president; Walter Green, second vice president; Albert Taylor, recording secretary. Courtesy ILWU Library.

Executive board and stewards council members, Local 207, 1947. Lee Brown is seated at the right. Others are Rose Robinson (seated, second row, sixth from the left), who became Lee's common-law wife; August Harris (standing, left); Andrew Nelson (standing, sixth from the left); and C. J. Meske, international representative (standing to the right of Nelson). Courtesy of ILWU Library.

Some of the women members of Local 207, including Rose Robinson (seated, second from the left). Rose was the mother of Lee's son Brownie. The women worked at Sunlight Mills in New Orleans. Courtesy of ILWU Library.

A Local 207 picket line protesting unfair labor practices at H. G. Hills Co. Courtesy of ILWU Library.

Lee Brown being fingered by FBI informer Arthur Eugene at a hearing by the House Un-American Activities Committee (HUAC), February 15, 1957. Brown was questioned about his membership in the U.S. Communist Party. Permission granted by the Times-Picayune Publishing Corporation.

Lee Brown is escorted from the HUAC hearing by U.S. marshals after he refused to answer the committee's questions.

Lee Brown with Grace Oliver at their wedding, January 21, 1976.

Lee Brown with Grace Oliver, 1976.

Lee Brown with Charles Lamb, a leader of Local 2 of the hotel and restaurant workers' union in San Francisco.

Lee Brown with Kendra Alexander (at left). She was a leader of the Northern California branch of the U.S. Communist Party.

Lee Brown at a demonstration with Angela Davis. Brown and Davis were active in the Northern California branch of the Communist Party and later the Committees of Correspondence.

Lee Brown acting as a bodyguard to Alfred Nzo (seated, second from the right). Nzo, a leader of the African National Congress of South Africa, was attending a public gathering in San Francisco.

Lee Brown holding aloft a Communist Party banner at a demonstration in California. The banner reads "Communist Party, U.S.A. Alameda County, Peace, Jobs, Equality."

Lee Brown addressing a gathering of senior citizens.

Lee Brown speaking at a seniors rally in San Francisco, 1986.

Lee Brown with Angela Davis at "Tribute of a Lifetime" gathering, June 26, 1994. The event, sponsored by the Committees of Correspondence, honored veteran activists.

Lee's son Brownie and daughter-in-law Bobbie.

Lee Brown's great granddaughter, Calisha Keyanté Brown, at age 5.

The companies tried to break the strikes by using strikebreakers, but that didn't work. They tried every trick but nothing worked. Finally after nine months, workers won the strikes in several locations in the state of Louisiana. The story of these strikes was told in a pamphlet that one union published called *The Black Fishermen in the South Are Organized.*

The next big struggle took place at Armour Packing Company in New Orleans. We tried to negotiate a new contract with the negotiating committee and employer. We was forced out on strike. The union threw up a picket line in front of Armour plant. A soup kitchen was organized. A picket captain was elected to carry on activities on the picket lines. There was both males and females on the picket lines.

Next a general membership meeting was called with workers at other plants where the union had contracts. They were informed about this strike that was going on at Armour Packing Company. Shop stewards and members from other plants made pledges to support Armour strike workers. Members set up a Strike Fund Committee. Every week the Strike Fund Committee went around to each union shop we had under contract and the members gave donations.

At this time, Armour Packing Company started using tactics against the strikers and myself. They called a police sergeant to warn the picketers that they was trespassing on Armour property. Cars loaded with policemen came and ordered us off the sidewalk in front of the company. I told the picket captain to take all picketers off the sidewalk and let them walk in the streets but be careful not to let passing cars hit any of the picketers.

In the meantime the president and I went to the Survey Department in City Hall to find out whether Armour Company really owned the sidewalk in front of the building. It wasn't long before we found out that Armour Company did own the sidewalk in front of their building. That was one tactic Armour used to temporarily win against the union and rank-and-file members.

We wasn't through yet. We had to use another strategy. Armour Company had several engineers who wasn't members of our union. Brother Nelson contacted the engineers union and explained the situation we were having with Armour Packing Company. Nelson and I explained the need for all workers in the South to unify, regardless of race, creed, or color, around bread-and-butter issues. A representative of the engineers union told us not to worry, that his members wouldn't cross our picket lines anymore. The engineers union members did respect the picket lines. But some of Armour's truck drivers went through the picket. Despite this, Armour Company really began to worry about the strike.

Someone tipped off Brother Nelson and me that Armour was sending several truckloads of meat to load on a ship at the docks. During that time we was carrying informational picket signs asking the public not to buy scab products: "Don't eat scab meat." Our local number and the name of the

Armour Packing Company was also on the signs. "Don't eat their products." The signs said we was on strike because Armour Packing Company refused to negotiate a new contract with our union, Local 207.

We went out to the dock where the ship was loading. It was Nelson, myself, sister Della Burton, who was a member of the union who worked at the feed mill, and some others. We threw up a picket line. The chief steward on the ship talked to us over the ship rail. "What's going on?" he asked. We told him the reason for our picket. Two picketers stayed on the picket line twenty-four hours, day and night.

When the ship's crew came onto the ship, they voted not to stay on a ship loaded with scab meat. The crew threatened to walk off the ship. Then the captain of this ship had to call the Armour Packing Company to get the meat off the ship and put the meat back on the dock. By the way, the name of the ship was *Looking Back.*

We started calling people on the telephone to ask them not to buy scab meat. We got numbers out of the telephone book. I remember one lady I called said she wasn't eating meat nohow 'cause she was sick! I said I was sorry she was sick but I hoped she would support us when she got well. She said she would. I talked to a lot of white people 'cause they was the ones who mainly had telephones. We got a lot of support.

Restaurants and people shopping at stores stopped buying Armour products. The public gave overwhelming support, particularly in the black communities. Black churches supported our union in their communities. The people knew we was fighting for the interest of all workers in the communities. This was one reason Brother Nelson and I was being attacked by the reactionary forces. Brother Nelson and I dedicated ourselves to the union struggle in the interest of the workers as a whole and believed a labor movement must be built in the South, even if it took our lives. We knew what we were up against.

Finally, after forty-five days of constant picketing, Armour Packing Company called our negotiating committee back in to start negotiating again on our contract. But we still maintained our picket lines around the building. None of our members on the picket lines ever weakened. The longer they picketed, the stronger and more militant they became. Our negotiating committee didn't get everything we wanted, but we obtained some agreements that was for the good and welfare of our rank-and-file members.

A special meeting was called with the brothers and sisters who was working at Armour Packing Company. Our negotiating committee brought the contract to the membership to accept or reject. A majority of members voted in favor of the contract. Our negotiators was able to get some improvements in the contract: job security, vacations, wage increases, upgrading and seniority. Any worker who got hurt on the job was sent to company doctors. We didn't win health and welfare plans or pension plans, but

Brother Nelson and I was thinking and planning about how to get health and welfare plans for the rank-and-file members on union jobs.

Contracts was signed between Armour Packing and Local 207 negotiating committee. The union brothers and sisters went back to work as usual and picket signs came down. This strike was over, but we continued the struggle as a whole.

At Inland Waterways Corporation, black and white workers worked on the docks. One day Brother Nelson and I was discussing some conditions that needed to be changed on the dock. We often talked at lunch at an oyster bar. (The waitress at the Elite knew just what I liked: a half dozen raw and a half dozen cooked oysters with some Miller High Life beer.) We felt it was time to upgrade black workers at Inland Waterways. Brother Nelson and I said, "We're going to put our talk into action." We wrote down our proposals on paper and presented them to the general membership on a Sunday. We thought these proposals should be added to the contract. Brother Nelson and I discussed these proposals with the membership in a very simple and plain way: As soon as new jobs come available, the company should place all vacancies on bulletin boards for five days, so employees can read them and apply for new jobs on the basis of seniority, regardless of race, creed, or color.

Black workers was placed in some of the dirtiest, lowest-paying jobs on the dock. Brother Nelson and I felt black workers should be upgraded, for instance, to working as crane operators, tractor drivers, watchmen, and sack sewers. These proposals was added to our contract to be negotiated. Our local also asked for other things in the contract: seniority, paid vacations, paid holidays, and pension plans.

The president and I got ideas from other unions and their contracts that was in the interest of our members. I've also got to say that we learned a lot about tactics and negotiating in the Communist Party. We had good district organizers, like Emanuel Levin. The party taught us a lot of things. To me the Communist Party was the party for the people, and I was a militant Communist and trade unionist.

We were ready—both black and white workers on our negotiating committee. When we asked Inland Waterways for a twenty-five-cent raise across the board, one of our union members brought a deck of playing cards and taped a quarter on the deck. When our negotiating committee walked into the negotiating room, the union member took the deck of cards with the quarter taped on it, slammed the deck of cards on the table, and told the company representative, Mr. Mooney, the big boss himself from St. Louis: "That means we want twenty-five cents across the board!" Mooney didn't know what to say. Then we started negotiating. The company representatives presented their proposal and union representatives presented the rank-and-file proposal. Now the battle was on! And we had a weapon we could use—slowdowns!

They didn't like that at all. We had them between the devil and the deep blue sea! We won the twenty-five cents across-the-board increase. We won upgrading and we won seniority.

Brother Nelson, the union president, was chief negotiator. By then I had been elected vice president, so I was second in line. Both of us black, heads of a negotiating committee in the Deep South! Even though we was facing the antiunion movement, reactionaries, Jim Crowism, and racism, we was determined to build a strong union, especially at cotton compresses, feed mills, fertilizer plants, packing houses, and among dockworkers and barge and boxcar workers. Our union, Local 207, New Orleans, Louisiana, was among the most militant, courageous, and active in the South. Our president and vice president was black but our rank-and-file was both black and white. We had white business agents, white shop stewards, whites on the negotiating committee. Our white members had overcome Jim Crowism and discrimination. White workers had become union conscious, and we were united on bread-and-butter issues.

This was a high point of our union organizing in Louisiana. I felt proud.

CHAPTER SIX

Fighting
Southern Injustice

In 1947 I and other workers rallied to try to defeat the Taft-Hartley law. Black labor representatives, religious leaders, political leaders, and black community leaders had mass meetings in Shakespeare Park. Ernest J. Wright, who was head of the Peoples Defense League, organized these meetings and asked me to speak. Crowds of people turned out to support the workers and to hear speeches against the Taft-Hartley law. All the workers knew this law was brought about to weaken and break the unions. We raised money to send telegrams to the president, as well as senators and congressmen from the state of Louisiana. Andrew Nelson sent me, his troubleshooter, to the meetings and to play a part in this fight against the Taft-Hartley law. We discussed where it was best for me to go to hit it hard. My union, Local 207, was behind me all the way. We discussed in the union how dangerous this bill was for workers. We rallied and sent telegrams from the local. I went to different meetings all around New Orleans.

President Harry Truman vetoed the bill, but Congress overrode his veto. Despite strong working-class opposition, the Congress voted this bill into law in the United States of America—against American workers!

Among other things, under the Taft-Hartley law no union officers could be members of the Communist Party. The officers of Local 207 called a meeting to discuss this law. Nelson then discussed it with the top officers of the ILWU [International Longshore and Warehouse Union]. During that time Harry Bridges was in trouble with the law. They was trying to deport him for being a Communist. We didn't want to add no oil to the fire. The international decided not to break the law but to go along with it to protect the international and the local unions. We decided to withdraw our membership in the Communist Party. Nelson and I also knew they wanted to get rid of Local 207 and put us all in jail. So this was a way to protect the international and the local. We stopped going to Communist Party meetings. But this did not mean we lessened our militancy; as progressive trade unionists, we continued fighting for decent wages, decent working conditions, seniority rights, pensions, welfare funds, better schools, and better health institutions in the communities. And I still felt deeply that socialism was needed to solve the problems of all oppressed workers.

Another bill came up in the state of Louisiana, the right-to-work bill. It was aimed at busting the unions. Andrew Nelson and I took a delegation to the State Capitol at Baton Rouge to speak against this right-to-work bill. Many speakers were lined up to speak against the bill. We had many businessmen, middle-class people, ministers, progressive labor leaders, and politicians who was against the bill, along with members of the unions. We was speaking before a nine-man committee and urging them not to pass this bill. Finally the decision came: five to four; five for the bill, four against. We lost the fight. We lived with that law for two years. However, the unions managed to survive through this struggle.

Later Earl K. Long, Huey P. Long's brother, was running for governor of Louisiana. The labor movement said it would support him, and he pledged to repeal the law if he became governor. We elected him governor. Earl Long did repeal the right-to-work law, and it was knocked out. However, the unions was still facing national antilabor laws like the Kennedy-Landrum law and the Griffin Act, as well as the Taft-Hartley law.

The employers didn't want progressive trade union activities being in operation. Naturally, that was one reason the Taft-Hartley law was passed. The aim was to break up union activities, particularly in the South. The workers was aware of these things from the start. This made us more militant in carrying on union activities. We started organizing the unorganized throughout Louisiana and Mississippi, fighting Jim Crowism.

During this time I was working at Federal Barge Lines. In June 1948 a letter came from the loyalty board of the Commerce Department saying that I was violating the loyalty rules by working for a government agency if I was a member of the Communist Party. They wanted to get me off the Federal Barge Lines, which was then a government-run agency.

Andrew Nelson and I discussed this letter to decide what I should do. We also wrote a letter to the international vice president of the ILWU in San Francisco.

I refused to answer the questions the Department of Commerce sent. I had until August 9 to answer the questions or be discharged from the job. But Federal Barge Lines changed hands from a government agency to a private agency. The private agency was named Inland Waterways Corporation, and the government rules didn't apply to a private agency. Companies and government agents was attacking us on all sides. Even so, we were determined to win demands for union members. Moreover, the Southern states was anti-union. This was one reason that union demands for workers was hard to obtain without a struggle. And my own job was often on the line.

Once before the Federal Barge Lines was trying to fire me. I was dismissed because I was too militant, although they didn't say that. The president of my union, Brother Nelson, took action immediately. My union local called an emergency meeting with the company's five shop stewards (I myself was a shop steward). Some workers called for an immediate strike action. Some workers called for a work slowdown. When the decision was put to a vote, the majority of workers voted for a work slowdown.

Next day, union members staged a work slowdown. Each member was slow going to their working position. Naturally, the company's superintendent, supervisors, and foremen objected to this move. Throughout the day, the work slowdown continued. Some workers was asked, "Can you work faster?" The workers answered, "We are working." Some foremen said, "You are on the job, but not working."

The work slowdown lasted a day and a half. Finally, the superintendent called the president of the local for an emergency meeting at two o'clock that afternoon. The shop stewards, the president of my union, and I went to the office. The company presented statements; the union presented my statements. A decision was made at company headquarters in St. Louis, Missouri. Finally, when the decision was sent back to Local 207, the company president in St. Louis recommended that I be suspended for thirty days before returning to work. The union accepted this decision with the understanding that no seniority was lost. The president and shop stewards notified the workers that "the work slowdown has been called off." That was a victory for the union. Most of all, this proved how strong and well organized Local 207 was in those days in the South.

In the meantime, I worked at Higgins Warehouse until the thirty days was up. Then I returned to Federal Barge Lines.

When I returned to work I was still dock steward and sat on the negotiating committee, the executive board, the trustee board, and the political action committee. And I remained a progressive trade unionist.

What Federal Barge Lines didn't know was that I was vice president of my local, and even if I was removed from the docks I would still be active on the negotiating committee, working on all contracts with all companies that had contracts with our local.

Every two years an election for union representatives of Local 207 was held. The general membership would elect a five-man election committee.

The election committee traveled in a car from plant to plant, so each member could get a chance to vote. This took two or three days traveling time. The election committee members who had to take days off the job to do this work would receive the same pay from the union as on the job. When all votes were collected, the election committee came to the local headquarters at 420 Gravier Street and counted each candidate's votes. Some union representatives would lose, some would win. This was trade union democracy. Both Nelson and I was reelected as president and vice president. I continued in my local fighting for better wages and better working conditions as a member of the negotiating committee facing the company, even while I was suspended from the job on the docks.

Other organizations besides the unions tried to educate black and white workers in the South. One of these was the Southern Conference Education Fund. SCEF played an important role in helping workers throughout the South. One time in 1948 they organized a three-day conference in New Orleans that I attended. At the conference I met Walter White and his wife, Gladys. Walter White was executive secretary of the National Association for the Advancement of Colored People. He was the guest speaker one night during the conference. I sat with his wife while he spoke. "Can't he speak!" she said. To tell the truth I never had any great confidence in Walter White. I respected him but he didn't seem too militant. He was very light-skinned and could pass for white. The best thing he did was go to Klan meetings in the South and get information on them. One time he nearly got caught and they was gonna kill him, but he got out. I respected him for doing that undercover work.

The next night I met Henry A. Wallace, who was also a guest speaker. The crowd was very responsive to him. It was black and white sitting together in the hall—no separation. Afterward, we shook hands and talked briefly about the need to register and vote. He was very friendly and supportive.

The third night, Mary McLeod Bethune, the educator and founder of Bethune-Cookman College, was guest speaker. She talked about problems facing black people in the nation. I was very impressed with the knowledge and feeling coming from her. When she was on her way out, coming down the aisle, I spoke with her and embraced her. I couldn't help but embrace her, I was so impressed. We didn't talk long because she had to catch a plane and her time was limited.

In 1951 I was acting executive secretary of the Louisiana Civil Rights Congress. This was a branch of the national Civil Rights Congress based in New York. The purpose of the organization was to fight for the civil rights and voting rights of black people, and especially people unjustly put in jail, and get lawyers for them. We fought against Jim Crow and segregation. Dr. Oakley Johnson had been the head of the Louisiana chapter but he got fired from his teaching job at Dillard University and he had to step down. It was just a few of us. Brother Nelson and I worked on different cases in the Civil Rights Congress. Its existence was a great comfort to black people—just by knowing hope was around and active in this time of violence, which was every place, especially in the South.

One example of what we did was a young black married man named Paul Washington. Washington, and another black man by the name of Ocie Jugger, was charged with raping a white woman in Algiers, Louisiana. Washington was in jail six or seven months before our Local 207 heard about the case. We learned about Paul Washington through another black man who was a member of our union. This union brother said he had talked with a black trustee in jail who told him about the case. Paul Washington and Ocie Jugger had received the death penalty.

Brother Nelson and I got in contact with the William L. Patterson, national executive secretary of the Civil Rights Congress in New York. We turned over the information we had received about the case.

William Patterson came to New Orleans and we went to see Paul Washington. He asked if the Civil Rights Congress could help him in any way because he was innocent of the rape charge and felt he didn't get a fair trial, since he had an court-appointed attorney and an all-white jury. President Nelson called our attorney, James McCain, and asked if he would look into the case.

After the attorney reported back, President Nelson presented Washington's case before our local's executive board to see if our local could help. I spoke before the executive board in favor of supporting Paul Washington. I said, "Lots of our black people have been railroaded on false charges of rape. Our people have been continuously lynched legally and it is about time for our people, especially our trade union sisters and brothers, to fight against this so-called rape charge that is attacking our people. I call it legal lynching and I ask the executive board to give us their support!" I also told the members of the executive board that I would work with Brother Nelson on this case.

In the meantime, our local set up a defense committee to raise funds to work together with the Louisiana Civil Rights Congress. William L. Patterson and lawyers from the national office started plans to have the case appealed. Louis Berry, a local black attorney, also worked on the case. Dances and raffles was given to raise funds for the defense appeal. We brought the case to the black communities and churches. Ministers gave us permission to come before their congregations to present the case.

In the churches and communities I made a speech that went like this: "There are a lot of Paul Washingtons and Ocie Juggers in the South being framed. This is a big fight and we are not fighting this battle alone. There are many organizations who are helping us fight for justice in the South. But we must also help ourselves if we want others to help us. Numbers of unions are with us in our fight. Local unions and international unions are with us."

When the attorneys came to New Orleans, I was with them in a local attorney's office when they prepared the appeal brief. I was part of their security. I went with the attorneys every place. I also went along when the attorneys went to jail to talk with Paul Washington. I had the opportunity to shake his hand and inquire about his health. Under the circumstances, Paul Washington was feeling all right at that time. When the time came for Paul Washington to talk to the attorneys about his case, the union brothers and I left them in privacy.

Union officials found out where Paul Washington's wife was living. They asked me to keep in touch with her. I visited his wife and little girl often. The only time Paul Washington got a chance to see his little girl was behind prison bars.

The attorneys got Paul Washington a new hearing with the State of Louisiana Supreme Court. The State Supreme Court upheld the lower court decision. So Paul Washington was still facing the death penalty. Then the attorneys made a motion to the United States Supreme Court, but the motion was denied. I can't recall on what grounds the motion was denied. We fought hard to save Paul Washington's life. Unfortunately, due to this unfair "justice," the death sentence was carried out. Paul Washington was executed on a Friday in July 1952. I felt terrible, especially for his wife and daughter.

Ocie Jugger's statement during the trial was that he had only asked this white woman for some food because he was hungry. The court attorney gave our attorneys this report about the case. They said the police had a written confession that was signed by Ocie Jugger. We knew this statement was a lie because Jugger couldn't read or write.

In court, before an all-white jury, Jugger was asked to read the name that was signed on the confession. He didn't know his own name on the paper. Then the attorney gave Jugger a piece of paper and asked him to write his name. He didn't know how to write his name. The attorney proved that point. Someone else had signed Ocie Jugger's name on the confession of rape. Ocie Jugger couldn't read or write, so it was impossible for him to sign a confession or any other thing.

During the trial, Ocie Jugger's lawyers kept asking the white woman had he raped her. During the whole trial, she never answered the question yes or no. Every time the attorneys asked her had he raped her, the woman pretended to faint.

The all-white jury found Ocie Jugger guilty as charged, based on circumstantial evidence. This judge sentenced him to death by the electric chair. Then the judge set the date for the execution. Our attorneys got involved in the appeal and made a motion for a new trial, which was denied.

In the meantime the date for Ocie Jugger's execution was getting closer. Four officials from different unions went to Opelousas on a Thursday to ask for a stay of execution. The state of Louisiana was going to execute Jugger that

Friday. Our attorneys went before a federal judge and asked for a stay of execution for Ocie Jugger. The federal judge turned down the stay of execution.

That Thursday before the execution a large gathering of white people—women, men, old, young, babies, and children of all ages—came to see the electric chair, which was being brought in a truck to the courthouse yard. I never saw the likes of it in all my life! It was outrageous. You should have seen those people's faces, all lit up like a Christmas tree, cheering, laughing, hollering, in a state of excitement, like they was in an amusement park.

Four of us union men was standing among the crowd. Everywhere I looked these white people was picking up their children and putting them on their shoulders so they could see the electric chair. Some white people I was standing near was explaining to their children, "That is an electric chair. It is for a nigger. That's what they are going to use to kill that nigger in tomorrow."

All the black people who lived in that town had left the courthouse yard. Only the white people remained. Only two black men was left there—a black union brother and myself. The other two union brothers was white—one from the leather and fur workers union and one from the tobacco workers union.

Our headquarters for that day was at a barber shop, so the Civil Rights Congress office in New Orleans could keep in touch with us. It was extremely dangerous in this Ku Klux Klan town. When the union brothers and I walked on the streets in this little town going back and forth to the barber shop, white people tried to provoke us by bumping into us on the streets. This was perfectly clear to us. We didn't say anything to these people. We didn't give them any reason to go into their violent act. The white union brothers walked ahead of the black union brother and me and kept their eyes on us for security. When we went back to the barber shop, Dr. Oakley Johnson, who was at the office in New Orleans, had called on the phone and left word with the barber for our delegation to leave that Ku Klux Klan town before dark for our safety.

The next day, on Friday, so-called justice was carried out; Ocie Jugger was executed.

Later, after the execution of Ocie Jugger, Albert Jones, one of our attorneys who defended him, was visiting his own mother in the country in Louisiana. Someone shot him three times with a .22 rifle. He was hospitalized at the Charity Hospital in New Orleans. Often I went to visit him in the hospital. Finally, he recovered and continued in the union and civil rights, fighting for the rights of the poor black people in the South.

The Louisiana Civil Rights Congress tried to help anyone who was seeking our help. But sometimes we lost contact with the people who needed help. We heard about a lady in Hattiesburg, Mississippi, who was seeking our help, so I wrote a letter that Mrs. Sims typed up and sent it to her. The letter said: "Dear Mrs. Bailey, the Louisiana Civil Rights Congress has heard about you from our national office in New York and we are interested in helping you, if we can. Since our office is in the South, it will be easier for us to get in touch with you than for New York to send someone down from up North. Now, we want you to send us more information about your brother and his wife. Please answer the following questions: What was the charge they was convicted of? Was it murder, robbery, rape, or what? Who was the lawyer who defended them? When was they arrested, when tried, when convicted? Do you have newspaper clippings about the case and will you send them to us? Could you or some other relative come to New Orleans later on and tell us all about the case? If we can get more information about the case, so we can know whether or not we can help, we will be very glad." I signed the letter: "Very truly yours, Lee Brown, Acting Executive Secretary, Louisiana Civil Rights Congress."

When I sent this letter and I didn't get an answer from the person, I thought maybe someone opened all their mail and they hadn't received that particular letter. I wouldn't have been too surprised, because the FBI opened all my personal mail and union mail, and letters containing civil rights issues on different people. Sometimes the FBI would wait at the post office when my secretary went to pick up the mail. The FBI told Mrs. Sims that they was FBI and that she had to show them the mail. They intimidated her into showing them the mail; this is what they did. Anyway, after I didn't get any answer from Mrs. Bailey, all I could do was close the case.

A black man who lived in Laurel, Mississippi, named Willie McGee, was in trouble with the authorities of that city, who claimed he raped a white woman. The Civil Rights Congress in New York was handling this case at the time. Since the Civil Rights Congress in New Orleans was closer to Laurel, Mississippi, I was asked if I would get in touch with Dr. Oakley Johnson to work with us on this case.

First, a defense committee involving the union and people of the community was set up. Dr. Johnson often worked along with the union. Dr. Johnson asked me, "Would you go to Laurel, Mississippi, and take Mrs. McGee (Willie McGee's mother) a bus ticket directly to her home?" A community meeting for Willie McGee's defense was being held in New Orleans and they wanted to bring his mother to the meeting.

Every precaution was being taken to keep Mrs. McGee from being followed and attacked by reactionary white people in Laurel. By taking a bus ticket directly to Mrs. McGee's home, we could prevent her from having to go to the bus station to buy a ticket.

Mississippi was dangerous for strangers to travel through, especially black strangers. Therefore, taking this under consideration, I discussed matters with Rose. She pleaded with me not to go to this small town in Mississippi. Despite all her pleading, I told her that this was extremely important, because it was a struggle for black people throughout the Deep South and I had to go contact Mrs. McGee and buy a bus ticket, so she could come to New Orleans to attend a meeting to be held that coming Friday night.

I bought a ticket for Laurel and took the train that Wednesday at eight a.m. Someone in New Orleans had notified Mrs. McGee in advance about the nature of my visit. Every possible precaution had been taken, so I wouldn't get hurt or draw suspicion from anyone in Laurel. When I arrived at the station in Laurel, quite a few poor black people was standing in the station. When I got off the train, all eyes seemed to be on me. I felt these people knew I was a stranger in town. Each one seemed frightened, like they wanted to tell me, "Go back where you came from, it's not safe here." But no one said one word to me in the station.

Outside a cab driver was standing, waiting. He asked if I was the fellow from New Orleans to see Mrs. McGee. I told him yes. I got in the cab and he drove me to Mrs. McGee's home. My plan was to catch the next train back to New Orleans. Dr. Johnson told me that if I wasn't back in New Orleans at ten p.m. that night, he would call to see if I had arrived safely; if not, he would call the FBI to investigate to find out what happened. I arrived at Mr. and Mrs. McGee's home. After an introduction, I didn't tell them I was from the Civil Rights Congress. Instead I told them I was from the union in New Orleans. The reason was that we had found out that Mr. McGee, Willie McGee's father, was giving out information about Willie McGee's case to the authorities in Mississippi. I was careful in discussing the case because he couldn't be trusted.

Mrs. McGee gave me a great deal of information about the case. Later, some friends of Mrs. McGee came to her house to talk with me. I didn't discuss the case with her friends, but I talked on other issues like the civil rights struggle. The main issue I spoke on was Jim Crowism in the South and how white oppressors were causing this Jim Crow system, which was keeping workers divided and preventing them from organizing into unions.

When my discussion with Mrs. McGee's friends ended, it was time to go back to New Orleans. I went to the bus station and bought Mrs. McGee a ticket to New Orleans. I wasn't under the suspicion of anyone in the station. I told Mrs. McGee that when she got on the bus, not to talk to anyone about where she was going. During that time the cab driver gave me his name and phone number, so he could come to the station and pick me up at a certain time. When I called the cab driver at that time, he told me we had to wait until the train whistle blew. Then he would take me to the station for security reasons and because I was a stranger in town. Everything went along as planned. I was back home in New Orleans at ten o'clock that night.

Mrs. McGee arrived in New Orleans on a Friday. Immediately Mrs. McGee was sent to a private home for security, where she stayed until the time for the meeting.

The Willie McGee Defense Fund meeting was held in the community center. At eight o'clock Mrs. McGee was brought to the meeting. A large number of people came to hear Mrs. McGee speak about her son. Before the meeting started, I was seated with Mrs. McGee on the platform. My job that night was to be a bodyguard for Mrs. McGee.

Despite the tight security and secrecy in communication, two plainclothes detectives found out about the meeting and was sitting in the audience. Some white workers found out about the detectives' presence and passed the word down. Dr. Johnson, who was in charge of the meeting, advised Mrs. McGee not to speak too much about the case because the detectives was in the audience. Several other people spoke on Willie McGee's case. Some speakers came from the civil rights organization, some from labor, and I spoke on the case also. Before Mrs. McGee spoke, we collected donations for Willie McGee's defense fund.

My subject was the struggle of black workers in the South. I called for freedom and complete emancipation for the working class as a whole.

Mrs. McGee's message was brave and strong. She told everyone to keep up the good work and continue fighting for the rights of the poor people because the people would win.

Some news reporters was present at the meeting. They took pictures of Mrs. McGee and all the people on the platform and the audience. After the meeting Mrs. McGee was taken back to a secure place to spend the night. The next morning she went back home to Mississippi.

After this period, I was no longer able to be involved in the case. I was facing problems and had to take extreme precautions. They were getting after me too. So I didn't know the outcome of the Willie McGee case. *[Willie McGee's conviction was appealed to the U.S. Supreme Court and two stays of execution were granted. But after a third trial and conviction all appeals were denied.]*

CHAPTER SEVEN

On the Road
for the Union

In spring 1955, I was elected in the Local 207 membership meeting to travel with Brother Andrew Nelson as a delegate to the Eleventh Biennial Convention of the ILWU in Long Beach, California, from April 4 to April 8.

I went home to get prepared and threw a few clothes in my suitcase and some necessary union credentials in my briefcase; then I was ready to leave. Brother Andrew Nelson and his family came to my house to pick me up for the trip. Before we started toward Long Beach, Brother Nelson had to drop his family off at his father-in-law's house, located in a small town near New Orleans. Afterward, we started on our long journey in his old model Oldsmobile.

Sugarland, Texas, was our first stop. Unexpectedly, we were shocked when we saw hundreds and hundreds of black prisoners working on a farm. Those black men, wearing white prison clothes, were being guarded by white guards riding horses and carrying shotguns.

Brother Nelson and I discussed why so many black men was in prison. One of the main reasons was being black; another reason was that they didn't have proper representation in courts. We knew what life was like in this racist, Jim Crow, discriminating society; seeing all those black prisoners made us more determined to carry on our fight for freedom for the poor workers.

We didn't sit there too long in the car cause we knew the guards would get suspicious of us; they liable to say we trying to break somebody out.

One thing for sure, at the convention we knew we would meet all our brothers and sisters from different parts of the country who was facing similar problems as those prisoners: maybe not at that moment, but they might be victims tomorrow, particularly black workers who are more oppressed than any other sector of workers. Not because of God or sin but because of monopoly capitalism!

Another time we stopped to rest and get something to eat, a sandwich or something, in a small place in Arizona. When we left and had driven for a while, Brother Nelson noticed that a car was behind us. He said, "Looks like that car behind us is following us." This car followed us a long way; then Brother Nelson stepped on the gas and speeded up his old model Oldsmobile. Then the car behind started speeding, trying to overtake us. It seemed to me we were speeding for hours. Finally the car turned off the highway and went back in the other direction. There was white men in the car, but we never knew who they was or their intentions. We knew it was dangerous to travel in those small towns. And out there in the desert they could kill you and nobody would know nothing about it. However, Brother Nelson and I was prepared to defend our lives. I had a little .38 pistol given to me by a lady named Momee (I roomed with her when Rose and I separated for a while). Momee was old and she used to send me on errands, like paying her dues at the Eastern Star, and she gave me a piece for protection.

Finally, having traveled on the road three days and four nights, tired but determined, Brother Nelson and I arrived in Los Angeles early on a Sunday morning. Brother Nelson had a brother-in-law living in Los Angeles on 54th Street. So we went to his home early that morning. Leroy and his wife was asleep. When we finally woke them up, they came to the door. I was introduced by Brother Nelson. Leroy and his wife said, "Andrew's friend is truly our friend! You are welcome!"

Afterward, Leroy's wife fixed our breakfast. Leroy went out and brought in some drinks. Leroy's wife started playing music on a combination radio, phonograph, and TV. This was the first time I had seen all these various forms of entertainment combined into one. Now this was quite a treat; in fact, we enjoyed ourselves very much that Sunday morning!

Later that evening I went out to take in the sights. Los Angeles was my old stomping ground. I lived there during the war and knew my way around. I didn't return to Brother Nelson's brother-in-law's home that night. Instead I spent the night with one of my old friends, a lady named Pat, and some of her friends. We sat up laughing and drinking and talking about old times. Pat used to work at Ella's café, where they called me Kokomo.

The next morning I left Pat's house. I took the Long Beach car to the auditorium where the convention was being held. I called Brother Nelson at his brother-in-law's home and told him to bring my briefcase and meet me at the convention.

Before Brother Nelson and I went into the convention we had to go before the credentials committee to prove we was legal delegates and get approval from the committee. I was accepted as an official delegate from Local 207. The convention activities started at ten a.m.

At the convention, I was on an important committee—the committee on publicity and education. During the convention I stood up and nominated a candidate for the international executive board, Brother Bernard Lucas, from Local 208 in Chicago. I knew him from the time when he came to visit our local and I invited him to speak at a meeting on the docks.

Later on in the convention a black caucus meeting was called together to discuss issues concerning the welfare of our members within the international. We had black brothers and Hawaiian brothers at the caucus meeting. Some locals was denying work to black brothers who was traveling and needed jobs. We brought a resolution to the floor. I believe the resolution was for all traveling members to be able to work out of all locals within the international, regardless of race, color, or creed. After it was brought before the convention body, this resolution was approved, except for one or two votes.

I saw ILWU President Harry Bridges briefly at the convention, just to say hello and shake hands. I had met him before when he came to New Orleans and had a chance to talk with him. I liked Bridges; he was honest and he believed in the rank-and-file. He said he tried to represent the rank-and-file. He used to sit on the floor and talk with us about the labor movement. I know he also liked oysters!

A resolution for world peace was brought before the convention and spoken for by Harry Bridges. The resolution said A-bombs and H-bombs should be outlawed, and it called for independence for colonial countries. After Bridges spoke, I decided to hit the deck and go to the microphone to speak in favor of peace. Here is the speech I made at the convention:

> I am from the city of New Orleans, in the state of Louisiana. I would like to say to the delegates here that we are facing a very important situation. It is very dangerous. That is why I stand here in this convention and speak for peace, because peace is very important to the American people and it is important to the peoples of the world.
>
> As Brother Bridges stated, it is true that 1 billion, 500 million people are on the march. I am speaking of the colored people of the world, who are crying for peace. And I urge every delegate when he goes back to his union to fight for peace in his community, in his state, in his city, in his church, in his lodge; fight everywhere you can and cry out for peace and tell the representatives of your state and national governments that we want peace; that we don't want bombs, we want schools; that we don't want pain, we want hospitals; that we want education for our people and we don't want war and that we are not going to stand idly by as American citizens. As citizens, my friends, we must speak for peace, and now is the time that we must go back and the ILWU must stand up and fight for peace. Thank you, sisters and brothers.

When I finished speaking on peace, there was loud applause from the delegates. This was an exciting moment for me, to be able to speak before this
convention and call for peace.

After I spoke, one brother named Maxey from Local 6 got up and spoke
against the resolution. Maxey seemed to speak against everything that came to
the floor. If we had brought in a resolution to give Maxey a raise, he would
have spoken against it. I couldn't figure him out. Anyway, somebody made a
motion and the peace resolution was approved by the delegates.

The convention continued with speeches about issues facing workers in
this country. I learned a lot from various delegates from different parts of
the country. I would be able to return to my own Local 207 equipped with
knowledge to help members of my local and members in other locals in
New Orleans.

I enjoyed the convention, where I met lots of trade unionist brothers and
sisters. I met a lady who was a Russian immigrant and we discussed many issues about workers in the South. She was there with her husband, who was a
lumber worker somewhere up north in Oregon. She belonged to the women's
auxiliary of his union.

Lots of pictures was taken at the convention. I met some white delegates
from Canada and they asked me if I would join their delegation and have
pictures taken with them. Another black brother from Los Angeles was also
asked. Both of us accepted this invitation. They explained that they wanted
to take pictures with us to show unity and good relationships with black
people. I put in an order for some of those pictures to be sent to our Local
in New Orleans.

I had an opportunity to talk with a very militant lawyer named Vince Hallinan from San Francisco. He told somebody he wanted to talk with me. He
must've heard me speak at the convention. He wanted to discuss issues that
blacks and other workers was facing in the South. I discussed many issues
with Vince Hallinan and gave him much information on how black workers
was being exploited by the bosses and how black and white workers was divided in the South by Jim Crowism and segregation. I explained why the labor movement was weak in the South—because the unorganized have to be organized. When we can educate white and black workers and achieve unity, it
will better for all issues that we are facing. I said this wasn't a race issue but a
bread-and-butter issue. The strategy that was used against the workers was
"divide and conquer." I preached unity to white workers and black workers as
well. Vince Hallinan and I learned from each other. He was outspoken and
seemed very militant and progressive. We had a good relationship when our
discussion ended. (Years later when I moved to San Francisco, Vince Hallinan
used to tell me that I should write my life story. He said there should be more
black trade unionists writing their life stories.)

Later on, a dance was given for all convention delegates. The Russian lady and I went to this dance together. We didn't dance because the floor was waxed and slippery. Shit, I couldn't walk on it, let alone dance on it! But I enjoyed the dance and got a chance to meet a lot of brothers and union members. We exchanged ideas. At the end of the convention, they gave a dinner for all delegates.

Brother Nelson and I stayed eight days in California. We left on Sunday morning on our way back to New Orleans. As we traveled, we was very careful not to stop in any Jim Crow towns. We ate cold cuts and slept in the car.

But when we reached San Antonio, Texas, we had a flat tire and was short of money. Brother Nelson and I, at that time, was members of the Masonic Order. I said, "Let's see if we can get some help from the Masonic Order." We decided to look for the worship master and secretary of the Masonic Lodge in San Antonio.

Someone advised us to go to a particular black funeral home. When we arrived at the funeral home, we talked with the funeral director. We identified ourselves as trade unionists and members of the Masonic Order. Afterward, the funeral director called the secretary-treasurer of the lodge and told him he had two brother trade unionists and members of the order who was in distress and needed some assistance.

The funeral director gave me the secretary-treasurer's address. Then he gave me his name and telephone number in case we got lost. Brother Nelson and I went to the brother's home. We identified ourselves as trade unionists and the brother accepted us with a warm welcome. He said he was Brother Smith. Brother Smith asked for our lodge number and the name of our worship master in New Orleans. We told him, "We are members of Noah's Ark, number 2. Our grand lodge is King James. Our worship master's name is Robert Jones."

Brother Smith's wife fixed us dinner, and then he went out and brought in some refreshments. We didn't sleep that night; we sat up all night discussing many issues, particularly the labor movement. When we was ready to leave, Brother Smith said he was able to raise some money to help assist us on our way back home. He also got us a tire for the car.

That morning Brother Smith's wife fixed us breakfast and lunch to eat on the way. We then greeted each other in brotherly love and sisterly love. This was our philosophy. Brother Smith wished us farewell, "May peace go with you." Then once again we was on our way back home.

We arrived back in New Orleans safely. About six that evening Brother Nelson and I went to pick up his family. We stayed overnight with his father-in-law and sister. We sat up late talking about our trip and the problems facing black workers. Next morning, after breakfast, we all left.

After this trip, I didn't return to work right away. I rested for a few days. In the meantime I prepared my report about the convention to bring before our general membership. I said that our trip was very successful and we talked with brothers and sisters from Canada and Hawaii and other parts of the country and learned how they were doing. The general membership accepted my report and congratulated Brother Nelson and myself for a job well done.

It was also in 1955 that a conference was held in New York City. Numbers of representatives from different unions was present. The purpose of this conference was to discuss human welfare and rights for the people. The conference was known as the Unity Conference, with trade unions and other groups. It was held at the Capitol Hotel on 55th Street.

I was selected by my local to attend the conference. I went on the silver train that runs from New Orleans square into New York City. You could sit anywhere on that train, white and black together, even in the South. When I was coming back to New Orleans, I met a white lady who was going to Arizona. She must have been going to college in New York or somewhere and was coming to see her parents. She and I was sitting at the dining table together when the train stopped in Mississippi. White people outside was standing there looking at us. I told her, "If I was to get off the train here, you wouldn't see me any more!" She looked and said, "You're right!"

I was very proud to be one of the speakers at the conference, representing the most militant union in the South, Local 207, New Orleans, Louisiana. I spoke on Jim Crowism and things that we was confronted with, particularly black workers, who worked on the dirtiest and lowest-paying jobs in the South.

This is the message I left with the other delegates: Jim Crowism keeps workers divided by low wages and bad working conditions. The majority of workers throughout the South are unorganized because of Jim Crowism. All trade unionists, and all concerned people of other organizations, should struggle around particular issues—better schools for our children, better health institutions, and decent low-rent houses for poor people. I stressed the struggle against police brutality and that thousands of black people are being sent to jail because of the lack of justice for poor people. I said, "We should encourage all working people to register and vote. We can achieve lots of things through the ballot. We can vote for candidates who will fight for the rights of working people and poor people throughout the nation."

During my stay in New York, I lived with Mrs. Mallard, whose husband was killed by some Ku Klux Klansmen in Lyons, Georgia. Mrs. Mallard related this tragic event to me. . . . She had left her older daughter at home while she and her husband and baby went to a registration meeting. On their way home three cars loaded with white people dressed in Ku Klux Klan robes was following them. When they stopped at the church, the Klansmen caught up with them. Mr. and Mrs. Mallard jumped out of their car and ran under the church house, leaving their baby behind in the car. The Klansmen started shooting inside the car. Fortunately they shot over the baby's head, but the car was shot up with bullet holes. Then they started shooting under the church. Mr. Mallard was killed. Mrs. Mallard stayed under the church too frightened to come out. When the Ku Klux Klan thought both of them was killed, they left. She overheard the Klansmen say, "We got both of the niggers. That will stop the niggers wanting to vote now."

When the shooting had stopped and the Klan left, Mrs. Mallard came out from under the church, went to the car, and got her baby. Then she ran to some friends' home. Her friends advised her not to go back to her home. They said they would send some friends to get her daughter. When this was done, her friends went out and made some contacts to get her out of town. They even had some white workers who came over and brought money to aid her in getting out of town.

Mrs. Mallard and her baby went to New York. She didn't take her daughter with her at that time because they didn't want to send them together. After the Ku Klux Klan found out Mrs. Mallard was still alive, they went looking for her. Someone put out a report that said Mrs. Mallard was on a bus with her baby. Another black woman was on the bus with her baby. The Klan took this woman and baby off the bus and they were never heard from again.

Mrs. Mallard's baby boy was about fourteen years old when I met him in New York. When I saw him, I hugged him and tears flowed out of my eyes.

Later Mrs. Mallard's daughter wanted to take me out and show me the town. One night we went to a club named Birdland. The star of the show was Dinah Washington. This was my first chance to see Dinah Washington in person.

The following night I was a guest at the Electrical Workers Union. A dance was going on. I enjoyed myself very much, dancing with the workers and talking about issues facing workers in the South.

The next night a white comrade from the Communist Party picked me up and took me to his home. There I met a group of people, including news reporters. They wanted to interview me about many problems in the South and what the workers was doing to better these conditions. I told them, "We are trying to organize the unorganized and build better relations between black and white workers in the South, so we can defeat the Jim Crow system that is causing major problems among the workers. I believe someday there will be a new South! Labor will have a voice helping to defeat the right-to-work bills throughout the South. Don't be confused by these so-called right-to-work bills. These bills should be called by their proper name: the right to destroy unions and lower your wages, no job security and no future for organized labor bills. We as trade unionists and working people in this country can change this whole picture by organizing ourselves for unity and doing away with the

Jim Crow system. We can build a strong rank-and-file union for action. I am very proud to be here with you and hope I will have the opportunity to come back and see all of you some more." Afterwards, some friends took me back to Mrs. Mallard's house.

The next day I went to another friend's who took me to his house to meet his family. They fixed me a southern dinner: mustard greens, cornbread, and lemonade. Then I was shown around New York and New Jersey. I enjoyed this very much. They wanted me to stay over in New York two more days. I could cash in my train ticket, and they would send me back on a plane. But I told them I didn't ride in planes because I didn't trust them, and I had to get back to the South—there was a lot of work to be done.

I was supposed to see Dr. W. E. B. Du Bois while I was in New York but I missed him. He invited me to his office, but the guy that was bringing me was late and by the time we got there Dr. Du Bois had gone. So I didn't get to meet him. I did go over to the office of the Civil Rights Congress, but William Patterson was out of town.

The following day I prepared to leave to go back to New Orleans. Mrs. Mallard and another lady who was Jewish came with me to the station to see me off. They both were sad and crying. When I left, I told them I would never forget my stay in New York and the things they told me. Also to Mrs. Mallard I said, "You gave me confidence in myself to go back to the South and continue on struggling, and my love will always be with you to the end of my struggle." I was kissed by both of them before I left.

When I returned to New Orleans, my first duty was to make my report to the president and the general membership of my union. I told them about my speech and the newspaper interview and the different people and trade unionists I met and talked with. President Nelson stood up and said, "Brother Brown's report was good. He brought us back some information helpful for us in this great struggle here in the South. I would like to thank Brother Brown for a job well done. He is one of our rank-and-file members who is always ready to do his duty as a trade unionist."

In November 1955, I was working with three hundred or more black and white workers on Galvez Street wharf at the Waterways Terminal Corporation (which used to be Inland Waterways). The company was trying to violate our working agreement. For the safety of the men, our working agreement called for the cranes to lift no more than 2,000 pounds at a time, which amounted to one pallet board. The pallet boards was lifted from the barge and swung over the men's heads to the dock. The company wanted to speed things up and hook up two pallet boards at one time, one on top of the other and weighing 4,000 pounds, to swing with the crane over the men's heads. This was extremely dangerous for the workers. It might break and fall and kill people.

Since I was union shop steward on the dock (as well as vice president of the local), I immediately took up this matter with the foreman and superintendent of the docks. That was step one, following our agreement procedure. We couldn't reach an agreement with the foreman and supervisor. So we had to take step two.

Step two meant calling in the president of the local and getting the general manager of the Waterways Terminals. A meeting was set. We discussed these issues like we had done in the past. The discussion went on over three days. But even then we couldn't reach an agreement. After this unsuccessful discussion, we came out of the meeting.

The following day, the local called a meeting with the workers on the docks concerning this matter. The double pallet boards was loaded up in St. Louis on the barges by workers who was in a different union. In the meantime, our local union members and officials discussed it among ourselves to see what action should be taken. The union members made a recommendation that I should go to St. Louis. I explained, "We should form a committee of three rank-and-file members to go along with me, so the committee would consist of four men."

Meanwhile the union members called for job action. Job action was one of our old weapons to get the demands for our union members from the bosses; job action was a slowdown — working in slow motion.

That Friday we called another meeting in the parking lot, not far from the docks. This meeting was called to raise funds to send three committeemen, besides myself, to St. Louis. I helped select the three other brother members who was to go along with me. The selected committeemen was all black brothers and rank-and-file members; one brother was a dock steward.

Since one of the committee brothers had an automobile, we made preparation to travel in it. When we reached St. Louis, I had a contact there who got us a place to stay.

Despite being strangers in St. Louis, we quickly made new friends. We were invited over to East St. Louis to a night club that had a floor show. A man was singing on stage and his voice sounded like a friend I had heard sing in New Orleans. When he finished singing, I went backstage and introduced myself and told him his voice sounded like a friend's in New Orleans. I told him my friend's name, Roy Brown. He said, "I know Roy Brown. He's a good friend of mine." I also told the singer that three brothers who came with me was sitting in the audience, but I didn't explain the nature of my business in St. Louis.

The singer came to the table and got the names of the three brothers. He introduced us to the audience by announcing, "These men are trade unionists and they are my guests." When the floor show finished, the singer invited us over to his mother's home for dinner the next day. We accepted his invitation. The singer said that when he was in New Orleans he was treated with such good hospitality, he couldn't let anyone from New Orleans leave without inviting them over for dinner. The brothers and I made new friends in such a short while because we knew how to relate with others very well.

The following day I contacted the dockworkers local. I think they were affiliated with the Teamsters. I asked the president of the local to set a meeting with the committeemen and myself. The president agreed and set a meeting the next day at ten a.m.

Later that day, the committee and I got ready for our seven o'clock engagement at our friend's mother's home for dinner. When the four of us arrived at her home, he introduced us to her. His mother was a very friendly lady. She told us to make ourselves at home while she finished preparing dinner. Once seated in the living room, we started discussing political issues and problems facing labor in this country.

During our discussion, we was called into the dining room for dinner by our friend's mother. This was the first time I had ever seen a table set up like this! His mother served us a southern dinner that included southern fried chicken, rice, cornbread, candied yams, and mustard greens; a quart of beer was placed at each plate. The food was excellent.

After dinner, we laughed and talked at the table. Then we went back into the living room and picked up our conversation where we left off. We spoke about why we must encourage black workers to join unions. The unions have played an important role in getting things we need and want: education, health, and decent homes. It was getting late, so the brothers and I decided to go back to the place where we was staying.

The next morning the three brothers and I went to a cafeteria and ate breakfast. Then we started getting ready to meet with the official in St. Louis at ten o'clock. We arrived and met with the president and his committee. We discussed the pallet board issue. I was the spokesman for our committee. The president of the St. Louis local was named Brother Hook.

We decided to have a look at their contract; all of us, committeemen and president, scrutinized their contract. They ain't had shit in there! There wasn't nothing in their contract to prevent them from loading double pallet boards on the barge. They had to load whatever the company told them to. Their hands was tied!

After we finished looking over their contract, I said, "If you send the freight on double pallet boards, we will not unload it in New Orleans. We can work this out so it won't jeopardize your contract with your company." Because we was more militant and had struggled, we had a good working agreement that protected our workers. The brothers in St. Louis was not experienced and did not have this kind of agreement. But we didn't want to jeopardize the jobs of the workers in St. Louis so we said, "Send it, but we're not going to unload it."

The committeemen and president received us very well. All of them, black officials and rank-and-file members of their locals, was glad to meet us. They told us, "We are glad you came. We rank-and-file members here in St. Louis can work together with your rank-and-file dockworkers in New Orleans. We can have unity and solve our problems."

I gave the officials and the members an invitation. If they was ever in New Orleans, they should look up our Local 207, and they would be welcomed.

When I returned to New Orleans, at our first general membership meeting, I made a report on the St. Louis meeting. I told the sisters and brothers I felt that this meeting was a success because we made friends and advanced unity with the St. Louis workers, although there was nothing they could do to help our situation because they didn't have a good working agreement. The members accepted my report and was happy that our committee had made contact with the St. Louis workers.

When the committeemen and I came back to New Orleans, the dockworkers was still on job action. So we called another meeting on the dock and worked out some plans and ended the job action because we had something else in mind.

Finally the brothers in St. Louis sent another barge from St. Louis, loaded top to bottom with doubled-up pallet boards. We hadn't asked the brothers in St. Louis not to load the barge up, since their contract stated that their local had to perform the work that the company had for them to do. But we also knew that no matter how they loaded the pallet boards, we didn't have to unload them when they was swinging over 2,000 pounds.

The company was persistent in violating our contract. The company tried to feel out our strength. We started to unload the barge that came from St. Louis. Our two men who worked with the crane down in the barge hooked on the pallet boards. The men hooked on one pallet board, living up to the working agreement.

The foreman shouted at the men, "Don't send up one pallet board, send up two!" So the men hooked on two pallet boards, following the instructions of the foreman. Then the crane operator, who was a shop steward, said, "I am not going to move my crane as long as the company is violating the contract!"

The men sent for me. The foreman told me, "The men have stopped working." I told the foreman the reason the men had stopped working was that the company had violated the contract and the men wouldn't work on this particular barge lifting two pallet boards. The men would carry one but not two.

Naturally, the foreman tried to put me on the spot by saying I was trying to stop the work. I told the foreman, "It's not me who's stopping the men from working. It's you stopping the men from working because you are trying to get us to violate our contract!"

The foreman called the supervisor. When the supervisor came, he asked me what the trouble was. I told him, "The only trouble is that the company is trying to get us to violate our working conditions." The supervisor called down the head superintendent from his office. He asked me the same question; I gave him the same answer. I wasn't going to encourage my union brothers to break the contract. So the head superintendent told the supervisor, "Fire all the men involved in working on that barge."

Finally, and most significantly, I spoke and asked the superintendent, "Are you firing these men on the barge?"

He replied, "Yes."

I told the superintendent, "You just fired over three hundred men."

The head superintendent asked me, "What do you mean?"

I said, "When you fired these brothers for refusing to violate the contract, then you fired all of the men working on the dock."

Immediately I went into action. I told each shop steward on the job to go to each gang and order the men to quit working and come in. I told them to tell the men, "We are having a work stoppage meeting. Come in under the shade on the dock."

I went on the docks to all the gangs working boxcars and told the gangs to throw in all their runs ("runs" was wooden planks placed in the barges or boxcars for tractors to run on), put them on the dock, and leave their equipment in good shape. Then we went under the shade where the other brothers was waiting. We had some brothers working at the Lower Fleet, but we wasn't able to reach them.

I started off the meeting by explaining why the work stoppage was being called. We had three or four workers on the company side. One of these men used to be a shop steward but he was removed. This particular man was trying to get the brothers to go back to work and wait to see what the president of our local would say about this work stoppage.

The majority of the union brothers replied, "We don't need to wait on President Nelson because Lee Brown, the vice president, is here and we are taking orders from him now!" All the shop stewards was with me 100 percent. When I finished telling the men about the work stoppage, they decided not to go back to work.

The company called in our president to set a meeting the next day at ten o'clock. At that time, our union shop stewards, the president, and I met with the company officials. The company officials insisted they wasn't breaking the contract. The company tried to convince us that they had a right to put in new equipment. Our union president told the company official that what they was using wasn't new equipment and that they was trying to change our working agreement.

So the argument went, pro and con, and lasted two hours. Afterward the meeting was adjourned. Then the general president of the company spoke and said, "I am going to call some other head officials in St. Louis and ask our president his answer on what position he would take on this matter."

Next day the company general president called on the telephone for a meeting with our union president, shop stewards, and me. In the meeting the company general president asked us to return to work and wait until the time came to negotiate a new contract; the workers would handle only one pallet board at a time until the contract expired.

The president and I and the shop stewards agreed to this because we was living up to the union contract. All the workers went back to work. This was another victory for the rank-and-file.

CHAPTER EIGHT

Andrew Steve Nelson's Trial

In the spring of 1956 the employers and the government got after us again to try to bust the union. This time the Waterways Terminal Company wanted to use outside men to bust the union. We had an inside gang and an outside gang. The inside gang was working at the Galvez Street wharf and the outside gang worked at other places where the company had work. The outside gang wasn't regular work; it was part-time. We had union men doing the inside work. But these outside men wasn't in the union and the company tried to use them against us. These men wanted to come back to the Galvez Street wharf and go ahead of regular union men with more seniority; they wanted their outside work to count toward seniority and the union said no. We said, "If you gonna work on the Galvez Street wharf while we got a contract, you got to be in the union." It was a union job but it wasn't a closed shop.

The company got one of these men to bring charges against Local 207 at the National Labor Relations Board. Matter of fact, the company spearheaded it, since he didn't know anything about the Labor Relations Board. The company was doing this to break the union so that it could use nonunion workers. The company told those guys to say that the union threatened them because they wouldn't join the work stoppage back in 1955, which was a lie. We tried to explain to them that if you work inside, you was supposed to be in the union like everybody else. Outside we gave them a break; if there was work on the outside we sent them there to work. We did not threaten a slowdown or strike against brothers; that was common sense.

In May the union wrote a response to the charges. We said we did not demand that the company stop hiring these men but that the company should live up to the seniority provisions of our contract.

The National Labor Relations Board subpoenaed me and the other unions officers in July, and I testified about our case. I told them that we did not threaten or harass those men. We was trying to win them over to our side. They was still our brothers working on the job and we wanted to try to get them to join the union to benefit their own selves.

Even so, the union lost the battle. The National Labor Relations Board ruled in favor of the outside men, that they could work at the Galvez Street wharf.

We lost that battle but we didn't stop there. Certainly the union wasn't going to take this decision lying down. We had a union agreement, a contract, but we needed to make it stronger. The president of the union and I got together and asked the National Labor Relations Board for an election so we could have a closed union shop. The NLRB set a date for the election and came down to the dock and handled the election for the union.

Members voted by secret ballot. Two hundred men voted on the dock in favor of the closed shop, except two antiunion workers, one black and one white. The company and the government wanted the workers fighting against each other, and they wanted to use those two to weaken the union. After that the men refused to work with the two. Struggling to keep the union in the South active, we wasn't going to let two men split the union. Still, the company didn't want to get rid of them. (For a time the company made the black worker some kind of watchman, a stool pigeon. Once he caught me drinking a beer and tried to get me fired.)

After the election the National Labor Relations Board gave the union permission to display a bulletin board informing the men that they had thirty days to become union members. All the nonunion members joined except the two antiunion men. Even a supervisor asked the two men to join the union, but they still refused. According to the union agreement, the company was forced to take the two antiunion workers off the job. The rank-and-file finally won this struggle against the company. It was another victory for the union!

But at the same time it was becoming much harder for the union. A federal grand jury was investigating Andrew Steve Nelson under the Taft-Hartley law. I was very concerned about Brother Nelson. Not only was he president of Local 207, but he was also a very good friend, including his family. Susie, his wife, and their five children treated me as one of the family. Every Sunday I went to his home and had dinner. He was a good cook and would prepare different salads for me to eat. I ate dinner with him and his children. Susie never had time to sit down and eat with us, but she would always be present and willing to help. After dinner, over a fifth of whisky, we discussed politics and important issues that confronted black people here in America and abroad.

Brother Nelson had wisdom and knowledge and a reputation for being fair-minded to both black and white workers. He often said, "We are the most oppressed people, more than any other people in the world, not because of any sin we have committed but because of monopoly capitalism."

I sincerely trusted and had confidence in his ability to work for the good and welfare of his fellow workers at all times when it should be done. I learned a great deal about labor from him; he taught me like a teacher teaching his pupil.

In May 1956 we learned that Brother Nelson was being indicted. We read it in a newspaper report. The federal grand jury indicted Brother Nelson and charged him with violating the Taft-Hartley law. They claimed he was a member of the Communist Party. He was charged on four counts of making a false affidavit of non-Communist membership and affiliation. Nelson was shocked and angry about this charge because at the time they was talking about, 1952 and 1953, he was not a member of the party. We had withdrawn our membership under the Taft-Hartley law.

Nelson's bail was $10,000. Members of Local 207 and friends of different unions helped put up his bail money. Brother Nelson pleaded not guilty. He was released on bail and was brought to trial in September. Brother Nelson got our union lawyer, James McCain, to represent him in the federal court. I was with him every day of his trial.

Brother Nelson suffered with asthma, and during his trial he had a serious attack. In court I sat close by and watched him suffer, and it hurt me to my heart that I wasn't able to do anything to ease his pain. The lawyer asked Judge Christenberry to give him permission to see a doctor for medicine and treatment. This racist judge refused. So I had to take him outside in the hall because he was gasping for air. I laid him on a long bench in the hallway of the court until he felt a little better.

I was Brother Nelson's security, seeing him back and forth to court and to his home. During the trial seeing my president, a good friend, being mistreated brought uncontrollable tears to my eyes and they ran down my cheeks.

Then, all of a sudden, I got angry with this whole evil capitalist system that preys on the black and poor people. I had seen Jim Crowism, segregation, and discrimination in action as well as hate. Then and there I made a pledge to myself that I would carry on if President Nelson was defeated in this long and hard struggle. I would become a dedicated trade unionist by further sacrifice and putting my life on the line. During this trial I was being educated. I took a solemn oath: it was my responsibility and duty to help educate the workers in the trade union and labor movement for complete freedom and a better way of life.

The majority of Local 207 members supported our president through his defense fund. We wasn't given too much time to set up a defense fund because the court speeded up his trial, which lasted over September 4, 5, and 6. Numbers of unions and friends came to his defense, including the international.

During the trial one of the witnesses for the government was a black man named Arthur Eugene. He said that Nelson was a member of the Communist Party. Anything they would ask him he would agree. He was an agent for them, a stool pigeon, just like he was when he later testified against me at the Un-American Activities Committee. He used to be on a ship in the marine cooks and stewards union but they kicked him out. I reckon that's when he first turned out to be a stool pigeon. I met him back in the 1940s at the union hall after they kicked him off the ship. He didn't have nowhere to go. He told me about his children, and I asked Lawrence Blanchard, the foreman at the docks, could he give him two or three days work to try to help him. I used to tell Mrs. Sims to give him a few dollars out of petty cash to buy some cigarettes. I tried to help him. He came to some of the party meetings but I didn't see him too regular. He was probably snitching on Nelson and me back then.

After he testified against Nelson and me, I heard that his mother refused to let him come to her house and his wife said she didn't want to see him no more. They knew I tried to help him.

Maybe it should not be a shock when a person ain't got knowledge and understanding living in this goddamn system, but you got to be cautious, cautious.

Brother Nelson did not testify at the trial. James McCain, the lawyer, decided he was too sick to testify. McCain tried to get the judge to issue a directed verdict of not guilty. He said there was no clear criteria for membership in the Communist Party and that Andrew Nelson did not believe he was in the party when he signed the affidavits. The lawyer also had documents showing that at least one of the government witnesses was a paid informer.

Of course, Brother Nelson continued struggling to survive to tell his side of the story, clinging to life but getting weaker and weaker with each passing day. He was an extraordinary man, with so much confidence in people. This was another reason I loved and respected him.

Finally the trial came to an end. The all-white jury went into the jury room, stayed a few minutes, and returned with a verdict of guilty on all counts. Brother Nelson was released on $7,500 bail but had to appear in court in a few weeks for sentencing.

When he came back for sentencing, he was given five years on each count running concurrently, which meant he would have to serve five years in a federal penitentiary. James McCain said he would appeal the case.

Shortly after the trial, due to his illness Brother Nelson collapsed and was rushed to the hospital in grave condition. Brother Peter Sheppard, second vice president, and I, first vice president of Local 207, kept in close contact with Brother Nelson's doctors so we could be well informed about our president's condition.

From his sick bed Brother Nelson issued an open letter to the members of the union:

> I am not guilty of violating the Taft-Hartley Act; this is just another reactionary, antiunion attack against Local 207 and the International Longshoremen's and Warehousemen's Union as a whole, a part of the continuous attack against our International Union and me as an individual. [I] have been chosen as a victim only for the following reasons or causes: (1) because I am a Negro; (2) because I live in the Deep South, where the prejudices against rank-and-file unionism and the Negro people will lay the full basis for an easy frame-up in the district courts against the ILWU by an all-white jury regardless of the circumstances. A jury that would be prejudiced against me or any member of the Negro race, or the ILWU, a jury not interested in the facts but a fifteen (15) minute verdict of guilty, regardless of the nature of the witnesses, stool-pigeons, paid informers, etc., and (3) a conviction, so long as the conviction was there to be used in furthering the attack against the International Union in its democratic rank-and-file policies.
>
> I am not a member of the Communist Party now, nor have I been a member of the Communist Party or affiliated with the Communist Party at any time since signing the Taft-Hartley non-Communist affidavit as President of the International Longshoremen's and Warehousemen's Union, Local 207, nor have I been at any time since the early part of 1948. Neither have I been active in any of the affairs, and further have made no contribution to its activities, and the frame-up organized against me by the Justice Department thru paid Federal Bureau of Investigation stool-pigeons is in its entirety a pack of ungodly lies and to let them go unchallenged would be a crime against everything honest and decent. And therefore I appeal to you the members of my union, both Local and International, to assist me to the height of your ability in my appeal to prove this frame-up for what it really is, and as I have aforestated it to be a continuance of the false attacks and charges against our International Union as a whole, its locals and their membership. Thanking you in advance for your cooperation, I remain Fraternally Yours, Andrew Nelson, President Local 207–ILWU.

In the meantime, I went before the executive board of our union and asked if Brother Nelson's salary as president could be continued so that his family could have money to survive and pay the note on his home. The executive board approved continuing his salary. Brother Nelson's daughter, Elaine, came every Friday and picked up his check.

I knew I was next in line to be investigated and put on trial, so Brother Peter Sheppard stepped up and took over as first vice president and I became second vice president of Local 207. With this method we kept the union functioning.

Brother Andrew Nelson lived about four months after his trial. He came home from the hospital but he had to go back. He died on Saturday, January 12, 1957, about eight o'clock.

After I got over the shock, I started calling up our key members of the union and rank-and-file members, as well as many of his friends, and told them that Brother Andrew Nelson had passed on. Everyone I contacted was very sad and shocked to hear of his death, knowing so well how he fought for the rights of his people.

Brother Andrew Nelson was a true Marxist and Communist, informed and dedicated to changing this system and transforming it to socialism. At Brother Nelson's wake many union members and lots of friends and workers came to show their last respects. Each and every one of them was dedicated to the cause, both black and white, throughout the city of New Orleans.

Many different union members was present at his funeral. Brother Andrew Nelson was buried with honor and dignity. His denomination was Methodist. I spoke the last words over his body; that's the way he would have wanted it to be. "Brother Nelson was a citizen, fighter, husband, and teacher. He fought with his life in his hands."

Finally, his body was laid to rest in a grave site outside of New Orleans. In addition to all his friends who came for the services many telegrams came from as far as New York, Chicago and San Francisco, California. All the telegrams was given to me to deliver to his wife, Susie.

After the funeral, Susie asked if I would stay at the house with her and the children. I agreed. They didn't want to be left alone that night.

The next morning the union secretary-treasurer, Mrs. Sims, came over to the house and also Brother Chester Langer, who was Brother Andrew's worship master from his lodge. We gathered around the family and discussed their economic situation with them and how to work it out for the best. We stayed with our late president's family all the way.

Now I will close on the activities of the late Brother Andrew Nelson. He will live forever in my mind and in my heart as a true brother in the struggle.

CHAPTER NINE

The Government Comes After Me

Brother Nelson passed, and the next thing I was subpoenaed. The government had decided to concentrate on the ILWU in the South. They didn't want that union there. That's the whole thing. After Nelson's conviction they thought about bringing me up on state charges (Louisiana had a law requiring members of the Communist Party to register with the Department of Safety), but they would have had to charge the stool pigeons that testified against Nelson too. So instead the House Un-American Activity Committee came after me. I'd gotten word that they was gonna investigate me. I was working at a cotton compress, and the U.S. Marshal served me one day with a letter, a subpoena, to appear before the Un-American Activity Committee, which was Friday, February 15, 1957.

An old doctor from the Charity Hospital, who was a member of the party, was called before the committee the same day. He said to me, "Let's go along with them, cooperate with them."

I said, "Man, cooperate with 'em for what? I ain't done nothing."

"I'm gonna cooperate with them," he said.

I say, "That's you. Don't come tell me what to do. I ain't gonna hand nothing over to them." See, they was trying to kill two birds with one stone. They was gonna try to get the international through me. But I didn't cooperate. They thought I was a troublemaker, but they didn't know I was a troubleshooter!

I ain't had a damn thing to tell them! Tell them what? I wasn't going to admit to nothing. Hell, I wanted to make a statement! That was the tactic I used.

I said I wanted to make a statement first. They wouldn't let me make a statement so I wasn't gonna cooperate with them. I wanted to know was Senator Eastland a member of the Klan. Hell, they wanted to ask me what I belonged to, but I wanted to know what Eastland belonged to! That was the statement I wanted to make. I wanted to throw that monkey wrench in there. I don't remember where I got that idea from, but I came up with something for them! I blocked them—they wouldn't let me make my statement, so that gave me reason not to answer their questions. I got as much right to know about Eastland as he got to know about me. Shit, I don't care who he represents! That's the reason I refused to answer, to let them know all black folks wasn't afraid of their bullshit. They asked me over fifty questions, and I refused to answer them. I told them, "Until I am able to make a statement."

The man what supposed to be the chairman jumped down and ran all around the damn chair. Shit, I just rolled back in my chair like I wasn't thinking about him. He was talking about, "You don't scare me!" I said, "You don't scare me either!" They figured they'd come down South and try to make a fool out of a black man. Try to make me act like an Uncle Tom, scratching my head. They didn't know I was ready for their asses! I'd had me a half pint of Grandad that morning and I was ready. I was looking good too. Even the guy on the TV, Bill Monroe, said I was well groomed. I had this *Quo Vadis* haircut and I had on a steel gray suit, white shirt, tie, and black shoes. I didn't come there with one pants leg rolled up like I just came in off the farm.

They brought that stool pigeon Arthur Eugene to testify against me. He said I was a member of the party. Arthur Eugene was sitting in front of me, and I was sitting behind him in a big chair, like a king. (And with that half pint in me I felt like a king!) They told him to point me out, and he turned around and pointed his finger at me and said, "That's him." That picture was in the papers the next day. First time I ever see a black man on the front page of the paper.

I don't know if they paid Arthur Eugene for his spying or what. I know they did pay him for testifying at the hearing. In fact, to my surprise, they sent me a check for being at the hearing that Friday. They sent me $25. I thought, What kind of shit is this! They probably had that check made out already, thought I was gonna collaborate with them.

After the Un-American Activity hearing I thought it was all over with. I happened to go to James McCain, the lawyer's office one morning. I was in that area, and I stopped. He said, "Brown, you walking around here? You have been indicted." I thought he was kidding because he used to kid with me a lot. I said, "Been indicted, Brother?" He said, "Yeah, you was indicted by the grand jury. They gonna bring you before court and try you for being a member of the party, the Communist Party of the United States, as a trade union officer." He said, "They claim that when you signed that non-Communist affidavit, you was a member of the Communist Party." I said, "I was not."

I was indicted March 7, 1957, and served with a subpoena, but it was mailed to the wrong address. Then on March 29 I reported to sign up for my unemployment insurance. I was served with the subpoena there at the office to appear before the judge the same afternoon to post bond. I was unable to obtain $5,000 bond and I was held until Monday, April 1, when Dr. Oakley Johnson posted the bond. I heard the bond money came from the ILWU in San Francisco. In the meantime the Division of Unemployment rejected my claim because they said that I was not available for work March 29. I told them what happened, that I was picked up at the unemployment office that morning, March 29. I was arrested later that same day. But it didn't make no difference to them.

I fought to the best of my ability, with support from unions, individuals, church members, and some other trade unions; even some Catholic priests helped me. Some black Catholics helped me. Some visited where I was in jail before I went to trial. I was proud to be a member of the ILWU, one of the few unions where Negroes had full emancipation and shared leadership responsibility with white workers. Anti-Communists like Eastland did everything they could to destroy the union. What they were doing was unfair. I figured there was no reason for me to be going to trial. For what? Because I was a trade union man, and when they brought me before the Un-American Activity Committee I refused to answer their questions? I wasn't in the party anymore. We'd gotten orders not to pay dues; we was out of the party.

After Andrew Steve Nelson died, I had a dream one night about him. He was sitting in the chair in my room. He told me to get away 'cause they'd come and get me. It wasn't two weeks after that and they had me before the Un-American Activity Committee. The next thing I was indicted.

When I was out on bail before I went on trial, I met this guy from Cuba, a brother. We talked about my case and I told him that if I went to jail I couldn't get no more than five years. He told me, "Hell, I wouldn't give up five minutes for these people!" He made me feel kinda bad. He said he could get me on the sea train going over to Cuba. Maybe he was right. I thought about all the work I had done in the trade union movement and civil rights and now this was what they was trying to do to me. Make me sacrifice five years! It made me mad, but I decided to stay here. The Cuban brother stayed a few days and helped me put together some flyers and things about my case, and then he left. I thought a lot about what the Cuban brother said, and I thought about that dream where Nelson told me to get to stepping.

When they was going to arraign me in October, I decided to jump bail. I had this lawyer who had been appointed by the judge until I could get my own lawyer. I told the lawyer what I planned to do. He didn't say nothing much. They kept postponing the thing and I thought maybe they wouldn't even look for me. Some people said they just wanted me out of New Orleans.

So I went to Hitchcock, Texas, and stayed with my cousin Celie and her husband. I got a job at the cotton compress loading bails of cotton onto a truck.

After about a month the FBI caught up with me one night at my cousin's house. They knocked on the door, and when I opened it a black deputy asked me was I Lee Brown. When I said yes, he told me I was under arrest. They let me go back in the house to put on some clothes. For a minute I thought about going out the backdoor, but something told me not to do it. The day after they put me in Galveston jail, the newspaper said they had the house surrounded by FBI agents. Good thing I didn't go out the back; they would have killed me.

They took me to the jail in Houston where they kept me four or five days. I started talking to the brothers in the jail and made friends. I found out that the black folks, the young black folks, was not scared of the word "Communist." They'd read it in the paper. Some of them asked me what it meant. I'd say to them I was fighting for the rights of my people, fighting for the rights of working people, for trade unions, decent homes, decent education, and decent jobs. And definitely to get rid of race discrimination.

So I made friends, and they hated to see me go the morning when the marshals come to get me. It made me feel good. The brothers was clapping, saying, "Good luck, Brother. Good luck." I liked talking to them. They would come in and talk and one by one ask me questions. I met all kinds. Some in there for murder, all kinds of crimes. I talked with them and they accepted my advice. It gave me strength, gave me courage. It was bit of love and respect from my people.

They took me back to New Orleans and put me in the parish prison until the time for my trial.

They finally brought me to trial on March 24, 1958, in front of Judge Skelly Wright. I was charged on two counts of filing a false affidavit saying that I was not a member of the Communist Party in July 1952. The Taft-Hartley law said that you could not be a member of the Communist Party and an officer of a labor union at the same time. If they convicted me on both counts, I could get ten years in prison and a $20,000 fine.

At first there was one black person on the jury, a female. The district attorney got her off, so it was an all-white jury. I was in court a whole week for the trial testimony. By then I had new attorneys appointed by the court, Edward Koch, James McGovern, and Earl Amedee, a brother. My attorneys decided that I should not testify. They thought they could make the case without having me testify.

During the trial I noticed that Mr. Mooney from the barge line was there every day. I guess he was watching to see what would happen to me 'cause I gave him so much hell!

They brought in a black woman by the name of Gladys Williams. She said I was a member of the Communist Party. Now I used to go to her house and sit down and we talked and had a few drinks, but we never did discuss political affairs. She was asking me about the Nation of Islam. We talked about Elijah Muhammad and black history, but we never did bring up the political issue or discuss the Communist Party. Still, she said that I was a member of the party. I knew her husband a long time ago. He belonged to the Progressive Party in 1948 and during the Henry A. Wallace campaign, which I worked on. I heard they later separated. Maybe she was snitching on him.

Then they brought in a Chinese guy to testify against me. I never had seen but one Chinese in New Orleans, and that was on the dock where he was running a restaurant. But they found some young Chinese to come to testify and say that I tried to get him to join the youth Communist Party. I'd never seen him before.

Finally they brought in Arthur Eugene to testify against me. He said I was in the Communist Party. They asked him how he knew I was a member of the party, and he said he used to attend meetings with me. He said we used to have meetings standing in the street. "You don't know those Communists," he said. "They meet standing in the street!" Hell, he was lying so bad! They was fools to listen to his lies. To tell the truth, Arthur Eugene surprised me. I thought about how I had tried to help him years before when he got kicked out of the Maritime Union and needed work. I used to tell Mrs. Sims to give him a few dollars so he could buy cigarettes. I got the superintendent at the barge line to give him work 'cause I knew Eugene had a family. I didn't think he would do what he did to me.

The Trial
of Lee Brown

ROBERT L. ALLEN

Lee Brown's trial opened at 10:00 A.M. on Monday, March 24, 1958, in the federal district courtroom of Judge J. Skelly Wright. The government was represented by U.S. Attorney M. Hepburn Many. He was assisted by two trial attorneys, Donald Salisbury and Robert Crandall, from the Internal Security Division of the U.S. Department of Justice. Brown's attorneys were James D. McGovern and Earl J. Amedee.

Brown was charged with one count of making, using, and filing a false affidavit in July 1952 with the National Labor Relations Board (NLRB) stating that he was not a member of the Communist Party, and a second count of making, using, and filing a false affidavit claiming he was not affiliated with the Communist Party. A provision in the Labor-Management Relations Act (Taft-Hartley Act) of 1947 stipulated that to be in compliance with the law officers of unions had to file affidavits affirming that they were not members of or affiliated with the Communist Party. Hence, the government, to make its case, had to prove that Brown had actually filed such an affidavit and that he was a member of the Communist Party at the time of filing.

A jury of twelve white people was sworn in to hear the case. If convicted Brown could face a maximum sentence of five years imprisonment on each count and a $10,000 fine.

Prosecutor Many in his opening statement declared that "the Government will show that at the time Brown signed this affidavit . . . stating in that affidavit that he was not a member of nor affiliated with the communist party, that he was, in fact, a member of that party and affiliated with it." Defense attorney McGovern asked the court to require the government to outline the overt acts that they were going to introduce to prove the charge against Brown. When this motion was denied by Judge Wright, McGovern said that the defense declined to make an opening statement, reserving the right to do so later.

The prosecution then called its first witness, Juanita F. Bunch, a compliance supervisor for the NLRB in New Orleans. She testified that her job was to check that unions filed the required compliance documents with the NLRB. She said her office received such documents, including affidavits, from Local 207 in 1952 and 1953, and she sent out a notice of compliance. The documents in question were presented for identification to the witness and offered for admission as evidence. On cross-examination McGovern sought to establish that the witness could not affirm that the documents presented by the government had in fact been transmitted to her office by Local 207—there was no letter of transmittal—and therefore they should not be admitted into evidence. "I believe the testimony of the witness that she received it back from the local union but there is no letter of transmittal or anything whatsoever to negative the possibility that this might be illegally secured evidence," McGovern contended. Judge Wright, however, ruled that since the documents had official stamps of receipt and came from official custody, that was sufficient basis to admit them into evidence.

The prosecution next sought to prove that the signature on the non-Communist affidavit was indeed the signature of Lee Brown. First Israel Augustine, a notary public, was called and testified that the non-Communist affidavit was signed in his presence, but he admitted that he could not identify Brown sitting in court as the person who had signed the affidavit. Consequently, the prosecution brought in another witness, Leonard Thomen, a loan officer for a local finance company, who said that in 1955 Lee Brown filled out and signed a loan application in his presence. Thomen said he "vaguely" remembered the person who signed the form: "I believe it is Mr. Brown, sitting right over here." On cross-examination Thomen admitted that he didn't have personal recollection of the person who signed the loan application. Another loan agent, J. R. Smith, with another loan company testified as to a "Lee Brown" signature on a loan application in 1955 that he handled, and he identified the signer as "the defendant in the brown suit" sitting in court. To further buttress its linking of "Lee Brown" signatures with Lee Brown in court, the prosecution brought in Frank P. Mooney, manager at Waterways Terminal Corporation and Brown's old adversary in waterfront struggles. Mooney produced a copy of a labor contract with Lee Brown's signature on it. He identified Brown as the signer.

The government now had signatures on documents that had been linked to Lee Brown, but were these the same signature as the one on the non-Communist affidavit? George F. Mesnig, an FBI handwriting expert, was called to the stand and testified that the signatures were indeed made by the same person. Defense attorney McGovern raised questions about how the documents were handled when processed at the FBI handwriting analysis lab and how the copies brought to court were verified, but his objection to use of the documents on the grounds that there was a failure to establish the chain of evidence was denied by the court.

Feeling that it had established that Lee Brown signed the non-Communist affidavit, the prosecution then turned to the second part of its case, to establish that Lee Brown was in the Communist Party at the time he signed the affidavit and therefore had made a false affidavit. Four witnesses would be called to offer evidence about the party connection: Gladys Williams, Robert J. Chan, Irwin S. Knight, and the peripatetic Arthur Eugene.

Gladys Williams was the most curious of the lot. Williams testified that she joined the Communist Party in 1944 and that she met Lee Brown at the beginning of 1946 at the Godchaux Building on Canal Street, where the party held meetings. During the course of that year she attended various meetings of the French Quarter club and classes that were also attended by Brown, she testified. The prosecution went into great detail about these 1946 meetings, inquiring about who attended and what was said. Even the judge grew impatient. "Well, sir," Judge Wright interjected at one point, "we've gone into 1946 pretty thoroughly. Can we get closer to 1952?" The government replied that other witnesses would augment Williams's testimony and go further.

On cross-examination by Earl Amedee, Williams admitted that she had joined the Communist Party at the behest of the FBI. "I was contacted by government representatives in 1943, and I was also schooled first about one year before I joined, actually joined the Communist Party."

"You were schooled by the FBI?" asked Amedee.

"I was taking studies to learn how to maneuver in the Communist Party."

Upon completing her training as a government spy, Williams was dispatched to join the Communist Party and inform on its meetings. Asked if she discussed this with her husband, she replied, "Well, no. He had his—he had what he liked as a hobby and he liked certain things and I didn't discuss his affairs and I didn't discuss mine's with him." Asked if attending Communist Party meetings was her hobby, she replied, "I said that he had his hobby and I had what I wanted to do. I mean those were secret things that we were entitled to. I was entitled to what I said was secret, or whatever secrets I wanted to have, and he was entitled to have whatever secrets he wants, and that was what I said."

While the party meetings may have been her "secret thing" as far as her husband was concerned, Williams kept the government well informed, providing copious written reports of each meeting. Amedee elicited that her efforts as an informer netted $100 a month. The defense requested an accounting of these payments from the government, and the documents provided revealed that as of February 14, 1958, Gladys Williams had been paid a total of $13,238.32 as a government informer.

Williams's written reports were also requested. These proved to be chatty and opinionated, though hardly revelatory of any violent antigovernment conspiracy. She reported that in party meetings much time was devoted to discussions of recruitment and fund-raising, "the same old story," as Williams complained more than once in her reports. Other topics of meetings included the unemployment situation, voter registration, the KKK and racism, the colonial situation, and current labor struggles. "The C.P. is moving towards a revolution[ary] period," Williams wrote of one meeting in which there was a discussion of repression against the working class. "There will be a set time but I think it is afar off yet," she opined. The greatest excitement, at least for Williams, was generated when the party's district organizer, Emanuel Levin (whom Williams referred to in her reports as "Big Shot" or "Big Chief"), ran for mayor of New Orleans. She thought that a "well-packed" meeting to discuss his campaign was "terrific."

In her last report made available to the defense Williams complained that "sitting there in the meeting having to listen to the same old story was just another hard day's work. . . ."

The only significant reference to Lee Brown in her reports concerned an incident "told by a young Negro upstart Lee Brown" at the February 12, 1946, meeting in which Brown recounted attempting to solicit funds from a white man who responded by threatening to run him in to jail. Williams mused in the report that "the kid" seemed frightened by the encounter.

Nevertheless, for all this Williams admitted that she did not know for a fact whether Brown was a member of the party. Furthermore, she had not seen him since 1946; that is, not until, ironically enough, Lee Brown, unaware of the role she would play at his forthcoming trial, came to her home in the summer of 1957 soliciting funds for his defense. She gave him a donation.

Robert Chan and Irwin Knight were equally unhelpful with regard to establishing whether Lee Brown was a member of the party in 1952. Chan, employed by the Civil Aeronautics Administration as a traffic controller, said that Lee Brown was a customer at a restaurant operated by Chan's mother. Chan claimed that his one and only personal contact with Brown occurred in the spring of 1946, when Brown approached him in the restaurant. "I was watching, tending the business for my mother, and other than Lee Brown there was nobody else in the place, and he approached me, motioned me to come over, and he asked me if I would be interested in joining, and then he indicated with a yellow slip of paper which had written across at the top of it, 'The Communist Youth Organization of the U.S.,' and to which I replied, 'No, I am a Catholic.' And then I walked away. And then I reported the incident to the FBI. That is the only—since then I have had nothing else personally to do with him." Earl Amedee objected that Chan's testimony was not relevant to events of 1952 since he had had no personal contact with Brown since 1946. The court overruled the objection. On cross-examination Chan said that he was not an FBI agent and that he volunteered to testify at Brown's trial.

Irwin Knight, a clerk at Waterways Terminal Corporation, reported significant encounters with Lee Brown in 1945 and 1946. Knight claimed Brown approached him after lunch one day in December 1945 and asked if he would join the Communist Party. "I told him that I did not know enough about it to even consider it." Knight continued that in early 1946 Lee Brown asked if he would support the Communist Party candidate for mayor, Emanuel Levin. Knight professed ignorance of Levin but agreed that Levin could give him a call. After talking with Levin, Knight told Brown that because of his religious beliefs—he was a Catholic—he couldn't join the Communist Party. Brown's parting comment, according to Knight: "He said that I could have made the party a good man." Under cross-examination Knight said he reported these conversations to his immediate supervisor. Two years later in 1948 the FBI took a written statement from Knight about these encounters. (This was when Brown's political affiliation was under investigation by the Department of Commerce.) Knight admitted that he had had no discussions with Brown about politics since 1946.

The government's star witness was Arthur Eugene, the man who at the HUAC hearing the year before had dramatically pointed out Lee Brown as a Communist Party member. Eugene had also played a key role in helping to convict Andrew Steve Nelson. Given that no other witness had connected Lee Brown with the Communist Party since 1946, if the government had a case against Brown for lying about party membership in 1952, Arthur Eugene would have to make it.

Eugene's testimony began on the afternoon of Tuesday, March 25. Eugene, who said he was presently employed as a warehouseman, testified that he joined the Communist Party in 1948, when he was a seaman. He said he was a member of the National Maritime Union but had been expelled for Communist activities. Eugene said he remained in the party until 1956. Eugene said that he was introduced to Lee Brown as "Comrade Brown" shortly after joining the party. He claimed to have attended twenty-five to thirty party meetings with Lee Brown from 1948 to 1949. He remembered collecting dues from Lee Brown and doing party work together. "We worked together on a number of assignments, such as selling the *Daily Worker,* running off leaflets for the Communist Party."

In May 1949 Eugene said he and Brown were present at a party meeting during which the new Taft-Hartley law was discussed. At the meeting labor leaders affected by the law were instructed to comply with the law: to go ahead and sign affidavits. "They were not told to give up their party membership," he said. "But they were told to cease being an open Communist, such as making outright speeches and trying to recruit or sell the *Daily Worker* and so forth and so on." Eugene said he left New Orleans and went to San Francisco for a time but returned in 1951. He claimed the party's membership had declined, but he said he attended six or eight party meetings in 1951 at which Lee Brown was present, as well as meetings in May, June, and September 1952. The latter meeting was chaired by Andrew Steve Nelson, Eugene testified. The subject of discussion was the Cagle Act, a recently passed Louisiana state law requiring all Communists to register with the state police. The party had decided not to comply, Eugene claimed, and Andrew Steve Nelson, who chaired the meeting, "told us that he would be in contact with a lawyer and for us to get rid of any Communist leaflets or literature or books that we had hanging around in case the state police was to pick us up." Eugene said that he and Lee Brown burned some copies of the *Daily Worker* and other leaflets and literature in a trash can at the union hall. He said that Brown told him that he had made arrangements to leave town if things got too hot.

Eugene recalled attending additional party meetings in 1952 and 1953. At one meeting he said Steve Nelson told everyone to "lay low" while things were hot. He said he ran into Lee Brown on the street in 1954 and they had a discussion about trying to rebuild the party.

Since Eugene was already known to be an informer from the Nelson trial and the HUAC hearing, the prosecution asked during what period was he "furnishing information" to the FBI. Eugene replied he started on Good Friday 1952 and that he continued "clean up to the Steve Nelson trial." He said he was paid for information by the FBI and had received a total of $1,500 or $1,600 since 1952.

In March 1952 the FBI launched an investigation of Lee Brown on suspicion of having violated the Taft-Hartley Act by filing false non-Communist affidavits. (Even earlier, as we know from Gladys Williams's testimony, the FBI had established a network of paid informers, including Williams, to spy on party meetings in New Orleans.) Over the next six years the Bureau accumulated a nine-hundred-page dossier on Brown. In a memo dated May 19, 1953, the FBI admitted that "there is no known evidence to establish" that Nelson and Brown were members of the CP subsequent to the dates they executed non-Communist affidavits. Another memorandum on the same date claimed to have identified unnamed paid informers who could testify that Brown was in the party after signing the affidavits. (One of these unnamed informers was probably Arthur Eugene.) However, the memo concluded that these informers were "precluded from testifying at the present time due to their paid informant status." The informers themselves, according to another memo, expressed "great reluctance to testify," contending that their exposure would diminish their usefulness as informants. (Left unsaid was their concern that their exposure would also terminate their enlistment on the FBI payroll. Noncooperation also carried its risks: in a fit of annoyance the FBI cut off payments to one uncooperative informant.)

The Bureau made great efforts to identify other informants who might be able to testify about Brown's post-1952 membership in the party, but with no success. FBI Director J. Edgar Hoover followed the investigation closely and occasionally sent memoranda to the New Orleans office expressing his concern about efforts to produce informants to testify against Brown. In the end the Bureau decided to use paid informers to make the case against Lee Brown, although some hesitation was expressed about the quantity of "extraneous information" in Gladys Williams's reports and her "tendency to include in the reports her personal opinions and comments of persons in attendance at various meetings and activities." Apparently the Bureau found ways to obtain the cooperation of reluctant informers.

Defense attorney McGovern began his cross-examination by asking about the alleged street meeting with Lee Brown in 1954. McGovern clearly found this scenario highly unlikely, but Eugene blithely replied, "You don't know the Communist Party."

McGovern also pressed Eugene about the meetings he claimed to have attended in 1948–1949 at which Brown was present. McGovern was trying to impeach Eugene's testimony because the original written report he gave to the FBI made no mention of the twenty-five or thirty meetings he said he attended in 1948–1949 with Lee Brown.

Seeking to undermine Eugene's credibility as a witness, the next day, March 26, McGovern hammered away at Eugene's testimony, especially inconsistencies between his written statement and his testimony in court. McGovern elicited that Eugene's first contact with the FBI was in 1952; Eugene was contacted by the FBI and called in for a meeting on April 11, 1952. After being questioned by FBI agents, Eugene signed a written statement describing his involvement with the Communist Party. The statement was later read into the record by Judge Wright. In it Eugene said that during the 1948 National Maritime Union elections in New Orleans he backed two candidates who were identified as Communists. After the election he was kicked out of the union. He said he started attending Communist Party meetings in New Orleans in 1948. He claimed that the "real reason" he went to the meetings was to get a union book and a job through the Marine Cooks and Stewards Union. Eugene's statement described party meetings and activities he attended in New Orleans and San Francisco and on ships on which he worked. The statement said that "in February of 1951, I was screened at Providence, Rhode Island, and came back to New Orleans. *[In earlier testimony it had come out that at this time Eugene could not get work as a seaman, having been "screened" from ship work. During the Korean War any known Communists were "screened" by the U.S. Coast Guard and prevented from working on American ships as seamen.]* I haven't gone to any Communist meeting or attended any Communist function since that time." A few lines later the statement has Eugene claiming, "I have not been a member since about September 1950 and have had no contact with the Party itself since I left San Francisco. I do come into contact with the Communist party members occasionally, but none of them have attempted to get me to rejoin the Communist movement." Although Eugene named many individuals in this 1952 statement, Lee Brown was not one of them.

In his cross-examination McGovern pressed Eugene on the contradictions between his written statement and his court testimony:

McGovern: So you state, "I have not been a member since about September, 1950" and this statement is dated . . . April 11th, 1952. Is that right?

Eugene: Right.

McGovern: So, you haven't been a member during 1951?

Eugene: Yes, I was a member.

McGovern: Well, which is accurate, Mr. Eugene, the statement you gave the F.B.I. right after you wanted them to hire you, . . . or what you are going to tell the Court and Jury now?

Eugene: Well, this statement here, (indicating) this was the first statement I made to the F.B.I. They asked me to come up there to the office to give a statement, and I gave this statement. This statement here (indicating) is not accurate.

McGovern: It sure messes you up, doesn't it?

Eugene: No, it doesn't. I mean I wasn't going to give the F.B.I., at that time, when I made this statement (indicating) something to chop my own neck off with.

McGovern: You wanted the money?

Eugene: I didn't get any money.

McGovern: I mean right after they hired you?

Eugene: Right after that is when they convinced me that they weren't going to do me anything for any Communist activities.

In his cross-examination and summation defense attorney McGovern accused Arthur Eugene of being a liar. McGovern pointed out that in his court testimony Eugene claimed he attended several Communist Party meetings with Lee Brown in 1951, but in his FBI statement he said he attended no party meetings in that period. "Arthur Eugene, out of his own mouth, under oath, is a liar," McGovern concluded. "He is a liar for pay."

McGovern moved for a verdict of acquittal on grounds that the government had not proven its case. His motion was denied.

McGovern then stated that he had recommended to his client not to testify. "We have recommended to the accused that he do not take the stand. The Government has not proved its case." Instead, he asked the judge to instruct the jury that the failure of the defendant to take the stand creates no presumption of guilt.

Realizing that his whole case rested on the credibility of Arthur Eugene, prosecutor Many in his closing statement argued that it was understandable that Arthur Eugene gave a "very guarded statement" to the FBI when he was first questioned in 1952. "As he said," Many added, "he did not want to put a hatchet in the hands of the F.B.I." "I say again," Many told the jury, "put yourselves in his place. I assure you that it would not be easy for anyone, for Arthur Eugene, or for anyone else, and to get up and say, 'Yes, I did not tell the truth. Although I made the statement to an official body, I did not tell the truth,' but yet he did tell you that. So, you have which to believe? His testimony under oath here over a period of days, or the statement made in the first interview he ever made?"

"There, in essence, you have it, ladies and gentlemen," Many concluded. "The only witness that has been brought before you whose testimony is in any way impeached or contradicted, is that of Arthur Eugene, and that by the one statement given when he was afraid, when he didn't know where he was headed, and when first interviewed by the F.B.I. at a time that he had reason to fear. The Government submits to you that the evidence is clear and convincing beyond any reasonable doubt whatsoever."

After reminding the jury of the presumption of innocence, that the burden of proof was on the government, defense attorney McGovern, in his closing argument, attacked weak points in the government's case. He first argued that it had not been proved that Lee Brown filed the non-Communist affidavit in question. Juanita Bunch, the government clerk, McGovern argued, could not state who brought or delivered the affidavits to her office; she assumed they came in from the union. As to the signature, McGovern reminded the jury that the notary public, Israel Augustine, could not identify Lee Brown as the person who signed the affidavit. McGovern also argued that the government's effort to link Lee Brown to signatures on other documents and then link these signatures to the signature on the affidavit was not convincing.

With regard to the Brown's membership in the Communist Party, McGovern argued that even if Lee Brown was a party member in 1946, as alleged by Gladys Williams, Robert Chan, and Irwin Knight, that did not establish that he was in the party in 1952, as alleged in the charge against him. As for Arthur Eugene, McGovern said he was "an admitted paid informer, who is also an admitted paid liar. He is either lying about this man in Court today, under oath, or he is lying to the F.B.I., or to you as members of the Jury and the Court. But he has got to be lying one place or the other, because he has admitted he is a liar, and he can't reconstruct his testimony."

After the closing arguments finished on March 26, the trial judge issued instructions to the jury on Thursday morning, March 27. Judge Wright in his instructions offered his own interpretation of the charges. In the actual indictment the first count read: "On or about the 21st day of July, 1952, Lee Brown, in a matter within the jurisdiction of the National Labor Relations Board, an agency of the United States, and in accordance with the Labor Management Relations Act of 1947, did unlawfully, willfully and knowingly make, use and file and cause to be made, used and filed with the said National Labor Relations Board . . . a false writing and document, namely an 'Affidavit of Non-communist Union Officer,' knowing the same to contain false, fictitious and fraudulent statement and representation as to material fact, to wit, that he, Lee Brown, was not then and there a member of the Communist Party. . . ." Count two contained similar language with regard to affiliation with the Communist Party.

However, Judge Wright instructed the jury that "it must be shown to your satisfaction beyond a reasonable doubt that this Defendant made, used, or filed or caused to be made, used, and filed, this document. Now, the indictment charges by using the word 'and,' and the Court uses the word 'or,' but under the law if it is shown to your satisfaction beyond a reasonable doubt that this Defendant made, or if he used, or if he filed this document, or if he caused the document to be made, used, or filed, then this particular element of the offense would be satisfied." In effect, the judge instructed the jurors that if they concluded that Lee Brown made a false affidavit by affixing his signature to it, then this was sufficient to find him guilty. However, the indictment itself required that it be proved that Lee Brown made, used, and filed a false affidavit, and the question of whether he filed it was the stickler, since there was no letter of transmittal. McGovern took exception to the judge's interpretation, pointing out that it "gives the Jury an alternative to base the conviction on the making of the affidavit alone." This is the issue on which the final outcome of the case would hinge.

The case went to the all-white jury at 10:10 A.M. At 12:30 the jury asked for additional instructions from the judge as to what constituted membership or affiliation. The judge listed a series of activities that could be construed as constituting membership in the Communist Party, including paying dues or making financial contributions, possessing a membership card, attending meetings, classes, conferences or other party gatherings, recruiting new members, distributing literature, or participating in any other way in the activities, planning, or actions of the Communist Party. Affiliation, the judge said, meant a close working alliance or association between an individual and the party. At 12:40 the jury returned to its deliberations, and at 1:04 P.M. the jury came back with a verdict.

The clerk read the verdict: "We, the Jury, find the accused Lee Brown guilty as charged under Count Number 1. We, the Jury, find the accused Lee Brown guilty as charged under Count Number 2."

On Wednesday, April 2, Judge Wright sentenced Lee Brown to three years' imprisonment in a federal penitentiary. The judge said he considered the two counts as one since they were in effect the same. Lee Brown signed a statement saying he did not plan to appeal and on April 16 he was delivered to begin serving his prison sentence at the Texarkana Federal Penitentiary. Subsequently, Brown's attorneys filed a motion for acquittal and an alternate motion for a new trial. Both were denied in early June, but the court granted the taking of an appeal.

Brown's attorneys filed a notice of appeal on June 14, and after several delays the appeal was filed in the spring of 1959. A year later, on April 21, 1960, the U.S. Court of Appeals for the Fifth District announced its decision. The court decided that the appeal "raises only one serious issue: was there reversible error in the Trial Court's charge that the making, using or filing element of the offense would be satisfied if the jury found that Appellant 'made, or if he used, or if he filed the document. . . .'"

The court noted that in a prior case (*Jencks v. United States* [5 Cir.], 226 F. 2d 540, 545) "the essence of the offense charged by the government is the filing of the affidavit and the burden rested on it to prove that the Appellant filed the affidavit or caused it to be filed." The court continued that "the jurisdiction of the NLRB is not invoked until the affidavit is filed and therefore the act of filing is as essential to the commission of the offense as is the act of making the false affidavit. It seems, therefore, too clear for argument that, standing alone, the charge here complained of left open to the jury the right to convict Brown without the proof of one of the elements which we and other Courts of Appeal have found a necessary ingredient, even the gist, of the offense."

One short sentence concluded the appeals court's legal analysis: "The judgment is reversed." With the growing civil rights movement changing the political climate and with HUAC and the anti-Communist provisions of the Taft-Hartley Act being openly challenged by college students, progressive activists, and labor leaders (the non-Communist oath would be declared unconstitutional by the U.S. Supreme Court in 1964), the government decided not to initiate any further legal action against Lee Brown. In May 1960 U.S. Attorney M. Hepburn Many signed an order dismissing the indictment against Brown. Lee Brown would be released from Texarkana, where he had been unjustly imprisoned for more than two years.

CHAPTER TEN

Prison and Release

They found me guilty at the end of the trial. Judge Skelly Wright said, "I'm going to give you three years on each count but I'm going to run them concurrently. You only have to serve three." They sent me back to the parish prison there in New Orleans, and I stayed there until they came and got me. I was speaking through the bars there to the rest of the inmates. In the night, the word got around that I was going to leave that morning. I was in a cell all alone.

During the trial while I was at the parish jail they didn't allow me to see no one, even when I went to the shower. They would clear the dayroom to put fright into the people that I was some dangerous character. By being a Communist you are dangerous! Especially if you're black, you're dangerous! But I spoke that night to a lot of the inmates. I had made quite a few friends 'cause during the time when I was going to trial, it would come on the radio inside the jail. And all the inmates there would clap for it and wish me good luck because I was standing up fighting for the rights of my people and working people as a true trade unionist. They knew I wanted to see better conditions. I wanted to see better health conditions. I wanted to see better houses, better hospitals, better schools, better education for our people, in particular to study our history, black history. As a matter of fact, I'd like to see all nationalities have knowledge of their history. That's what I was fighting for.

After I talked that night there was one little guy who couldn't understand too much. He didn't know what he wanted to say. Sometimes he'd start off right, and then he'd forget. I said, "Let him talk. Let him bring it out." He clapped his hands after he couldn't get out what he wanted to say, he just, he clapped. Other brothers in there clapped with him. I learned that they was not afraid, like I had learned in Houston.

After that they taken me to Galveston. We laid over a night and a day in Galveston and then went on to Texarkana prison.

When I arrived at Texarkana, one of the officers talked with me. He was very friendly. He was telling me that he had been to all the institutions. He was kind of old. He said, "I'm fixin' to retire." I was talking to him about a new trial. My attorneys, James McGovern and Earl Amedee, had filed for a new trial. The motion for a new trial was rejected, but my lawyers filed an appeal. The officer advised me, he said, "If I was you, I would serve my time. I would not accept a new trial because you may go and come back with more time than you got." He said, "You don't have too much time left, all but three years. Do these three years. I would just advise you cause I've been around these institutions, and I have some knowledge."

When I first arrived at Texarkana, they put me in solitary confinement for thirty days. They gave a book of rules and regulations to study.

When they released me from solitary, I didn't have any real problems. In fact, that prison was like a school. I started going to the library and reading. I enrolled in some classes and eventually got my school diploma.

I did a lot of reading, going into different subjects—the labor movement, the religious movement, the political movement. I had taken up reading a large book they called *Social Science Encyclopedia*. That covered everything dealing with human beings—psychology, sociology, archaeology, biology, socialism, communism, colonialism—every subject that human beings was connected with. I was learning it from this book, studying it, studying many things. I would study history, some black history that I would find in the institution. Not very much. But I studied labor history there. Not the kind that I was able to get on the outside. Political history. I studied about communism, socialism. And it was very interesting. I learned a lot and studied hard. I went to school. Some of the inmates was teachers, and some of them was very good. They would take their time with you and help you, and I was concerned in that institution that I learned. I talked to people there. I learned from people. We sat down and had discussion with each other. And it was very good that I learned many things.

I studied and I put down notes. They had a young fellow there from New Orleans. He worked also in the education department. He knew how to use the typewriter. I asked him would he type these notes up for me, what I marked off and what I printed. I wasn't a good writer, but I could print a lot of stuff. I put it together. And he took it and typed it up for me. In some ways that prison was the best school I ever went to.

One time they threw me in segregation, solitary. They said I was causing some kind of conflict, trouble. I was talking, discussing with some of the other inmates. We were discussing different issues when a guard walked up. About six of us was sitting on the grass. Some other men was playing baseball. The six of us was discussing issues that was confronting us when one of the guards walked up. We were discussing our own opinions about our living conditions, the conditions that we were confronted with outside, and why so many of us black people was in the city jails, and the state prisons and the federal institutions.

Then this guard walked up and broke in and said, "How's the weather? How you all fellows doing today?" One of the young men said, "It's cloudy." He didn't know I had some Masonic knowledge and I understood that symbolic talk. His saying "it's cloudy" meant that somebody in there was bad news, that they was talking against the system. I realized then that he was an informer. He just pretended to be interested in what we was saying so that he could inform on us.

The next morning, one of the guards came to my cell and blew his whistle and said, "Brown, now, all the way out." They were going to take me out. He said, "You going this morning. We're going to put you in the segregation." I guess they decided I was stirring up trouble. They locked me in a cell by myself.

While I was in segregation, one of the inmates came by who was a trustee. He said, "You need any books or whatever you need, commissary, just let me know, I got the slips. I'll put it down, you sign the slip and I'll bring it to you, your books and anything you need from the commissary." So the segregation was not so bad. The worst thing about segregation was that I couldn't go out on the yard.

After a while they let me work in the garden. There was a little garden that they had on the outside. I had taken up vegetable growing. I got some books on that. I wanted to study vegetables because in my studies and research I began to learn that vegetables was similar to humans. They had to have food, water, and oxygen, same as the human being. I said if I studied vegetable life, I can have greater knowledge of human life. So I took it up and completed it, and I received a certificate for vegetable growing. I also took up general education, and I got my diploma. *[Lee Brown earned two certificates of achievement at Texarkana, a certificate for having "satisfactorily completed the course in elementary classes" awarded by the Education Department on May 20, 1960, and a certificate for having "successfully completed the prescribed course in vegetable crops" awarded by the vocational school on July 5, 1960.]*

I was imprisoned at Texarkana over two years, from spring of 1958 to July 1960. (And I was in prison from the time I was brought back from Texas in November 1957 through the time of my trial.) Finally came the day when I was released. My attorneys had won the appeal. The appeals court ruled that Judge Skelly Wright had made a mistake in his charge to the jury and my conviction was reversed. About five days before I was to be released, they called me in and measured me for a suit, gave me some shoes (new shoes), new hat, and gave me, I think it was either $75 or $100. The chief classification and parole officer, I think his name was Mr. Anderson, he said, "We'll take you to the bus station in Texarkana and put you on the bus for Hitchcock, Texas." They gave me my ticket and a change of clothes.

One thing they did not give me was my notes from my reading. Now it tells you right in the little booklet they give you when you arrive that you can bring out notes or even your life story when you are released from prison. But when I went back before the warden, he looked at my notes and said, "You can't take this with you." He said it would cause trouble if I took my notes, so he kept them. That made me mad, but there wasn't anything I could do about it.

They released me on July 12, 1960. They asked if I had any relations who would take me in while I did some parole time. I told them about my cousins in Hitchcock. They wrote my cousin Celie's husband—we called him Boss—and asked him if they would take me in for a while. He wrote back and said yes.

When I got to Hitchcock, Texas, I went over to my cousin Celie's house, and I knocked on the door. They was so glad to see me. But my cousin Celie had had a stroke. They was supposed to come up to the institution on that Saturday to get me, but that Friday another cousin had an automobile accident and was killed. They were very close, and when Cousin Celie was told about the accident she had a stroke and never said another word. When I went to the house they asked her, "Do you know who this is?" She began to laugh and smile. She knew who I was because our family was very close.

So I stayed at Celie's house. They prepared a dinner for me that evening, and we sat down and talked. The next morning I went around to see other relatives who was living close by. I had some in Galveston, some in Hitchcock, some in Lamar, and some in Texarkana. I went around and visited those I had scattered all over Texas—Port Arthur, Houston, Beaumont. I let them know that I was back, and all of them was glad to see me.

I stayed there a while, about a month or so. I worked and helped Cousin Boss and Cousin Celie 'cause they needed help. I prepared her food. She had to eat liquid food. While Boss was gone to work, he was glad for me to be there to help her. I was glad to do it because they had helped me. Sometimes I would go and stay with one of my other cousins like Aunt Bernice. I could do that 'cause Cousin Celie had quite a few friends and relatives who would be there all the time. Her daughter would stay there at night. So I could help take care of her and go back and forth to see other folks as well. I was trying to do the best I could with what I had.

CHAPTER ELEVEN

Starting a New Life

I stayed in Texas two, three months and finished out my parole. Then I decided I would go down to New Orleans, see my son, Brownie, and his mother, Rose, who was my former common-law wife. Brownie must've been about eight or ten years old then. I went down to New Orleans, and I went over to some friends' house there, and I said, "Well, I'm going over and see Rose." I went to my brother's house and called Rose. She had a telephone, and I called her, asked her could I come over and see Brownie. She said, "Sure."

My nephew Skeet happened to be at my brother's house that day. Skeet was a musician and he played with Fats Domino's brother, Freddie, in a small band. Skeet said, "I'll take you over, Uncle Lee." So him and I got in the automobile. One thing about Skeet—he happened to have in his glove compartment a little paper bag, a small bag of quarters. He said, "Here, Uncle Lee. This will help you some." I said, "Thank you, Skeet, for being so nice to your uncle."

This is hard, too hard to talk about. It's emotional, 'cause of the struggle I went through and the struggle I experienced from the depth of my heart when I went through it. I went there and I met Rose, and she was glad to see me. When I was there talking to her, I could look outside and see Brownie sitting all alone. He reminded me of myself when I was young working on the dry docks in Texas, how I used to sit by myself at lunch time. Rose called him, "Brownie, come here." He come and he saw who I was. He was young when I left, but he was growing up. Brownie may have been around ten years of age or a little older. He called me Lee. He ran to me, embraced me, hugged me. He was glad, very glad to see me.

I was emotional. Sometimes I get very emotional because it come from the depths of my heart. We sat there and talked. So Skeet say, "Uncle Lee, I'm going." And I thanked him for the gift of quarters, thanked him for bringing me over, and he says, Skeet say, "You in good hands now, Uncle." And I say, "So long, Skeet, take care of yourself."

Rose fixed me a dinner for that evening and we sat up and talked. I was so glad to see Rose and Brownie. I wanted to help Brownie, so I decided to stay around a while and try to get a job.

I bought Brownie a few books—there wasn't too many books in New Orleans on black history. I don't even think they had a black bookstore in New Orleans, not to my knowing. I bought him a set of *World Book* encyclopedias— a set of red books. I told him to study, to read. I picked out a subject dealing with Islam, and I told him, "You study that. Learn about and study your history." I told him that because before I left New Orleans to go to prison I was trying to learn more about black history and getting involved with the Nation of Islam.

Before my trial sometimes I used to buy the *Pittsburgh Courier,* an Afro-American newspaper, and I began to read it. And I kept seeing a picture of a bald-headed man talking about freedom, justice, equality, and black history. To me he looked Chinese. And I kept wondering, I said, "What Chinese is so concerned about black folks?" This was Elijah Muhammad. And what he was saying—he was talking about my history, talking about my freedom. I was very much concerned, and finally one day I had my "play sister" (we resembled each other so much that people thought we was sister and brother) and I said to her, "Levoya, I want you to write to this place in Chicago: 5335 South Greenwood Avenue, Chicago 15, Illinois." I wanted to know about him and his organization, the Nation of Islam. Finally I got back an answer. During that time I was living at 2017 Jackson Avenue in New Orleans. His secretary wrote to me as Mr. Lee Brown at that address. The letter, which she wrote on July 31, 1957, said,

As-Salaam-Alaikum:
   In the Name of Allah, the Beneficent, the most Merciful, the Lord of the Worlds; and in the name of His Divine Messenger, the Honorable Elijah Muhammad.
   Dear brother:
   Your letter has passed the Laborers' inspection. I hope it will be approved by Allah.
   Enclosed are two forms and a small Muslim prayer book. Fill out the forms and mail. If married have wife sign her own name, or if under 18 have parents sign form.
   May Allah bless you.
   As-Salaam-Alaikum
   Your Sister,
   Susie Hussein

I was interested so I filled out the application form and sent it in. The prayer book was compiled by Elijah Muhammad and published by the University of Islam in Chicago. I still have it. I wasn't so much interested in the religion but what they had to say about history. Sometimes when you want to be free you'll catch hold of anything talking about freedom.

It wasn't until I got out of prison in 1960 that I was in contact with Elijah Muhammad again. I had written to him telling about getting out of prison and trying to find work. I received a letter addressed to "Mr. Lee X Brown." He told me, "I received your letter of October the 26th, 1960, and it is my hope by this time you have found a job. I am very sorry to learn of your difficulty in finding a job, continue to strive hard and pray to Allah, and you will be successful. I am returning the clippings and notices of your trial, which I think you would like to keep. I pray to Allah for your success and blessings. As-Salaam-Alaikum. Your brother, Elijah Muhammad, Messenger of Allah."

When I got to California, Elijah Muhammad wrote to me again to confirm my registration in the Nation of Islam. He said I could take this letter to any mosque. I went to the mosque here in San Francisco off and on, but mainly I was interested in history. I joined the Nation of Islam because of my interest in black history. In the party I learned about the class struggle but I wanted to get some black history, and that's what Elijah Muhammad talked about, Africa and black history. I didn't see no contradiction between being a party member and being a Muslim. True Muslims (and I wouldn't call myself a true Muslim), true Muslims could also be revolutionaries. The prophets was revolutionaries.

I wasn't interested in prayers and all that 'cause like my grandfather taught me, you got to do something for yourself. "Wasn't no pie in the sky": that's what I believed. You can use religion to get some of the things you want, like certain kinds of knowledge. But you can't use religion to get to Los Angeles. If I want to go to Los Angeles I can sit down here and pray 'til I fall out, and I ain't gonna get to Los Angeles. I'm gonna need to get a ticket and bus to get there. Praying won't do it. Like my grandfather said, the Lord helps those who help themselves. But I did learn more about black people's history from talking with people in the Nation and reading their books.

In New Orleans our union, Local 207, had merged with the United Packinghouse Workers Union. I needed a job so I went there and talked to the president of the packinghouse union, Thomas West. He said "Brown, we don't have anything here. Maybe you ought to think about going to San Francisco, California. I will give you a letter, give you a traveling card, to go to other places." He wrote a letter praising me as a fine union brother. By then I knew I couldn't get a job in New Orleans. During the trial my picture had been plastered in all the newspapers; they made a lot of propaganda about me. Now when I went to the unemployment office, they waited on everybody but me. I thought I might have a better chance of getting a job in San Francisco, since that's where the ILWU was based. In August, when I was still in Texas, I had written to the ILWU in San Francisco asking for help. In November I wrote another letter to Harry Bridges about my situation. I told him about the Un-American Activity Committee and getting convicted and sent to prison under the Taft-Hartley Act. I told him, "It is extremely hard for me to find work because of the trouble I was in. In the meantime, I am asking for some financial aid to help me until I find employment, which assistance of course will be returned. I would appreciate it very much if you would state my case to Local 10 because I am very much in need of help. My ten-year-old son is in school and I really need assistance."

About that time I got a letter back from Bill Chester, answering my first letter to the ILWU. Bill Chester was the ILWU regional director for Northern California at the national office on Golden Gate Avenue in San Francisco. He said he couldn't promise me a job but he'd do everything possible to help me. He also sent a check for $100.

I knew the lady that I was living with from before my trial. She had a house and rented rooms. Her name was Mrs. Matilda Poplar; we used to call her "Mommee." She had about eight people living in her house. Each of them had a room. And I had mine. When I came back to New Orleans, she told me, "You always, Brother Lee, have a place to live here. Money or no money." That's the same sister, Mrs. Poplar, who wanted to put up her house for bond for me during the trial, but the lawyer told her it wasn't necessary; they already had the bond. I stayed with Mrs. Poplar while I was looking for work. She said, "I have a friend named Mr. Preston Holmes. He has a son in San Francisco. I'm going to talk with him when he comes."

Preston Holmes came in that evening. He was an old longshoreman with the ILA there in New Orleans. Mrs. Poplar started talking. She says, "Mr. Holmes, don't you have a son in San Francisco?"

And Mr. Holmes says, "Yes, I do."

She says, "Brother Brown is planning on going there pretty soon to find work. He can't get any here. It's very hard for him, and he said he'd rather go there and maybe be more successful."

And he says, "My son is named Joe Holmes. I will give you his phone number and his address, and you tell him so he can know you talked to me that he sent me two shirts, and the shirts had the initials J.H., meaning Joe Holmes. Soon as you get to San Francisco, you call him, and he will take care of you."

So I left New Orleans. Rose and Brownie stayed there. Rose and I had been separated since before I went to prison. I told Rose I might send for her and Brownie when I got to San Francisco, but I didn't know what would happen. I had my few clothes that I took and I left some of my books in a trunk with Mommee on Drive Street. I told Mrs. Poplar to take care of my books and some of the newspapers from the trial. All the people in the house who knew me greeted me and wished me good luck. They prepared me some fried chicken to take on the bus. All of them got together and gave me a little money. It made me very proud. I felt like I was going on to continue, coming into San Francisco to continue my struggle, continue to fight.

I came to San Francisco on the Greyhound bus. When I got here, I called Joe Holmes on the telephone. I spoke to him and explained myself and told him about the shirts, and he told me to wait at the bus station. "I will come right away," he said. And I waited there in the station on 7th Street between Market and Mission Streets.

About twenty minutes later Joe drove up. He took me to his home on Neptune Street. When we got there, he introduced me to his wife, Florence. He showed me a room and said, "This is your room; you can live there as long as you want." He put my luggage in the room. I was tired and I just went to bed.

The next day was a holiday. I think it was Thanksgiving. The Holmeses took me with them to the house of a friend called Della. She was a member of the ILWU Local 6, the warehouse workers. She worked in a coffee factory here in San Francisco. They had something like a party, Thanksgiving dinner. Lots of her friends and neighbors was there. It was very nice. When I got there, they started introducing me to their friends and telling them why I came. Most of the people there was from the South and New Orleans. They started talking to me and asking me questions, and I was very happy. They even passed the hat and said, "We heard about your case."

That made me very proud to be with working people and the struggles of working people. I feel that the world I live in is the university of learning. The people are teachers and the best teachers are at the grassroots level. I've learned many things in the labor movement, learned a lot in the struggle.

The next morning I got up and went over to the ILWU hall at 150 Golden Gate to seek assistance in finding a job. I talked to one of the ILWU representatives there. He sent me over to the Warehouse Union Local 6 to talk to one of the union representatives to get work. I met some of the union brothers in the hall, and we started talking. The brothers took up a collection and gave me some money to help me out until I could find work. I came around for a few days, and I went over to the hall several times during the period. One of those workers sent me to his good friend to ask him for some financial assistance. When I got there, they gave me one hundred dollars. Another friend gave me ten dollars, another one gave me twenty-five. I was treated very well by the brothers, and I appreciated it.

One day I went to the culinary workers union on Sixth Street, which was Local 110. I had a letter and my card from the packinghouse workers local in New Orleans. The secretary told me, "You wait. The business agent will be in here, and his name is Sam Daniels." She said, "You sit down in the union hall and get you some coffee. If you care for any, you're welcome to it. You're amongst friends." That made me feel very good.

When Brother Daniels came in, a very short, dark-skinned fellow, she pointed me out. He walked over to me and said, "My name is Sam Daniels, the business agent here, and I learned that you was looking for me. Would you please step into my office?"

I said, "Thank you, sir." So I went into his office, and he looked at papers I had and he looked at my traveling card. He said, "You're a union man."

"Yes, sir, I am. I have been in the union for a number of years. Local 12, the Los Angeles Packinghouse workers, and from there I went down to New Orleans, Local 207, where we had some problems."

"I heard about it," he said, "and I read about some of the problems you had under the Taft-Hartley law. Fortunately, we ain't never been attacked so far. I'm going to see what I can do for you." And he asked what kind of work I wanted.

I said, "Any kind. I can do anything 'cause I need work." He said, "What about working in a hotel? Have you ever washed dishes?"

I said, "Yes, I washed dishes. When I was in L.A., I used to ride the Union Pacific, Los Angeles to Nebraska, washing dishes and whatnot."

Then he said, "Maybe I can put you on at the Fairmont Hotel at night until we see what we can do."

There was another brother there. His name was Willie Bible. Sam Daniels said, "I want you to come back here tomorrow evening. Be sure to be here before five o'clock and go over to the union hall. I'm going to write out a work slip, and Brother Bible is gonna take you to the Fairmont Hotel and to see the kitchen steward there, and I'm gonna call him and talk with him."

When I got to the Fairmont Hotel, which was one of San Francisco's grand hotels, Willie Bible took me into the office of Mr. Johnny Ward, the kitchen steward who did the hiring. Mr. Ward said to me, "I heard some about you, Brother. I once was in the Marine Cooks and Stewards Union. I heard you been in the union quite a while."

I said, "Yes, sir."

Mr. Ward was a tall, brown-skinned fellow, very friendly. He said, "I can put you to work around here washing dishes. You go to work tonight." He told me I had to get a uniform to put on. I started washing dishes that night. And I stayed washing dishes maybe a month or two.

One day Ward said, "You a good worker, Brother Brown." (He called me Brother Brown.) "I'm going to put you to work in janitorial, a regular job, working at night. You're a night porter now."

I said, "Thank you kindly, sir." That made me feel much better. I felt good that I had success enough to get a regular job. And I had two off days each week.

After I had been in San Francisco a while, I was thinking about the party. I heard from someone that there was a party bookstore on Market Street. I went there and I happened to talk to the fellow who ran the bookstore. I introduced myself to him, and we started discussing political conditions. I bought some party literature, but I told him I was not in the party at that time on account of the Taft-Hartley. I told him that they had brought me up before the Un-American Activity Committee and I refused to cooperate with them. They brought me to trial under circumstantial evidence and found me guilty as charged of being a member or an affiliate with the Communist Party.

So we talked and he told me some people there to contact. I started going to the bookstore, and I started going to party meetings. I met some people who was from the culinary union—about five or six party members who used to meet and discuss the issues in the culinary industry.

Then I started to going to other meetings, different meetings concerning jobs or fighting racism or issues around housing—issues that benefit the people. Later at one of these meetings I happened to meet Kendra Alexander, a sister who was a leader in the party. She seemed very nice. I would go to meetings where I would hear her talk, and I was very much impressed with what she said. I liked the way she talked. I learned a whole lot from her. She inspired me very much.

When the bookstore moved to Valencia Street a couple of years later, I happened to meet another person, Sam Gold. Sam and his wife, Molly, came from Chicago. He had been in the party a long time and ran the bookstore. We became good friends. I remember one time him and Molly brought me some chicken soup when I was living on Third Street. I told Sam I had doubts about getting back into the party. He begin to argue with me. I said, "I will support the issues. I have faith in the program. I have faith in the party—in the principles—but some of the people, some of the leadership, I cannot understand." I read party literature. They would have conventions and they would pass resolutions, resolution on top of resolution concerned with Afro-Americans, and I still couldn't get the understanding of what was going on. It created doubt in my mind. I felt that the party leadership didn't follow through. They'd pass resolutions on racism and jobs but then they wouldn't follow through on the program. They didn't do what they said they would. The program was good but some of the leadership was bad; it didn't carry out the program. That caused me to have doubts.

There was also a problem with white racism. Some white party members would not speak to you on the street. There was a white woman who attended party meetings, and one day I saw her on Seventh Street. I spoke to her but she wouldn't even speak. She completely ignored me. I wanted to make sure, so I ran back and caught up with her and I spoke to her again. She acted like she didn't know me. So I brought it up at the next meeting, but they wasn't too much concerned about it. Hell, they did better than that in the South! We used to bring party members on the carpet so we could solve the problem. I told Sam Gold about it. He said he didn't like it either, but he begged me to keep coming to the meetings. I said I still supported the program but the leadership seemed weak. I stopped going to the meetings.

Fifteen of us was night porters at the Fairmont Hotel, and all the brothers, was very friendly. We talked. We had lunch together. The lunch that was given to us was precooked food, and not very good. We started talking about how we would like to stop, have time to cook, to fix our own food, because the men didn't want the precooked food that the cook left there for us. The cook had leftovers made from other food, and he gave it to the help. I began to look in the union books, and I saw that you had the right to have job stewards—I call them shop stewards—shop stewards to see that the company carries out the working agreement and that the workers get fair treatment. I said, "We need a shop steward. We have some problems that we need to solve." One of the brothers said, "What about you, Brother Brown? Would you take it? Seems like you have some experience." I said, "I had a little experience working in New Orleans on the docks and working in the union. I had a little experience, and I'll be willing to try to work so we can solve some of these problems. We'll talk to Mr. Ward, bring him our problems, our grievances, and ask him to work with us."

So we did. Ward told us, "You have to sign your names on a sheet saying you want a shop steward, and then I'll call the business agent, Mr. Daniels."

Daniels said, "You all want a shop steward?"

I said, "The men have signed."

He said, "Yeah? Bring in all the men, and we will elect a shop steward, and we will notify the company, notify Mr. Ward. I'll be there early, so you all can have the meeting." So we went to the union hall on 6th Street the next morning when we got off work. Daniels came about eight o'clock and we had the meeting. We proposed things that we wanted to discuss with Mr. Ward. Brother Daniels asked, "Now who you all elect for your steward?"

The men said, "We elect Brother Lee Brown."

"Now, Brother Lee Brown," Daniels said, "you're a shop steward at the Fairmont Hotel to take care of the grievances and see that the company carries out the contract and that none of the brothers will violate the contract." He said, "This will work both ways."

I said, "All right, Brother Daniels. I will do the best I can to work with the brothers, and I hope the brothers will work with me."

I was elected shop steward on April 17, 1963. I was the first shop steward among the culinary union workers at the Fairmont Hotel. In fact, I became the first shop steward in any hotel in San Francisco. This was the beginning of my involvement in the trade union movement in San Francisco.

CHAPTER TWELVE

Struggles in San Francisco

While working at the Fairmont, I became aware of some very poor working conditions. It was similar to a nonunion house. Personally I felt compelled to attempt to straighten up some of the discrepancies and conditions at the hotel.

I noticed that it was mainly Afro-American women working as housekeepers cleaning the rooms. They were often mistreated and abused and discharged from the job, with no follow-up to reinstate them from their union, Local 283 of the room cleaners union. I raised that question at a meeting of the joint board of the hotel workers unions. One of the representatives, Charlie Gricus, got angry with me, telling me, "You don't have anything to do with it."

I said, "I'm a member of the union and I'm going to speak out when I see anyone abused." So I took up the fight for the room cleaners. I was concerned about them and I wasn't afraid to speak up. I had knowledge of being a shop steward from working down South, and I was able to give support with the experience and knowledge that I had to struggle for better working conditions on the job.

As a result of my opinions and oppositions that I submitted to my superiors, the hotel representatives began to harass and make trouble for me. They made false accusations against me and said I was drinking on the job. Consequently I was discharged from my job in 1967, but the real reason was because of my union activities and my efforts to rectify the working conditions.

After being discharged, I went to Sam Daniels, the business agent of Local 110. I explained the situation and he went to talk with representatives of the Fairmont Hotel to question my dismissal. I was not present at the confrontation between Daniels and the Fairmont. The problem wasn't solved at the meeting, and after the meeting I asked Daniels to file an action with the adjustment board, which was made up of representatives from the unions and the employers. But my request to be reinstated was denied. I felt that Daniels was more or less collaborating with the hotel; he was very close to the bosses.

During the time I was working at the Fairmont Hotel I met and got married to Moselle Mayfield. Moselle belonged to the union too, but I didn't meet her on the job. She was working at the Holiday Inn. I met her on Third Street at her former husband's place. Her husband had married again. He had a cafe close to the shipyard where he sold barbecue. She was there one day with a lady friend, her roommate, and we got to talking. Moselle was active in a church on Newhall Street. She tried to get me to donate to the church but I wasn't too interested in that. After a while we decided to get married, but her roommate, whose name was Candy, decided to stay there with us in the house on LaSalle Street. I didn't like that too much. When we was shopping in the supermarket, Moselle would ask Candy what she wanted before she asked me what I wanted. I didn't like that either. Sam Daniels used to come around and visit and said he didn't think it was right for Candy to be living there and causing conflict. So he came and talked to Candy. But Moselle got angry and said, "If Candy is going, I'm going."

"Well," I said, "there's the door, sister. Get to stepping."

We didn't get along too well, and we decided to get divorced after two or three years.

Around the time I was discharged from the Fairmont, they had just opened up the Jack Tar Hotel on Cathedral Hill. I knew the kitchen steward, an old fellow in his seventies by the name of Mr. Smith. He was a nice fellow, brown-skinned fellow. He and I talked. I asked, "Do you have any work you can give me?"

He said, "Where you worked?" I told him I came from the Fairmont and what had happened. He was an understanding man. We was Masonic brothers. He said, "Brother Brown, I can put you to work around here cleaning walls until something opens up and you can get a regular job." That's how I started at the Jack Tar.

I got a regular job first washing dishes and then as a night porter. The working conditions at the Jack Tar was very bad, and I began to voice my opposition to such conditions. I organized a group of the night porters. We had a racially mixed crew, including some Spanish people, working there, and they said, "We want you to be shop steward." They had never had a shop steward on the job, but it was in the contract. Nobody had the experience or the guts to be shop steward. I said, "I accept," and they elected me shop steward on January 16, 1968.

The porters and the bar boys and vegetable cleaners was being overworked and I spoke up about it. The chef didn't like what I was doing, and that's when they made me assistant steward to Mr. Mitchell—figured I would sell the men out. Mr. Mitchell was the executive steward of the Jack Tar; he was really just the head dishwasher. He was over the store department. He was also in the union. On Sunday when Mitchell went to church, I took his place on the job, helping get the plates to the waiters.

One time when we had a union meeting of the men in the store department, the chef and the personnel manager showed up. I said, "Y'all can't come in here. This is a union meeting." They said they had come to meetings before. I guess Mitchell used to let them come in, but I wouldn't. They saw that I was shop steward and we had rules, and they got mad. I also told all the brothers to wear their union buttons to let them know we was organized.

Once again I was told to mind my own business or I would be dismissed. Mitchell told me that the kitchen chef and the manager, plus others, wanted me fired because of my union activities. But they couldn't directly fire me for my union work and they couldn't fire me for incompetence, so they accused me of being drunk on the job and discharged me on January 26, 1969. They wanted me off the job; I was too hot. They never had a militant person who would speak out, particularly for the black room cleaners. I wouldn't let them get away with abusing and discharging the room cleaners with no follow-up. They never had anybody who would stand up and tell them that they was doing wrong. The black room cleaners was not getting meals. All the rest of them, even the doormen and the bar boys, got meals. They was after me, and they also wanted to get rid of all shop stewards in hotels, which they hadn't had before I came along even though it was in the contract.

My case went to an arbitration hearing on June 2, 1969. Mitchell testified against me to save his job. When they had the hearing, he was sitting up there crying. He really hated to do it, but he did. He got caught in a trap. He said that I had to relieve him on a Sunday while he went to church. He claimed that he came back and I was drunk, said he smelled alcohol on my breath. What actually happened was that Mitchell wanted to fire a brother named Jefferson because he said he was drunk. I told Mitchell he didn't have the right to fire Jefferson. Mitchell said, "I'm going to fire you too; I'm going to fire both of you." That's how it started. Then at the hearing Mitchell said I was drunk too. That was a front to keep from saying that they was discharging me for my union activities as shop steward. I told them I hadn't had anything to drink. They wasn't bringing me anything I didn't know. I knew all about their "tricknology." I give them all hell up there, told them that I was discharged because I had made complaints about the conditions. I gave them a list of the demands I had raised: stop mistreatment and unfair discharges of maids, provide free meal tickets to maids in all hotels, organize hotel and restaurant workers throughout the nation into unions, and end all discrimination against black people in the hotel and restaurant industries.

The room cleaners went on strike in the fall of 1969. Since I was out of work, the business agent of Local 110 called me down to Commercial Street to be picket captain. I was picket captain for three years. I worked for the four locals—Local 44, the cooks, Local 48, the waitresses, Local 30, the waiters, and Local 110, my local. The room cleaners Local 283 was on strike over working conditions, and the other locals supported them by sending pickets.

My job was to sign the picket slips. They was supposed to picket for four hours, and then I signed the slip. I had my little book with the names and made them sign. Each week I worked for a different local. Each local paid me to be picket captain, and the one that paid me the most was Local 30. The whole three years we had no fights, no arguments, and no drinking on the picket line. I knew how to handle it.

The room cleaners finally won the strike after three years. One of the bosses who was at Harpoon Louie's diner on Commercial Street came out at noon one day and told me, "We're folding up. You got us."

I said, "What do you mean?"

He said, "We're gonna sign the contract." He shook hands with me, and I told the rest of the pickets that we had won a victory.

I got a job with the Western Addition Black Security Guards. Black Security Guards had been set up by the African Descendant Nationalist Independence Partition Party, the ADNIP Party, of which I was a member. I had got involved with the ADNIP Party during the time I was angry with the Communist Party because of racism in the party. I read Wilson Record's book, *The Negro and the Communist Party*. I felt that the party leadership, not all leadership but the national leadership, was not carrying out the program to fight racism and discrimination. The party wasn't fighting to build a left center in the trade union movement. The party should have been more effective against these right-wing unions and racist union leadership. The party was only serving the intellectuals, not helping the grass roots. I didn't feel like the party was serving the interests of the masses, of the black workers.

The ADNIP Party had an office on the corner of Fulton and Fillmore in the Western Addition. I joined them because I liked their program of building up the economic program of black people, and I figured that was one of the solutions to the problem. I think we should have our own community with our own stores, hotels, and whatever.

When I was working at the Fairmont, I tried to start a business of my own, Brown's Foot Formula. The idea had come up in New Orleans when I was staying at Mrs. Poplar's. She had trouble with her feet and had come up with a formula to help soothe them. Years ago I heard from her adopted daughter, Levoya, that Mrs. Poplar got run over in a car wreck and eventually passed. After I got out to California, I worked on the formula that she had told me.

Another fellow named Buddy McNeil worked at the Fairmont and helped me. It would help if you had bad feet, aching feet, corns, athlete's foot. You put it on and rubbed it in and it soothed your feet. A pharmacist named Mr. Reid helped us get it past the Food and Drug Administration. We took it to a company to put it on the market. It cost us a thousand dollars apiece. But I made a big mistake because I didn't get a lawyer to follow up on it, and I didn't keep a copy of the formula. Somebody probably got it out there on the market now under a different name. I learned from that to never do nothing in business without somebody to represent you and to keep copies of everything. It cost me $1,000 to learn that.

Al Sultan Shabazz was head of the ADNIP Party, which was founded in 1962. I met him at a community meeting when I was working at the Jack Tar. He was from New Orleans and had been in the army. He was very intelligent and well informed. He read a lot and he wanted to teach ancient African history. We discussed black nationalism and Africa and how we should have something in our community. I believe they did that in the Soviet Union—had different communities. I believe we would be better off if we had a community, something we could identify with, that would give us the right to teach our history. I don't believe that we are getting our complete history, particularly our ancient history, in the educational institutions. We talked about racism and white supremacy and how we wasn't getting a fair shake. So I got interested. I knew a little bit of my history and I knew we was a long way from getting a fair deal. People in church say to "forgive them, for they know not what they're doing." I say any time a son of a bitch is mistreating people, he knows he is doing wrong.

The ADNIP Party said they wanted separation, two separate republics— one for blacks and one for whites. They had a list of nineteen states they wanted. They had set up a provisional government with Al Sultan as prime minister. I was more interested in the trade union movement and was struggling to get the unions to deal with racism. I told Al Sultan I was in the union, so he appointed me minister of labor. I wrote articles for their newspaper and gave speeches at meetings.

The ADNIP Party had different businesses. They had a moving business and the black security guards. Al Sultan Shabazz had contracts for security guards at a building on Geary Street and in the Martin Luther King housing projects and other places. He had about twenty people working as security guards. Not all of them were members of the party. I was put in charge of the guards. I was the supervisor and I had to check on them. I would go around to the guards at night and check to see if they were at their posts. If they had problems, they would come to me. If they had a problem on the job or wasn't doing the job, I could suspend them or give them a few days off; but I had to know both sides. We also had families that would come over to the office with their problems. People didn't want to take their problems to the police. Black people have enough intelligence to solve their own problems, but they need help. I know I worked with about three or four families that came there. We helped solve their problems and they got back together.

We tried to stop people from being violent 'cause that wouldn't solve the problem. We talked to people. I learned that from my grandfather. I remember him saying, "When you get into violence, you ain't gonna solve the problem. You gonna make it worse." He taught me that if you get in an argument, before it gets violent, say, "Let's have a recess; let's table this and cool off." Then you come back and solve the problem. We were building the black community, showing what black folks can do. We advocated for the community and tried to clean up the community. The police didn't give us any trouble. Chief Cahill said, "I don't have anything against the Black Security Guards. Everywhere my police go, they see them."

We had general membership meetings and served dinners. We passed out flyers in the community. We had education meetings. One time we sponsored a meeting to commemorate the birthday of Marcus Garvey.

I was in the ADNIP Party four or five years, until it broke up. Al Sultan left the country and went to Guyana. There was a stool pigeon in the party and Al Sultan was accused of hiding some guns somewhere. I never did see anything like that. He didn't want to go to court, so he left the country. I never did see him again. I heard that he wrote two books and opened up a bookstore over there. Then I heard he was going to come back to the United States but he was assassinated. I think the snitch was working for the CIA. After that the ADNIP Party just fell apart. My work for the Black Security Guards was the last job I had before retiring.

While I was working at the Jack Tar, Dr. Mitchell at UC told me I had to stop working in the kitchen, that the heat was too much and I was getting high blood pressure. I took some high blood pressure pills for a while and later I got partial disability.

From the time I first arrived in San Francisco, I was meeting people and going to meetings and getting involved. When I first came here, somebody told me to go see Dr. Carlton Goodlett for help in finding a job. He had an office on Fillmore between Sutter and Bush. Dr. Goodlett was also the publisher of the San Francisco *Sun-Reporter*, a black community newspaper. He gave me $25 to help me. I saw him again at the Cow Palace at a big civil rights rally where Martin Luther King was speaking. There was thousands of people there and I was sitting way in the back. Dr. Goodlett was passing out copies of his newspaper, and we talked for a while. A few years later while I was working at the Fairmont Hotel I met Dr. Goodlett again. I was at a meeting on Van Ness Street and I run up on him. They had a lunch break at the meeting and he said, "Brown let's go get some buffalo meat." I was surprised. I said, "Doctor, don't be pulling my leg." I never heard of eating buffalo meat. We come on up to Tommy's Joynt at

Geary and Van Ness. We sat upstairs and he ordered buffalo stew. I ordered the same thing. It was good. We talked about different things and got to know each other. After that I used to go by his office sometimes and talk.

In 1966 Dr. Goodlett decided to run for governor. He asked me to support his campaign. I said I would and he gave me a letter authorizing me to collect funds for his campaign. I used to go around to meetings to talk about his campaign, raise funds, shake the bushes, and talk to people one-on-one. I didn't do a hell of a lot, but I helped out because I thought he was a good man, very progressive.

He and I stayed friends. I used to go to his office to talk about issues. When I got my medications from the Kaiser health clinic, I would take them to him to look at and tell me if they was any good.

I was sorry when Dr. Goodlett passed in 1997.

I also was involved with the Auto Row protest. All the car dealers was located on Van Ness Street, and they decided to protest against the racism of the car dealers. I marched down there with Dr. Bourbon, who organized the demonstrations. They wanted the dealers to hire black salesmen to work there on Auto Row. I think they got two, three jobs for some black salesmen. That wasn't a grassroots issue; it was about upgrading the professionals, just like fighting for better parts in the motion picture industry years before.

Another time we picketed the hotel there on Market Street, the Sheraton Palace, to try to get them to hire more black workers. Like all those damn hotels, it was very racist about hiring black folks. I remember one night a busload of Africans pulled up while we was picketing. We started talking. They wanted to know what we were doing. We asked them not to go in there, and they didn't. We did get the hotels to hire more black people and improve conditions for the room cleaners, but only a few people went down there to the union to apply for the jobs. I don't know why more people didn't go for those jobs.

In 1968 I worked with the Peace and Freedom Party in Eldridge Cleaver's presidential campaign. Kathleen Cleaver asked me to work on the campaign. Kathleen had heard about me from a girl named Tracy Sims. We used to march in demonstrations down at City Hall. One time we marched down there when Cahill was chief of police. This was when Sam Jordan was running for mayor. Sam was a retired longshoreman who had a bar on Third Street, and he was very active in the community. I spoke at the rally. Chief Cahill had brought out police dogs to scare the people. I said, "Turn those dogs loose! Goddamit, we'll eat 'em up!" I would probably have been the first one to run, but it worked. I scared the chief and he didn't let those dogs loose. Maybe Tracy told Kathleen about that.

Kathleen and I had a long conversation. She wanted me to join the Peace and Freedom Party and help them out. So I went around talking to people, handing out literature. I stayed involved with the Peace and Freedom Party right into the 1980s, when I was on the central committee.

I also worked some with the Black Panther Party chapter in San Francisco. I met some of the members, a guy they called "D.C." and some others. This was a young group, and I used to give them advice on handling security. This was when I was working with the Black Security Guards. We used to meet upstairs at the Panther office on O'Farrell Street. Some of them acted like big shots in the community. But I remember one time the Panthers from Oakland came and took their money. Showed they was just selling wolf tickets.

I worked with the Panthers until they broke up. I was there when Betty Shabazz came to San Francisco. I was in charge of her security. I told the security guards how to search people, pat 'em and check for weapons. I was her personal body guard.

So I was involved with the Communist Party, the ADNIP Party, the Peace and Freedom Party, the Black Panther Party, and sometimes the Muslims and some other groups. I kept up my membership in the NAACP and went to their meetings on Divisadero Street. I was busy in those days, brother. That was my trouble; I was trying to do too much. It was crazy. On Sundays I would leave one meeting and go to another. And I didn't stop when I retired. I worked more, with the NAACP and with the Senior Action Network and housing groups. That's how come I started to have high blood pressure and heart problems. I'm lucky not to be dead.

Through it all I was working to get freedom. I wanted people to be free. I thought it would come through socialism. I thought socialism was coming right away. We still need socialism, but we also need strong unions, low-income housing, health care for the people, social security, day care centers, and rest homes for the old people. We need all of this.

What disappointed me about the Communist Party was that the leadership didn't follow through on the struggle against racism, white chauvinism. I think there was some truth in that book by Wilson Record. The party was mainly using intellectuals and didn't go to the grass roots in the trade union movement. The intellectuals and professionals messed up the party and they divided the people. To me the party members in the South was more dedicated, and there was more trade unionists in the party. What we need is a strong party and a left-wing movement in the unions. The biggest mistake they made was not building the left wing of the unions, not moving the unions to the left center. That's why I liked V. I. Lenin and William Foster. Build the unions. That's the key. That's where the masses are.

The other organizations I worked with over the years, I wanted to get in there and bring up issues. Raise issues and let the people know what's going on. A good left-wing trade unionist will get in there and bring issues to the floor, like I used to do in the NAACP and the other mass organizations. Be a sparkplug, and at least some of the people will go along with you.

CHAPTER THIRTEEN

Grace in My Life

In 1967 I met the person who would mean the most to me for many years. I first met Grace Oliver at the Fairmont Hotel. She was working there as a room cleaner.

Every Christmas Ben Swig, the old man himself, the owner of the Fairmont Hotel, would give a big party at the Fairmont, and all the staff went to it. Grace liked to dance. Not me. She was doing a dance called the Jerk or something. Even Mr. Swig was clapping. She had on a black dress and she looked sharp, brother! I went up to her and told her how good she looked. That's when we met.

Grace and I used to meet in the cafeteria and talk. We talked about the work at the hotel and the labor movement. I liked her looks and she seemed to be very intelligent. She was very concerned about trade union activity. She was a member of Local 283, the room cleaners union. I didn't know if she ever carried the ball for the union, but she understood what it was about. We talked a few times and she invited me to come over to her house. Grace used to live on Sharon Street. I was living at 2502 Third Street. She seemed to be a very good woman, and we got into a relationship.

Grace was born in Shreveport, Louisiana, but her family came to San Francisco and she grew up here. She had six children—two girls, Ruby and Gloria, and four boys: Larry, Jerry, Alfred, and Luke Jr. The youngest was still in school. She was separated from her husband, Luke, and later she got divorced. I saw him a couple of times when he came by the house. I helped her with the children. They wasn't angels, but they respected the way I treated them and the way I carried myself. She was honest and made them respect me. I was buying food and helping to pay the rent.

When we got married on January 21, 1976, Grace moved in with me on Third Street. By then the children was on their own. They would come visit on holidays and Grace would prepare a big dinner. Larry was married and he would come and bring his children. Ruby had got married and Gloria was living with her aunt. Luke wasn't there and Alfred was locked up. Him and Luke was in trouble a lot.

Grace and I met when Terry Francois was the president of the chapter here of the NAACP. She told me that one time he and Dick Swig, Ben Swig's son, was going around asking the room cleaners how they liked the job. That's when Francois call himself fighting discrimination in the hotels. Quite naturally, she wasn't gonna bad-mouth the job in front of Dick Swig. She said, yeah, she liked the job. But they did have some trouble with racism, and I was telling her that they could do better.

Before I got to know Grace well, I remembered there was a lady named Mrs. Brown who worked there in the linen room. She was a room cleaner, and I was telling her they should have black inspectors. At that time I was on the local joint board for the hotel workers unions up on Market Street. At that time there was separate locals for different hotel workers. The room cleaners, cooks, waiters, waitresses, and bartenders was in different locals. I had raised the question in the joint board about how if they discharged a room cleaner they had no follow-up. The business agent wouldn't take up the case to get them reinstated. I was telling them that there should be a change. To get back to Mrs. Brown and the black inspectors, she called Bert, the head of Local 283. We wanted the black room cleaners to be able to advance to inspector. This was like the same thing I had fought for in the South, to upgrade the workers on the docks. When you have an opening, it should be open to anyone to apply and upgrade. I told Mrs. Brown to threaten to march on the local if they didn't demand that they put on black inspectors. Bert called Mrs. Bennett, the head housekeeper at the Fairmont, and got them to hire black inspectors 'cause he didn't want the room cleaners marching on the local. Mrs. Brown and I was talking about the march sitting in the cafeteria. They thought we was drinking coffee but we were organizing!

Grace got involved in union activities after she left the Fairmont and went to work at the Mark Hopkins Hotel. In the cafeteria the room cleaners were being served precooked food that was left over from the restaurant, and they had to pay for it. I told her that wasn't right. The workers should get the food for free or bring their own. Grace discussed this with her fellow workers and they decided to boycott the cafeteria to protest. She organized them to bring their own lunch from home in a brown bag. The negotiations took a while but finally all the hotels agreed that the room cleaners could eat free in the cafeteria after they had worked so many hours. I gave Grace the ball and she ran with it. She had the consciousness to become an activist; all she needed was a little guidance in the right direction. If somebody has a little spark and you develop it, it will grow. I learned that through the struggle in the trade union movement.

While this struggle was going on, the manager of the hotel tried to discharge Grace two, three times, said she was drunk on the job and falling out. The bosses will try to pull anything, and they'll get away with it if you don't have the strength to fight back. Grace went to the union. The union had a meeting of the grievance committee and Joe Belardi, who was head of the local joint board, went and fought for her. I knew Joe Belardi. He was born in the same town as my mother—Bolton, Mississippi. He got Grace's job reinstated.

They kept on harassing her at the Mark Hopkins Hotel. One day they discharged her again. Grace did drink but not enough to be falling out on her job. Grace got a statement from her doctor saying that she wasn't drunk. She was suffering from seizures and taking a medication called Dilantin. *[Dilantin is a drug commonly used for management of seizures in patients with brain cancer.]* They called her at home and told her she was reinstated and to come back to work. But they continued harassing her. She finally decided that she would quit because she was tired of being harassed.

For a time Grace worked with other women in an organization called the Committee For Jobs. The Committee initiated a struggle for jobs for women on the waterfront. They faced a barrier of male supremacist harassment without much support, but they continued to sit in the hiring hall and to speak out. The committee didn't really get off the ground, and only later did this struggle gain the visibility and support to break through.

Later she got a job at a small hotel on Turk Street. She worked there close to five or six months. The hotel owner sold out. He had only two black room cleaners there, one of whom was Grace. He called the two into the office to give them two weeks' notice and a recommendation and two weeks' pay.

I suggested to Grace that she should get on disability because she was ill. She was still having seizures. She would never tell me what exactly was the problem because she said she didn't want to worry me. But it worried me more that she wouldn't tell me. She stopped drinking but she didn't get any better. I took her to the social security office on Mission Street to apply for disability and social security. When we went down there I told Grace don't go there like some people, who dress in one shoe or a blue sock and a green one or a red one. Go there looking neat. Dress well. I had learned that when I was negotiating in the South and meeting people. If you want to be successful, look successful. When we went to the office the lady told Grace, "Don't worry. I'm going to put you on right away." I was there observing, and I had on so damned many union buttons that maybe the lady was thinking, "We don't want no trouble!" Grace started receiving social security on September 13, 1982, and I was named payee so she wouldn't have to go out to cash the checks.

During the time Grace and I was together I was involved with the Communist Party and the ADNIP Party. I was interested in any organization I thought could help black folks. Grace wasn't too interested in the ADNIP Party. I think she attended a couple of meetings with me, but that was about all. She didn't have any connection with the Communist Party except what she knew about it from me. She wasn't against the party and she didn't oppose me being involved with it. Grace would go along with some of the issues, like fighting racism and working on the job situation. We used to go to the *People's World* fund-raising event every year. But I think her attitude to the party came out one day when I told her the FBI did not seem to be bothering the party anymore. She said, "Well, that's because you all ain't doing nothing!"

Although she wasn't well, Grace did some work in the community. I had to raise hell to get a polling place put in Dog Patch at the bottom of Potrero Hill so old people wouldn't have to climb up the hill to vote. We worked together on that. Grace worked on registering people to vote, and she worked at the polls. Meantime I was learning and she was learning; we were learning to work together around issues.

Grace wasn't no Harriet Tubman but she did the best she could, and I respected and loved her for that. We could work together and she gave me inspiration to move forward. She encouraged me to write, and she helped me. I had faith in her, I had confidence in her, I could trust her. If she was living today, she would still be out there.

Her drinking was pretty bad sometimes, but we worked on that, and she finally stopped two years or so before she died. But she couldn't stop smoking. I used to buy her three, four cartons of cigarettes a month. She said she just couldn't quit.

Toward the end we had a fire at the apartment building where we were living on Third Street. The fire broke out early one morning. Grace was sleeping in her son's apartment, number 3, because I had a big Belgian shepherd that she was allergic to. A lady passing by saw the fire and warned people. Grace was sick, but she got up out of bed and went into the hallway, which was in total darkness. Two other tenants saw her going the wrong way—toward the fire—and they took her outside of the building. The firemen came and put the fire out before it did too much damage.

The fire started on the back porch. That made me suspicious because a fire had started there once before. We believed maybe the landlord had started the fire. So I started staying up and watching, and I got a couple of the tenants to act as security at night.

On Monday, January 13, 1986, I had to attend two meetings. When I got home, the lady at the store told me that Grace had passed. The ambulance came and got her that morning and took her to General Hospital. She had gone there once before to get operated on. I didn't have too much faith in General Hospital, but a lot of people said it was a good hospital. I didn't trust those white doctors. Maybe they gave her too much medication. Grace wouldn't tell me what the operation was for; I believed it was cancer.

Grace had started going to the Metropolitan Baptist Church and that's where the funeral service was held. A lot of people attended the service, and I got hundreds of cards and telegrams.

I loved Grace. We had a good relationship, and I had a good sister I could trust. I had a lot of faith in her and she had faith in me. I'm sorry that I couldn't save her.

Grace was very much loved and highly respected in the community. Perhaps one of the finest tributes showing this is demonstrated in this letter from the San Francisco Board of Supervisors, dated January 23, 1986:

Dear Mr. Brown:

This is to inform you that, upon motion made by Supervisor Doris M. Ward, the Board of Supervisors adjourned its regular meeting of January 21, 1986 out of respect to the memory of the late Grace Oliver Brown.

The members of the Board, with a profound sense of civic and personal loss, are conscious of the many fine qualities of heart and mind which distinguished and brought justifiable appreciation to Mrs. Brown in the community.

The Supervisors realize that mere words can mean so little to you at a time such as this, but they do want you and the members of your family to know of their deep sympathy and heartfelt condolence.

Sincerely,
John L. Taylor
Clerk of the Board

Over the years I have faced other deaths among my loved ones. My mother passed years before I left New Orleans to come to San Francisco. She died before I went to the penitentiary. She was sick. I remember the doctor called me and my brother and sister into her room. He said, "I can't save her, but I can keep her alive a little longer." She had a slow leak in her heart. He wanted to do something that would keep her alive. She lived a while longer but then she passed. This was when I was working on the barge lines, around 1951, when she passed.

After I got to San Francisco, I used to call and talk to Rose and the children—my son, Brownie, and Rose's other children, Yvonne and Theodore. I went back to New Orleans on the bus one year before Brownie passed, and I spent about five days with him. He drove me around in the car and we talked a lot. Instead of sitting in the front of the car I always sat in the back because I didn't believe in using those buckles, putting on the seat belts. He always wanted me to talk and said, "Talk to me, tell me something." He wanted to know about different things I was doing.

I was staying with my cousin from my father's side, Sugar Duck, who I stayed with before when I was living in Los Angeles and went to visit New Orleans. She was the daughter of Joe Reece. She was sixty, seventy years old and used to strut all over. We went to the store and she wanted to buy three Irish potatoes. I said, "Cuz, put that back." I got the basket and started to dropping chicken, meat, and other things in there. I was gonna stay there a week or longer and I wanted to help out. The lady at the counter looked at me when I pulled out a hundred-dollar bill. She acted like she ain't never seen a black man with a hundred-dollar bill.

Brownie had a job driving a water truck, delivering bottled water. He said he liked the job. That was the first time I had seen him since he was small, after I got out the joint. I was glad to see him. He was married and had three children: Donald, Derrick, and Darwin. His wife was named Bobbie. I think he was doing good. That was one year before he drowned. He was twenty-six years old, I believe.

Brownie drowned in the swimming pool at the place where he lived. Yvonne's son found him in the pool late one night. I don't know how it happened, but I thought something was wrong. I asked Rose's brother-in-law to investigate, but he never found out anything.

When Brownie passed, Rose called me and I returned to New Orleans to go to the wake. Cousin Sugar Duck left the key with a neighbor. I got there and took a bath and went to the quiet hour. Sugar Duck was there, and as long as I could look back and see her I felt strong. I knew I wouldn't have no break down. I knew she was there to protect the family if anybody fell out. My sister and my brother was rubbing me on the head and all that. Brownie's wife was whooping and hollering. Sugar Duck carried a bottle of camphor oil. She needed it the next day at the cemetery. Rose's daughter, Yvonne, fell out when they was lowering Brownie down into the ground. Cuz stuck the camphor bottle under her nose and she came back.

Rose and Moselle have passed too. Rose died a few years ago. I didn't know nothing about it until my sister sent me the news. Rose had been sick in the hospital. She used to smoke a lot. I think that's what killed her.

Moselle got killed in an automobile wreck. Last time I was passing her cousin's beauty shop on Third Street four or five years ago, she called me and told me. I couldn't believe it. That was the second time Moselle was in a car wreck. She and her Uncle Doc was in another car wreck when they was on their way to Florida.

Brownie's wife got married again, but her and her husband separated. She raised the children and kept me in touch with them. One of the boys came out here and stayed, but he was bad news. He was living in Union City and always getting in trouble. That was Derrick. Brownie's youngest son, Darwin, got married, and now he has a daughter named Calisha Keyanté Brown, my great-granddaughter. They sent me a picture of her. She's five years old now. They say she's a "real Brown." I don't know exactly what they mean by that, but it sounds good.

CHAPTER FOURTEEN

Retirement:
Activism and Writing

I retired on disability when I left the Jack Tar, but I worked some for the Black Security Guards, as I said. When Grace and I lived on Third Street shortly after we got married, that's when I got my first social security check. I got it first and then she got social security.

Trade Union Activism

After I retired, I remained active in the trade union movement. I worked with my union and supported progressive labor organizations like the Coalition of Black Trade Unionists. In 1975 all of the hotel workers locals had merged into one local, Local 2, the Hotel Employees and Restaurant Employees Union. I was active in the Local 2 Retirees Association, and in 1979 I ran for the executive board of Local 2. We had a progressive slate called Action Thru Unity. It was headed up by Charles Lamb for president, Larry Tom for vice president, and Sherri Chiesa for secretary-treasurer. The union had been losing membership and we wanted to organize the unorganized workers. Membership had dropped from 24,000 when the locals merged to only 17,000 in 1979. Our ticket won that election, and I got the most votes of any executive board member.

I was on the affirmative action committee of the executive board. I wanted to get more black people working in the hotels, and as members in the union.

By 1982 we only had 1,379 black members out of a total of 16,000. I was very concerned. I said there was a great need for the affirmative action committee. I tried to encourage young people in the black community, as well as all un- employed workers, to seek employment in the culinary industry.

I ran for the executive board again in 1981, along with Jean Damu, a young, progressive brother that I knew in the union. In our campaign for the execu- tive board Damu and I pointed out that we had fought for unity and democ- racy in Local 2. We had kept the rank-and-file affirmative action committee alive. During the hotel strike in 1980 we called on the union leadership to de- mocratize the conduct of the strike and get support from other unions. We urged the local to support freedom struggles in South America and South Africa. We called on the international to organize workers in fast food restau- rants like McDonald's and Kentucky Fried Chicken and to push for the thirty- five-hour week. We opposed the firings of many minority business agents by the current administration of the union. We wanted a strong executive board, but our opponents was doing everything to split the progressive vote in that election and kept us from winning.

Even though I wasn't on the executive board any more, we kept the unity and democracy caucus going and I continued on the affirmative action com- mittee. I was also second vice president of the Retirees' Association. When time came to negotiate a new contract for hotel workers, I issued the follow- ing press release:

> Trade Unionist Lee Brown's views and report on Local 2 Hotel Workers sent a loud and clear message to the hotel owners in San Francisco. No sweetheart con- tract. For a good contract, we vote 'yes.' They voted 94% for a good contract. Some workers voted 'no', but the majority voted 'yes.' No takeaways. We will strike again, if necessary. We will not go backwards. They say that we will sup- port the rank and file negotiating committee; we will support the staff of Local 2, for we all learned a lesson in the first struggle for a decent contract.
>
> They also threatened to take away some holidays: July 4th and Thanksgiving Day. They threatened also to take away the union hiring hall and that made the workers angry. And I repeat they will not go backward, they will go forward. These threatening issues united and made the rank and file much stronger. And these are the issues: We demand a decent working contract around wages, vaca- tion, holidays, meals for all employees including roomcleaners. . . . From my point of view, the hotel workers are much stronger than they were in the first strike, when they [employers] threatened to take away the hiring hall which is the backbone of the hotel workers. The real source of the union's power is its rank and file membership. We are united behind the negotiating committee and the staff of Local 2 struggling for a better and a fairer contract in the culinary indus- tries. Struggles will teach us a lesson. Labor must get involved in American pol- itics. The bosses are scheduled to present before the statewide elections Decem- ber 13th a bill by Assemblyman Don Sebastiani (R-Sonoma)—author of the scheme. This scheme is designed to make California become an open-union-shop

and a right-to-work state. So, we must fight back and organize a united front. All community members should be encouraged to seek work in the culinary industries. There are many job classifications, briefly, from cooks, food servers, buspersons, bartenders, including dishwashers, roomcleaners, and telephone operators. Now I want to encourage the Black community, in particular, and all unemployed workers to seek employment in the culinary industry. . . . As a former member of the Executive Board and appointee of the Affirmative Action Committee and second vice-president of the Retirees' Assoc. (Local 2), I will continue fighting for a progressive, democratic Local 2 and a strong, fighting, militant union in the culinary industry, for a training program to upgrade and/or promote the workers, [and to support] the rank and file negotiating committee and chief negotiator, Charles Lamb. The rank and file membership has been well-informed through bulletins, leaflets, speeches, newsletters, etc.

I will repeat: we will not go backwards. We will continue going forward. Local 2 members speak with one voice for trade union unity and democracy. I, Lee Brown, will remain your brother in struggle until the emancipation of the workers in the United States of America.

Senior Activism

After I retired, I had gotten back into the Communist Party. Sam Gold had first asked me to come back into the party. I did go to some party activities. I was a fellow-traveler, and that's how I met Kendra Alexander, a sister who became chair of the party in California. Kendra impressed me as a sincere person and I had respect for her. We used to discuss trade unions. She also encouraged me to get back into the party. To me Kendra was a Harriet Tubman and Elizabeth Gurley Flynn. It was a great loss when she died in a fire in her home in 1993.

Although I had my criticisms of racism in the party, I started going to meetings again. By 1979 I was a member and was paying dues again. I paid dues through 1991.

Kendra Alexander put me on the party's senior commission because they didn't have any blacks on it. One of the people I met on the commission was Billy Allan. I think Billy was the chairman of the commission. I liked Billy. He was honest, he wasn't racist, and I respected him. A tribute was held for me in 1982. Billy was out of town, but he sent a statement that Lee Brown "brings to the organized working class movement a dedication, militancy, and clarity needed so much in these complex times, when the class is under such fierce attack by the Reaganites and Reagonomics. He speaks loudly, valiantly and with passion against the twin sources of disunity, red-baiting and racism. No red-baiter or racist will get away with their divisiveness while Lee Brown is able to get to the floor and rebut that splitting tactic of the bosses. In the senior movement he has made his mark. A vice president of the retirees organization in Local 2, he sends out the call to all seniors to unite and get with it, to beat back the attacks on their rights and needs by Reagan. Onward and upward I say to Lee Brown."

Billy died in 1988. I wrote to Billy's wife, Stephanie, and his family to express my wholehearted sympathy. Billy was very knowledgeable of the trade union movement. He tried to connect the party with seniors and the trade union movement. I learned a lot from him.

I was a member of many different senior organizations, including the Senior Action Network, the National Council of Senior Citizens, the National Caucus and Center for the Black Aged in Washington, and Legal Assistance to the Elderly. I was a member of different committees and boards that studied issues and policies and whatnot and made recommendations and reports. Starting in 1986 I worked on the senior advisory committee of the Legal Assistance to the Elderly, and in 1990 their newsletter published an article profiling my life and my work in the trade union movement.

I was a member of the board of directors of the Senior Action Network but because of health reasons I had to resign. But I continued on the crime committee that met once a month. In 1992 I was nominated for an S.A.N. Senior of the Year Award. They gave a trophy. They also gave me a certificate of honor for volunteer service to the San Francisco community.

In addition to serving on committees, for many years I went to the annual senior rally in Sacramento where we would raise issues concerning the needs of seniors. I was a monitor at the demonstrations and I was on the board of the California Legislative Council for Older Americans that sponsored the marches. I would still be going now except that in 1997 I had a heart attack and my doctor, Dr. Arthur Coleman, told me I had to slow down.

I also wrote many articles and letters to editors about issues affecting seniors, including an article that was published in the *People's World* newspaper on May 19, 1984.

BLACK SENIORS—DOUBLE WHAMMY

As a Black Trade Unionist, I call for an end to the discrimination against Black seniors on a national level. This means all those in senior organizations, retiree groups, community groups, churches, etc.—minority and white senior elders—should fight for equality of all seniors.

Black seniors are also suffering as part of the working class for being Black, so that means they are doubly oppressed. Therefore, all of us—seniors and non-seniors—must work together to bring about equality for all minorities, seniors and especially Black seniors in this country.

Poverty continues to increase for older Blacks. There are nearly 800,000 older Blacks among the poor in the U.S., according to the Census Bureau statistics for the '80s, which are some two of every five Blacks who are 65 years or older. This includes a high number of elderly Blacks who are living below the poverty level.

Black Americans are living in health hazard housing, fire hazard housing and overcrowded housing. Some older Black couples are living on an income of $4,954. Among older Black women, three out of seven are poor.

Cutbacks in programs such as Social Security, food stamps, Medicare, and escort services mean older Blacks will be hit hardest and suffer worse than they already do.

It is the great fear of race in the minds of Americans which is causing crisis and conflicts among citizens in this country, where they suffer from this great fear of racism and people have to suffer. For example . . . Black senior women suffer doubly from being exploited on account of being part of the working class and Black. So, Black seniors are second-class citizens, definitely; because of this, it must be on our agenda to fight for all minority seniors, particularly Black seniors.

As a trade unionist speaking for the grassroots seniors in this country, I know it is Black senior organizations who are representing (and not very well) the masses at the grassroots level. And I'm speaking from the experience of collecting information and personal investigation and scientific research and talking to people well-informed. And I am a member of national senior groups as well as local.

Now is the time for seniors to demand their rights: food, shelter, health care, energy, transportation and decent homes that we can afford. We must demand that no more cuts are enacted in social programs. And this means that seniors must also fight for peace and jobs for all.

—Lee Brown

My wife, Grace, helped me start off writing after I retired. She encouraged me and assisted me. She would type up my articles and letters and help me with the writing. My friend Tom Dunphy also helped me. He would interview me and write it down. Both of them also helped me with starting to write my life story. I wasn't no fancy writer, but I tried to express my ideas, what I think needs to be told, because other writers and editors wasn't getting down to the grass roots. I wrote many articles for the *People's World* and I wrote a regular column called "Diary of a Black Trade Unionist" that was printed in the *New Bayview News*. My articles and letters were sometimes printed in other publications like the *Sun-Reporter* newspaper and *The Black Scholar.*

Housing Issues

Another issue I worked on was trying to get decent housing for all people. When Grace and I lived on Third Street, I worked with the Tenants Union and I was chairperson of the Committee for Fair Rent.

I also wrote about the housing crisis and possible solutions. Here are some excerpts from an article I wrote that was published in the *New Bayview News*, May 28, 1981.

HOUSING CRISIS

By Lee Brown

As a Trade Unionist I fight for the right of housing for working people in this country. I would also include the seniors, retirees, the disabled or handicapped, and housing especially for the poor and working class youth. Because the young who want to have their own decent place to live cannot find anyplace to live, they are forced to live in overcrowded homes. Mostly these "homes" are a health hazard and a fire hazard. These traps are indecent and immoral. WE NEED HOUSES FOR PEOPLE, NOT FOR PROFIT. It is a human right. Houses for people is a basic human right.

In California we are 210,000 housing units short, and that is not including the unlivable housing. By not having adequate houses for the people we have lost over 175,000 jobs in California. . . .

Those who can well afford to get housing get more help, and the poor, working class and low income continue to cry out for a decent place to live. The only thing they ask for is a decent place to live. A place that we can afford. And especially hard hit are our single women with children. . . .

I now would like to present a solution to the housing crisis in the USA as follows: A battle for rent control. Because we have a serious fight ahead. (Rent control law is in serious jeopardy in Calif., if not the whole country.) We need a national rent control law. The poor people are living in worse houses in the central city areas. The landlords only use a small sum of their profits, which they receive from the pockets of their tenants, to patch up the falling down housing, and then use any repair as an excuse to raise the peoples rent. This then forces the seniors and us poor out. The hardest hit are on fixed incomes. Those of us on fixed and slipping incomes have to give up food for higher rents and utilities. . . .

We must act, we must turn talk into action, and form housing committees for immediate action. We can then form community organizations on a block by block basis to do something other than just talk about this problem. Go after your churches, your labor organizations, and your neighbors to form committees. . . .

The NAACP

I have a lifetime membership in the NAACP. Since my days in Houston I have always been a supporter of the NAACP, and after retiring I continued to be active. I was very concerned about senior issues, housing, and health care. For a while I was the chair of the NAACP's senior citizen committee. Sometimes I had problems with the leadership of the San Francisco chapter of the NAACP, but I always thought it was an important organization and I worked along with other progressive members like Julianne Malveaux and Harold Treskunoff to do what I could to support it.

I feel that the local leadership hasn't been democratic about choosing delegates for national conventions. They pick delegates they want, but the delegates should be elected by the general membership, as we do in unions. The chapter I attended in New Orleans was more democratic. And the leadership here doesn't follow through on issues we need to be fighting on—that's housing, health needs, jobs. You could build the NAACP if they worked on these issues. That's the way you build an organization—around issues.

I tried to sum up my views on the NAACP in an article that was published in 1984 in the *Sun-Reporter* newspaper.

IN SUPPORT OF THE NAACP

By Lee Brown

I would like to express my concern regarding the National Association for the Advancement of Colored People and my involvement in the association. In 1939 I became aware of the NAACP in Houston, Texas, and later became a member of the NAACP Youth Movement in Los Angeles. I was involved in fighting for better roles for black Americans in the motion picture industry. Mrs. Charlotta Bass, editor and publisher of the *California Eagle,* the major black newspaper in Los Angeles during the Depression, was the Executive Director of the Youth League of the NAACP.

We must continue the fight for better roles in the motion picture industry, television, and other entertainment fields. We must not treat the subject lightly. We have made some gains in the Negro and Hollywood films, but not enough. Hollywood must take a new look at the black American and continue the fight to eliminate the roots of racism in the industry. In the past a number of black films were made which told about the struggle for a better life in the U.S. Several films such as "Home of the Brave," "Lost Boundaries," "Intruder in the Dust," and a number of other films were made but they did not tell the complete story of black people in helping to build America—that's one reason why we should encourage more people to join the NAACP because the NAACP is the oldest civil rights organization in America.

We should help build the NAACP, help build the people's movement. I acted in the labor movement for over 46 years and sold a number of memberships in our Local 207 in New Orleans. Our union staff and executive board worked very closely with the national organizational branch of the NAACP to maintain rights of organized labor and the field of health, housing, education and jobs for youth and adults and in other areas as well. . . .

The NAACP must change in order to grow. Some must come down off their high horses and be human!—respect the rights of the people, regardless of what level they've attained. Those of us concerned with the NAACP and conscious of the struggle in America must learn to relate and listen to each other, because no matter what level, we're all victims of racism in America.

I would like to say to the leadership of the NAACP that we must call upon our friends in labor, religion, and other areas to help secure freedom. The struggle for freedom of black Americans is the struggle for freedom for all America.

Join the NAACP today, not tomorrow, for tomorrow may be too late. First recruit your family into the NAACP, then your neighbors. I feel that this is our duty and our responsibility that we must sacrifice in the cause of freedom. So let it be on our agenda, for time is running out.

We're going into 1985 and I propose that we study the history of black workers in America and black history in general. We must have knowledge of where we came from in order to know where we're going. I propose also that you become a nation of readers! We have been in a storm in the struggle for liberation of oppressed people in the U.S. And we must become allies with all organizations that fight for freedom for all oppressed peoples in the U.S.

We must also study the history of the NAACP, from the beginning of the Niagara Movement in 1905 to the present. . . .

I remain with you in the struggle, and continue the unfinished march for justice.

Peace and Solidarity Work

When the movement against apartheid in South Africa started I got involved in it. I participated in marches and demonstrations and I spoke at rallies. I went in 1981 to New York City to the Conference in Solidarity with the Liberation Struggle of the People of Southern Africa. I was the representative of Local 2, sent by the president and the executive board. Thousands of people came to this conference.

When I returned from the conference, I wrote an article reporting on it. Here is an excerpt from the article, which was published in the *People's World*, November 7, 1981, and reprinted in the *New Bayview News,* December 1, 1981.

SOLIDARITY CONFERENCE

By Lee Brown

The purpose of the conference was to establish a plan of action to educate and organize the U.S. masses against the racist apartheid regime of South Africa. Apartheid is the racist system of government whereby the white minority (17 percent of the total population) owns and controls over 85 percent of the wealth. The 70 percent Black majority suffer atrocities most North Americans find difficult to comprehend.

The distribution of wealth in South Africa is itself a reflection of how these atrocities are possible. Blacks in South Africa are among the world's most poverty-stricken people.

The declaration submitted by the New York delegation was adopted by the conference delegates; it included the following:

- To organize mass support in the U.S. for the liberation movement of South Africa;
- To expose the U.S. government and corporations' leading role in the South African apartheid system;
- To mobilize the people in the U.S. from the grass roots in the anti-apartheid struggle.

I will report back to Local 2, demanding ongoing assistance to the liberation struggle in South Africa. I urge everyone to fight this system of genocide against South African Blacks.

"An Injury To One Is An Injury To All."

I continued to be active in the antiapartheid movement, and in 1985 I marched in a demonstration with Alameda County supervisor John George. A photograph of us marching together was published in the *California Voice* newspaper. I'm proud that I marched in demonstrations. I'm also proud that I helped provide security when Alfred Nzo and Nelson Mandela came to the Bay Area. I got to meet Nzo but not Mandela.

In an article that *The Black Scholar* published in the May–June 1981 issue I discussed the different social issues and connected them to the trade union movement, peace, the military budget, and political involvement.

VIEWS ON THE MILITARY BUDGET

By Lee Brown

I am writing on behalf of the lower and moderate income workers, on how Reagan's military budget affects us as working people. Reagan's interest is not the worker's interest. Escalating the already bloated military budget only robs the people of services necessary for their survival. Senior citizens, retirees, the disabled, handicapped: all standards of living are reduced when money is taken from social programs and used instead for MX missiles. Poor people, youth, single mothers are all victims of a needlessly inflated military budget.

The workers cannot afford to rent decent housing, let alone buying a home; food and utility prices are far more than many people can pay; schools are being closed, denying young people any kind of education. Poor people face over-crowded living conditions with severe health and fire hazards.

Do U.S. workers really know what's happening? I say that Reagan is anti-people. He represents pro-monopoly and pro-military spending, serving the interests of big business and putting profits before the people's well-being. We face tough years ahead. Reagan has given the green light to bust unions in the U.S.A. The resurgence of racism is being used to divide the ranks of labor. The threat of a sub-minimum wage for youth is an attempt to separate young people from organized labor. Unemployment continues to rise as workers are repeatedly bombarded with plant closures and runaway shops; hospitals, clinics and schools are being closed, which not only denies communities of needed services, it also adds to unemployment. The U.S. is in an economic crisis and the people must act now.

Organized labor has the ability to lead in the struggle for the rights of all workers. Trade unionists must participate in coalitions with representatives from religious groups, senior citizens, youth, community and political organizations. We must build a united front which serves the interests of working people in this country. An enormous military budget and constant threats of nuclear war do not serve our interests.

Trade unions must become the vehicle for workers to struggle in their own interests. Labor's goal must be to organize the unorganized. Unions need study circles and union classes to educate workers on trade unionism and practice unionism, teaching workers trade union consciousness, with a knowledge of trade union democracy.

Free education and health services and decent housing for all people in this country must be struggled for. We must fight for rent control and lowering of utility prices. We must close tax loopholes of the monopolies. We must fight against unemployment, inflation, runaway shops; we must demand jobs for all with effective affirmative action for nationally and racially oppressed people. I feel this is a people's program. And we must not forget those on Social Security and S.S.I.

There is a solution to high unemployment that trade unions can become involved with: workers' fightback is the answer. We can demand more houses for poor and elderly people. Housing increases will create jobs for construction workers throughout the country. Keeping schools open will employ vast numbers of people from janitorial and food service workers to clerical workers and teachers, as well as educating the nation's youth. Keeping hospitals and clinics open also offers an abundance of jobs. Trade unions can fight the devastating effects of plant closures by supporting and participating in public and government joint takeover of closed plants. The time has also come to demand a shorter workweek with no cut in pay. Railroads can be re-opened in large cities, putting Americans back to work at union wages and working conditions. The possibilities are endless if we organize to stop Reagan's war economy and demand that our needs be met.

It is time to put talk into action. I call upon today's youth to turn out in masses to register and vote for candidates who work for peace and the people's needs. We must become politically conscious by building relationships with one another in all working-class communities. We must have faith and confidence in one another and strive for peace throughout the world.

I say that labor must be in the forefront of this struggle and call for unity for all organized labor in the U.S.A!

"Doctor of the Working Class"

I have worked in many organizations and have learned many lessons. As a worker and a trade unionist I'm struggling, I'm trying to do the best I can to call up the needs of the people. I have worked and lived in the midst of the workers. I must know everything that I can about working people, the union people, that I work with at the grassroots level. I must try to understand the poor and the masses of the people. I must find the correct approach so that I will be able to work with them and they will help and work together and help themselves and help me. I must win the confidence of working people as I struggle in community service.

It was in July 1981 that I became a "doctor of the working class." I gave myself the Doctor of the Working Class degree. My university is the university of the world, and the people are the best teachers. I feel that through my experience in the struggle I earned that degree. I'm proud to be Lee Brown, D.W.C. *[Lee Brown obtained a Certificate of Registration for an unincorporated nonprofit association from the state of California. The association name is Doctor of the Working Class with Lee Brown listed as founder and director. The registration certificate was issued on July 21, 1981, and is signed by March Fong Eu, Secretary of State.]*

CHAPTER FIFTEEN

Looking Back, Facing Forward

My grandfather always told me that God helps those who help themselves. That told me something—that you had to help yourself, that you didn't have to look up, since there wasn't no god up there; god was down here within you. You got to move the situation, struggle to change things, and have faith in the people.

Sometimes people at the grass roots get to fighting each other. The problem is shaky leadership, even in the labor movement. They collaborate with the bosses. They mislead the workers. That has got to change. We need to have a new labor movement, a new struggle.

When I look back, I see that the trade union movement gave me inspiration and knowledge and the experience of fighting for freedom. I learned that the workers wasn't getting complete freedom and justice. We had to combat racism and fight for better working conditions, jobs, upgrading, health needs, and housing.

I learned that to build any organization you have to fight for issues. If you want a strong organization, you pick out issues to organize around. We fought Jim Crow as one issue to build the union. The union did an extraordinary job in the South on this and other issues. We dealt with social issues like voter registration, as well as job issues. In 1948 we was fighting like hell to get people registered in the campaign for Henry Wallace.

Racism is still a problem, and it's a problem in the unions. I remember when they was talking about merging the hotel and restaurant workers unions

177

in San Francisco back in the 1970s; Charlie Gricus came to my house one day. He was telling me that we would have a better chance of fighting Jim Crow. He wanted me to work with him in bringing together the unions so we could merge. I thought it was good. But after they merged into Local 2 they still had problems with racism, not getting more black people into hotel work and into the union. They also didn't have many black people working on the staff of Local 2, only one brother on the staff. I talked to the president about that but they didn't follow through. So racism is still a problem in the labor movement. It was better when we had Charles Lamb and Sherri Chiesa as the union leaders. We had more blacks in the union then. Now it seems like the leadership of the union is working with the company to keep blacks out. So you got to fight the union and the company both.

I also think that the CIO merging with the AFL in 1955 was a deadly mistake. We had bad leadership. We could have had strong unions throughout America. But the bosses wanted to block the organizing of a lot of businesses. There are a lot of places that are not organized. When the CIO was around, it organized the textile, automobile, fur and leather workers, dockworkers, packinghouse workers, and many other workers. But when it merged with the AFL, the organizing drive stopped. I blame the party for that. The party should have built a left-wing movement in the trade unions to keep the unions from going to the right. We needed a left-center movement to hold the unions and fight around issues like racism, health needs, and housing. That could have moved the masses of the people. So that was a mistake.

I know some people look to [AFL-CIO president] John Sweeney to make things different, but I say the power comes from the rank-and-file. The people themselves got to speak out. I don't give a damn how good your leader is if you ain't got a strong rank-and-file to fight around issues and build the organization.

We got to build a new, strong labor movement around issues. We need to be very militant and fight for issues. Blacks should study the history of progressive movements. We need to study how to mobilize the people. Reparations is one issue that we can use to mobilize black people of different classes. We need to talk about redistributing the wealth. We can get brown people and some white people to unite with black people around that kind of issue.

We need an international labor movement. They need to make international contacts in other countries like South Africa, where there is a strong union movement. We need to start here first, but we also need to make contacts and have dialog with workers about issues we can use to build the labor movement. You got to have a new labor movement. That means talking with progressive-minded workers, black, white, brown, all kinds of workers, to support a new labor movement. Women need to be involved, like in the room cleaners' struggle. It's like taking a ball and rolling it. You got to start it off. People need to know the truth. As long as you got the capitalist system you ain't going to make it here, not the poor. They may get a few crumbs, the middle class may, but not the poor. We need a big movement here around issues. We need to get out there and hit the streets. When you start an organization, you need organizers and you need to be able to protect them when they get thrown in jail, like we did in the South. If you get arrested, you have somebody to get the people out before things get vicious in the jails.

In New Orleans I worked with the NAACP and civil rights. I met Martin Luther King when he came to New Orleans. I was introduced to him by Rev. L. Davis. I talked with him a little bit around issues. He was down-to-earth. When I told him I was for peace, freedom, and socialism, he didn't flinch. You know he went to a socialist school, quiet as it's kept, the Highlander School. I think Dr. King was correct in fighting for civil rights, and I think we made a lot of progress, but I think we should have been working to educate the working white about racism and how he is hurting himself by trying to maintain white supremacy.

I think Julian Bond and Kwesi Mfume are good top leaders of the NAACP, but you still got to wake up the membership. They need to mobilize the young people to build the NAACP. They can't let it just get conservative, middle-class, petit bourgeois. They'll be satisfied as long as they get a dollar but that won't solve any problems. You need the masses, poor people, in the membership. That's where the power is. As I told them in the labor movement, the source of power is the rank-and-file membership. Listen to them and you can't go wrong. I have faith in the masses.

I believe the Muslims helped to enlighten people too, especially the brothers, to get them to come out and stand up like a man. They taught them how to treat one another right, to get off dope and alcohol, to respect women, and to treat everybody right. They said the Muslims was antiwhite, but I never read anything by Elijah Muhammad where he said to hate anyone.

I worked with the NAACP and the Muslims because they can bring out issues and help the people, and you need to reach all people to educate and motivate them.

Issues and conditions will move the people, but they need somebody to carry the ball. You got issues here—you got people hungry, people sleeping in the streets. You need somebody to get out there and mobilize them, wake them up, shake the bushes. Conditions will move anybody, but you got to have some leadership.

You need good leaders—people who are militant, have some experience, and are willing to fight back. You don't want leaders who gonna go along with the bosses and collaborate like some of these preachers. At the same time you have to be careful when you make criticisms because you can divide the people. You have to lead by bringing out issues. That was how I tried to lead, throwing out issues and getting people to support the issues.

In the Communist Party I learned to be more militant. The party gave me a militant consciousness. I learned the issues we need to fight for and how we need to organize to fight for jobs, housing, and health needs, and to fight against discrimination, particularly white chauvinism. But I also came to see there was racism within the party, like in the trade union movement, and I read books—Wilson Record's book and Bill Gould's book, *Black Workers in White Unions*—that opened my eyes.

I felt the leadership of the party in the South was more militant, more struggling. We had some militant white leaders here in San Francisco, like Archie Brown, Billy Allan, and Mickey Lima. But in the South we had to stick together, and some went to jail like the sixty-four. We never did have that kind of problem with white chauvinism.

The party gave me experience and knowledge, but we had some bad apples, some bad leadership. I studied Marx and Lenin, historical materialism, dialectical materialism, and bringing the workers together. I read books by William Z. Foster, Herbert Aptheker, and Elizabeth Gurley Flynn. I learned to see errors in how we was fighting and how to fight to move stones out of the way in our everyday struggles. We studied and had classes on the labor movement and all kinds of issues. I also used to meet with the black party members from other unions to talk about job issues, racism on the job, and other issues. If you know and know that you know about issues, and if you observe and learn from the struggle, from books, and from people, then you can help find a solution to the people's problems. I learned a helluva lot about the capitalist system from studying in the party.

When they called me before the Un-American Activity Committee, I think they was trying to use me against the ILWU. Maybe they figured I was a weak man who didn't know nothing. They didn't know I was studying at night, my head in the books, reading Karl Marx and V. I. Lenin.

So they put me in prison. But that was like throwing the rabbit into the briar patch. I was at home. You'd be surprised at the people you meet in prison from the left. We were discussing Marxism and socialism. Hell, I think I read more about communism in prison than I did outside.

I supported the program of the Communist Party, but over time I thought the national leadership became weak. You could have built a left center in the labor movement. You could have built a strong trade union movement. When they passed that damn Taft-Hartley law, that should have been stopped by the labor left-center movement. The Communists could have played a very important role. Then when the AFL and CIO merged, that should have been stopped. That's why they stopped organizing the rank-and-file. The leadership sold out to big business.

In February 1992 the Northern California party members split off from the party. I wasn't at the national party convention a few months before the split, but I understand the national party leaders wouldn't let Angela Davis,

Charlene Mitchell, Carl Bloice, or Herbert Aptheker and other people, speak and raise issues about democracy in the party and the fight against racism. I supported Angela Davis and the others, but Gus Hall, the national party chairman, kicked them all out of the convention. That's when I stopped paying dues and quit the party.

I also thought that Gus Hall was against the senior movement. That's another reason I didn't care too much for him. Henry Winston, an Afro-American who was national chairman of the party before he died in 1986, was a strong supporter of the senior movement. We used to talk about issues whenever him and his wife came to California. When Henry Winston died and Gus Hall, who used to be general secretary, took over the chairmanship, that ended black-white collective leadership at the top level of the party. A lot of the black party members didn't like that.

Kendra Alexander and the Northern California party members formed a new organization called the Committees of Correspondence. But the Committees of Correspondence had their own problems. They set up a steering committee to put together the program. But a few individuals came up with the program without discussing it with the whole steering committee. We didn't know a damn thing about it. We should have had a chance to discuss it before it was brought to the general membership. That's democracy! I talked to Kendra about that and she agreed with me that it was wrong. After that I still supported the Committees of Correspondence, but I wasn't so actively involved anymore.

If we don't get ourselves together, we gonna move back. I remember one time I made a speech and I said we gonna have creeping fascism in this country. One guy got up and said, "No, you ain't got creeping fascism, you got running fascism in this country." That's what we gonna get if people don't wake up.

I still believe that socialism is the only solution to the problems of working people. They say that socialism failed in Russia, but the people in Russia still want socialism. That's a lot of propaganda coming out there. The people ain't finished yet. They're gonna rebuild the party. The party fell apart but the people still want socialism.

Same thing here. The people need to get some knowledge about issues and we need good leadership. That's what it's gonna take to build the movement for socialism. You got to get some people who will stand up and build an organization around issues. You got to bring in people from the Democratic Party, the Republican Party, anywhere you can find people willing to stand up and mobilize. I know some middle-class people may think everything is all right, but you got to fight that. Raise issues! Education, health care, housing.

Some young people today only think about making money. I say to young people, try to get an education. Not just to get a good job, but you need to also know how to help your people. You can work for business or the government, but you should put something in the community too—a community health center or community schools to teach our history and teach the history of the struggle. Build something for the people.

Today big business controls everything. Big business controls the educational institutions, controls the churches, controls the penitentiaries, controls the government, and controls the laws. There's got to be a change. It's gonna be hard, but the workers got to do it. No child should go to bed hungry at night. That's wrong. People are not gonna stand around and starve. People need to wake up and fight to survive. They have to fight for bread-and-butter issues, and when they see they can't get that under capitalism then they gonna move toward socialism. You just got to educate 'em, motivate 'em, and agitate 'em.

That's my opinion, brother. You can tell 'em Lee Brown said it.

Afterword

ROBERT L. ALLEN

In recounting his life and struggles as a militant trade unionist, Lee Brown contends that issues and leadership are keys to building any organization. Although issues arise as a consequence of the circumstances in which people find themselves, how does leadership emerge? In the following pages I want to examine this question by looking at the formation of Lee Brown's character in relation to his self-described emergence as a leader in the trade union movement. I would suggest that the interplay between Lee Brown's personal qualities and his development as a grassroots leader was characterized by (1) an openness to learning from role models, mentors, colleagues, and his own experiences, (2) a willingness to act on the basis of this new knowledge, and (3) a bedrock belief, growing out of his experiences, in the capacity of ordinary people to change their circumstances through struggle.

Early Years

Several factors appear to have been formative in Brown's development as a leader. One of these was the example of his grandfather. Brown makes it clear in his remarks that his grandfather had a great impact on the formation of his character. His experience with his grandfather gave him the beginnings of a social consciousness and a set of values and principles that would stay with him for life.

The elder Brown, for whom young Lee was named, is remembered as a kindhearted, generous, gentle man who tried to help poor people. His home was a gathering place for local people who came to talk and get advice on issues of farming, church business, money matters, and health. The elder Brown also taught young Lee to share his toys with other children and to be concerned for others generally. "He taught me how to get along with people," Brown remembers.

Grandfather Brown was an industrious man who owned a small farm and had a small drayage business. His hauling service brought him into contact with whites. Brown always maintained his dignity and bowed to no man. To young Lee, Grandfather Brown was a role model and teacher whose influence was made all the greater by the evident love that young Lee felt for and from the older man. The two were constant companions for the few years that young Lee lived with him.

While life on his grandfather's farm may have been pleasant, young Lee was soon introduced to the realities of racial segregation in the South. He realized that his grandfather died partly because in segregated Louisiana a hospital that would treat black people was many miles away. He also saw that many black families, unlike his grandfather who owned a plot of land, were poor, struggling sharecroppers, subject to exploitation and mistreatment. When he started school after his grandfather's death, he discovered that black children were not allowed to ride on the school buses but had to walk six miles to school. Although black farm children attended school only three months out of the year, Brown gained an early love of reading that would continue through his life.

Living with his Uncle Tot and Aunt T-Babe, he learned of another racial reality of southern life: the sexual harassment of black women by white men and the precarious situation of black men. When Uncle Tot's sister, Bernice, was harassed by a white man in a bar, Tot was forced to flee after someone shot the white man. Later Brown would reunite with Tot in Galveston and be introduced to the labor movement.

With his grandfather dead, his mother and Uncle Tot out of the picture, Brown remained with his Aunt T-Babe. At age fifteen he decided to strike out on his own, evidencing an independent streak and a desire for new experience that would keep him periodically moving for the next eight years. Like many young men during the Great Depression, Brown hopped a freight train and rode the rails in search of a better life.

Working as a live-in servant for a white family in a small town in Louisiana, Brown saw that white racial attitudes were not monolithic but might vary even in a single family. When the mother in the family forced Lee to take his meals outside in the backyard, the daughter objected that this was wrong and got permission for him to eat at a table in the kitchen.

His housing was a small shack out back. He was allowed to plant a small garden and sell anything he grew to supplement his small salary. He shared part of his harvest with the family and industriously sold the rest from a red wagon he pulled through the streets, an enterprising spirit that, no doubt, would have made his grandfather proud.

After two years Brown decided to move on to Galveston, Texas, where Uncle Tot and Aunt T-Babe had settled. While looking for work in Galveston, Brown visited the local courthouse to listen to trials. He noticed that more black people than white seemed to be brought to trial and sent to jail. He concluded that equal justice was not being dispensed.

Uncle Tot worked at Todd Dry Dock, and after a while Brown managed to get a job there doing common labor. There was a union of the black common laborers at the dry dock. A strike was called in 1938 that lasted three months. Uncle Tot was a strong union man, and he and young Lee both walked the picket lines. White workers honored the picket lines. The strike lasted three months and resulted in a wage increases of thirty-five to fifty cents per hour. Brown was elated and inspired by this union experience. For the first time he saw the possibility of change through organizing. "The union made me feel that I could do something for poor people like myself and my cousins. The union gave me a way to go forward, to help change things."

Work was slack in Galveston and Brown could find only a poorly paid job at a brickyard in Green Bayou. Here he encountered Old Man Henderson, who introduced him to the NAACP and the idea of an organization fighting for freedom. It had immediate appeal to Brown. "We was searching for freedom," he said of himself and a friend, "young men who wanted to be free. I know I wanted to be free and wanted to join something to get freedom." The youthful search for freedom emerges here as an early theme in his life. The meaning of freedom—and unfreedom—would become more clear with time and experience.

As a railroad worker in Arizona, Brown faced his first challenge as an organizer. When a foreman tried to fire a worker named San Antonio over a minor incident, Brown intervened. He called a meeting of the workers and organized a strike. "At the meeting I said that we shouldn't go back to work until the foreman put San Antonio back to work. All of them agreed." The next morning the workers refused to work and Brown, acting as spokesman, told the foreman the men would not go back until San Antonio was put back to work. The foreman said he couldn't do it. Brown threatened to go to the road master in Yuma. The foreman caved in and agreed to San Antonio's return.

Reflecting on the experience, Brown said, "After this experience was over, I realized that unity with other employees was what made the foreman act. If all employees united together on jobs, there would be less trouble and less firings would come from the employer." There is more evident in this incident in that it anticipates and is characteristic of his emerging leadership style. Drawing on his experience in the Galveston strike and improvising when needed, in this confrontation Brown used four tactics: (1) mobilize and unify the workers, (2) seize the initiative from the boss, (3) refuse to accede to the boss's definition of the situation, and (4) if necessary, raise the stakes. These organizing tactics would serve him well as an organizer and union shop steward in years to come.

Brown was also able to listen and respond positively to criticism that challenged him when he failed to manifest his values and principles. His would-be acting career provides a ready example. He enjoyed taking bit parts in movies and being a player, acting as though he were a rising star. The parts he took, however, were the same demeaning roles to which most other black actors were confined. Brown did not hesitate to berate these roles and the actors who took them as Uncle Toms. When he took his girlfriend Mildred to see a film in which he had a bit part—in a cotton picking scene—she was appalled. She let him know in forceful terms: "You should be ashamed to play in scenes that are so degrading to black people because you fight in the NAACP for better parts for black actors." Surprised at having this contradiction revealed, Brown felt ashamed. A person with less integrity might have dissimulated or attacked the bearer of the message. But Brown took Mildred's criticism to heart and he refused any more parts in movies.

In other ways Brown's relationships with women partly reflected and partly shaped his political maturation. His youthful relationships with girlfriends were casual and opportunistic. As he grew older, his relationships matured into thoughtful and productive partnering with women who were fellow trade union activists. A deep commitment to mutual encouragement and support in the struggle was most evident during his marriage to Grace Oliver.

Adulthood

Brown's life in New Orleans from 1944 to 1958 witnessed the maturation of his character, the growth of his leadership skills, and the enrichment of his social consciousness and political vision. His work with Local 207, his involvement with the Communist Party, and his relationship with Andrew Steve Nelson, who bridged the two organizations, would dramatically change his life.

In Andrew Nelson he met a black man, a Communist, and a militant labor organizer who would become his closest friend and mentor. Brown started attending executive board meetings and speaking up about conditions on the waterfront, especially the issue of upgrading black workers who mainly worked as common laborers, whereas whites had access to more desirable, better-paying jobs. Soon he was elected shop steward. Nelson, older by several years, began grooming Brown for a leadership position. Their Friday lunch meetings and Sunday dinners became occasions for political discussions, informal instruction, and union strategizing as well as enjoyment of delightful New Orleans cuisine, which Brown clearly relished. Nelson was like an older brother, a man whom Brown admired much as he had admired his grandfather. In time Brown would become vice president of Local 207 and coleader with Nelson.

His work with Local 207 gave him rich experience with a militant union dedicated to improving the lives of working people, especially black workers. Along with Nelson's mentorship, it gave him the opportunity to learn new skills and rise to a leadership position based on his skills, militancy, and courage. As an interracial union with black leadership, Local 207, struggling in the midst of a society based on white supremacy and black subjugation, also gave Brown an inkling of a different kind of society that might be created through struggle.

Nelson also introduced Brown to the Communist Party. Brown had been favorably impressed by a Communist organizer he met in Los Angeles, but he had not attended a party meeting until invited by Nelson. Nelson said the party could train him to work with and organize people.

What impressed Brown about the Communist Party in New Orleans was its commitment to building a militant trade union movement, its advocacy and practice of racial equality (including black leadership), and its anticapitalist stance.

Brown was not particularly interested in the intricacies of party politics or doctrinaire debates over party line. What drew him was the party's active involvement in working to improve the lives of working people, especially black people. But the party offered more than the union because it also gave him a vision of a new society based on socialism and racial equality. Brown already understood, based on his own experience, that the interests of the bosses and workers were antithetical. The party gave him an analysis of capitalism that deepened his innate understanding of boss–worker conflict. The analysis further gave him an appreciation of racial segregation (Jim Crow) as a deliberate ruling-class strategy to divide and weaken the working class by fostering racial hatred. For Brown the party gave him another militant, fighting organization with a program (as Brown saw it, fighting Jim Crow, building strong trade unions, supporting voting rights and progressive candidates) and a vision (racial equality, socialism) that coincided with his developing social consciousness and working-class values.

As with his experience in Local 207, the party gave him new skills. "I learned how to run meetings, set up committees. Sometimes we had all-day meetings on how to organize people, how to get them to register to vote by educating them, how to work with politicians, and how to fight Jim Crow."

The party also introduced Brown to individuals who strongly influenced his outlook. He found himself in an organization with whites who shared his commitment to racial equality and treated him as an equal. He was impressed by the party's district organizer, Emanuel Levin, and he became friends with C. J. Meske, the international representative who was also a party member. Brown and Meske enjoyed talking about conditions facing black and white workers in the South, and what could be done. The Communist Party encouraged and gave direction to Brown's intellectual development. He loved to read. The party introduced him to socialist literature and comrades with whom he could discuss and debate political ideas. The values he learned from his grandfather and Uncle Tot and from his experiences in workers' struggles were shaped by his reading and discussions into a coherent socialist worldview. His intellectual development was motivated fundamentally by his desire to change the world. A largely self-educated activist/thinker, Brown is an example of an authentic working-class intellectual.

During these years, Brown came to see in the trade union movement and the Communist Party the keys for improving the lives of black people and combating racism. His faith was reinforced by his own experience. The eight months he worked with black and white striking sugar refinery workers in the towns of Reserve and Gramercy was a powerful experience. Drawing on his union and party training, Brown managed to break down racial divisions among the workers and unify them, with the result that the strike was won. Clearly, in his mind, a program of actively fighting Jim Crow could succeed. This was the way to unite the working class and win victories, but it demanded commitment and action.

Brown was impressed by the commitment of white party members to practice racial equality in their personal lives. To Brown, personal integrity is a measure and indicator of political integrity. That is why the case of the sixty-four—black and white people, many of them party members, arrested for having an interracial party in New Orleans—was so important to him, especially the fact that the group successfully fought the original convictions and got them overturned. "We helped establish the right to associate and visit each other's homes and attend meetings or demonstrate together regardless of race, color, or creed. To me this was a victory for the working class in the South—not just black workers or white workers. It was the working people as a whole that won. We put a nail in the coffin of Jim Crowism!"

Brown's biggest disappointment came years later, when he was living San Francisco (he had moved there to find work following his release from prison): he felt that the party and the trade unions were capitulating to racism. A significant incident for him was being snubbed on the streets by a white party member and his feeling that the party failed to deal with this instance of "white chauvinism." This may appear to be a minor event, but to Brown it was symptomatic of a deterioration of political consciousness and militancy in the party. That deterioration was reflected, in Brown's view, in the party's failure to stop the AFL–CIO merger and in the failure of newly created Local 2 to stop the growing discrimination against black workers in the hotel and restaurant industry in San Francisco. Brown concluded that the party's leadership had retreated from the struggle to build a strong antiracist left center in the labor movement.

His attraction to forms of black nationalism reflected both his continuing interest in the problem of black unity and freedom and his sometimes doubt about the Communist Party. He made it clear that his attraction to the Black Muslims owed less to their religious doctrine and more to the fact that the Muslims taught that African Americans had a unifying history linked to past civilizations and cultures, a history not limited to slavery and savagery. His involvement with the African Descendant Nationalist Independence Partition Party came during a period when he was disillusioned with the Communist Party and had been fired from his job at the Jack Tar. The ADNIP Party, through the Black Security Guards, provided him with work and a sense of organizational activism on behalf of the black community.

Lee Brown saw no fundamental contradiction between being involved in black nationalist groups, trade unions, the Communist Party, and the NAACP. He asserted that he was always interested in anything that would help working-class black people and, in his mind, all of these organizations offered possibilities for improving the lives of black people. For example, his involvement with the NAACP—an affiliation that continued throughout his life—grew from a powerfully felt commitment to being part of a struggle specifically aimed at gaining civil rights in the present society. At the same time he brought to the NAACP a militancy and concern for working-class issues that was informed by his trade union and party activism. These interventions were not always welcome, leading to a sometimes fractious relationship with the more bourgeois NAACP leadership. Nevertheless, he never abandoned his commitment to the NAACP and his hope that it might emerge as a militant, progressive organization.

Finally, it is worth noting that Brown's affirmation of his support of the Communist Party program, despite what he sees as the failures of its leadership, reveals his fundamental faith. It suggests a basis for his continuing optimism and activism in the face of setbacks. The failures of leadership may be all too common, but this does not negate his commitment to the struggle for racial equality and socialism.

For Lee Brown it is his sense of "the people" that grounds his commitment—his abiding faith in the agency of ordinary people. "I have dedicated my life in the service of poor people," says Lee Brown. "I got faith in the masses."

Whatever one makes of Lee Brown's character and the qualities of his leadership, he stands squarely within a long and rich tradition of black radicalism, a tradition that insists that issues of race and class must be simultaneously confronted if there is to be any hope of fundamental change in American society.

This radicalism is premised on the deep interweaving of racial inequality and class exploitation in the history of this country, from the establishment of slavery in the colonial period to the dismantling of affirmative action in the present. The construction of race has been fundamental to the structuring of class divisions, and without class divisions, race would be meaningless. Generations of black radicals have sensed this peculiarly American nexus. They have insisted that without a determined struggle against racism the class struggle will fail, and without a struggle for economic justice the fight for racial equality will be subverted.

I honor Lee Brown for keeping the faith and for his courageous and enduring commitment to the tradition of black radical struggle.

Awards and Honors

Letter of Appreciation from Congressman Phillip Burton, July 7, 1982
Tribute Meeting, Women's Building, San Francisco, July 17, 1982
New Bayview Newspaper Publishers Award, 1985
Certificate of Appreciation, Coalition of Black Trade Unionists, San Francisco, June 26, 1985
Commendation, San Francisco Board of Supervisors, July 28, 1990
Certificate of Appreciation, San Francisco Coalition for Low Income Housing, February 21, 1992
Certificate of Life Membership, National Association for the Advancement of Colored People, September 1992
Certificate of Honor, Senior Action Network, San Francisco, November 19, 1992
Tribute of a Lifetime—event sponsored by Committees of Correspondence to honor senior activists, June 26, 1994
Certificate of Appreciation, San Francisco Coalition for Low Income Housing, December 7, 1996

A Note on Sources

The primary sources for this autobiography were a series of interviews that Robert L. Allen conducted with Lee Brown between 1994 and 1999, as well as earlier texts prepared by Grace Oliver Brown and Tom Dunphy. The personal files of Lee Brown contain a wealth of source materials, including letters, articles, leaflets, newspaper clippings, pamphlets, books, copies of speeches, and official documents of various kinds.

The prologue is excerpted from the published transcript of the hearing by the Committee on Un-American Activities of the House of Representatives, February 15, 1957 (Washington, D.C.: Government Printing Office, 1957).

The chapter entitled "Black Workers on the New Orleans Waterfront" is based on material in John W. Blassingame, *Black New Orleans, 1860–1880* (Chicago: University of Chicago Press, 1973); Daniel Rosenberg, *New Orleans Dockworkers: Race, Labor, and Unionism, 1892–1923* (Albany: State University of New York Press, 1988); Bruce Nelson, *Workers on the Waterfront: Seamen, Longshoremen, and Unionism in the 1930s* (Urbana: University of Illinois Press, 1990); and Philip S. Foner, ed., *Organized Labor and the Black Worker, 1619–1973* (New York: International Publishers, 1974). The history of Local 207 is drawn from a master's thesis by David Lee Wells, "The ILWU in New Orleans: CIO Radicalism in the Crescent City, 1937-1957" (Baylor University, 1979).

Materials on the trial of Andrew Steve Nelson and the transcript of the trial of Lee Brown were obtained from the National Archives, Southwest Region, Fort Worth, Texas.

Other published sources that were helpful in understanding the background of the story were Ann Fagan Ginger and David Christiano, eds., *The Cold War against Labor,* 2 vols. (Berkeley, Calif.: Meiklejohn Civil Liberties Institute, 1987); Jean Damu, "Economic Repression: The San Francisco Hotel Workers Strike," *The Black Scholar*, January–February 1981; and various articles in the *New Orleans States,* the *New Orleans Item,* the *New Orleans Times-Picayune,* the *San Francisco Chronicle,* the *Sun-Reporter,* the *California Voice,* the *New Bayview News,* the *People's World,* the ILWU *Dispatcher,* and newsletters of organizations with which Lee Brown was associated.

About the Authors

Lee Brown was born on May 28, 1921, in New Orleans. Mentored by his grandfather, a farmer, and his uncle, a shipyard worker and union member, young Brown soon found himself organizing railroad workers in Arizona, fighting for the rights of restaurant workers and black actors in Los Angeles, and in the 1940s and '50s, organizing waterfront workers in New Orleans as a leader of an interracial union and a member of the Communist Party. Hauled before the infamous House Un-American Activities Committee in 1957, Brown refused to cooperate and was imprisoned for more than two years after being convicted under the Taft-Hartley Act. Released in 1960, Brown moved to San Francisco and organized hotel workers until his retirement. Since then he has worked with senior citizens and civil rights organizations.

Robert L. Allen is author of *The Port Chicago Mutiny*, a book about a group of African American sailors who were unjustly convicted of mutiny during World War II. Allen is also senior editor of *The Black Scholar*, a national journal of black studies research, and co-editor (with Herb Boyd) of *Brotherman: The Odyssey of Black Men in America*, which won an American Book Award in 1995. His other books include *Black Awakening in Capitalist America* and *Reluctant Reformers*. He is presently a visiting professor of African American and ethnic studies at the University of California, Berkeley. A native of Atlanta, Georgia, he graduated from Morehouse College and holds a Ph.D. in sociology from the University of California, San Francisco.